A
LATIN EXERC

ESPECIALLY ADAPTED TO

Gildersleeve's Latin Grammar;

WITH PARALLEL REFERENCES TO THE GRAMMARS OF ALLEN AND GREENOUGH; ANDREWS AND STODDARD; BULLIONS AND MORRIS; AND HARKNESS.

BY

B. L. GILDERSLEEVE, PH.D. (Göttingen), LL.D.,

Professor of Greek in the Johns Hopkins University, Baltimore, and late Professor in the University of Virginia.

UNIVERSITY PUBLISHING COMPANY,

NEW YORK AND NEW ORLEANS.

1897.

Educ T 918.97.425
✓

HARVARD COLLEGE
7 Mar. 1921
LIBRARY
Gift of
Prof. Ephraim Emerton

Entered according to Act of Congress, in the year 1871, by the
UNIVERSITY PUBLISHING COMPANY,
in the Office of the Librarian of Congress, at Washington.

*** 1821

PREFACE.

In the preparation of the first three courses of this little manual, I have followed in the main the guidance of Prof. J. Lattmann, an experienced teacher of boys, whose *Lateinisches Uebungsbuch* commends itself to my judgment as an excellent introduction to the study of Latin. The fourth course has been compiled from various sources.

This new edition of the Latin Exercise-Book has been brought into substantial harmony with the revised edition of my Latin Grammar. In order to make the exercises more generally useful, I have added, wherever it seemed practicable, references to the grammars of Allen and Greenough, Andrews and Stoddard, Bullions and Morris, and Harkness. These references begin with the second course and embrace the leading phenomena of Latin Syntax. The special references in the text are briefly explained at the back of the book.

B. L. Gildersleeve.

University of Virginia, *April*, 1873.

A. = *Allen and Greenough.*
A. and S. = *Andrews and Stoddard.*
B. = *Bullions and Morris.*
G. or Gr. = *Gildersleeve.*
H. = *Harkness.*

CONTENTS.

FIRST COURSE.

PART I.

PART II.

SECOND COURSE.

THIRD COURSE.

PART I.

PART II.

FOURTH COURSE.

SYNTAX OF THE VERB.

THE COMPOUND SENTENCE.

FIRST COURSE.

PART I.

VOCABULARY.

☞ TO BE LEARNED BY HEART. ☜

Rules of Gender, Gr. 18–20—First and Second Declension.

1. NAMES OF PERSONS.

Deus,	*God.*	**rēgīna,**	*queen.*
pater (patris, 3),	*father.*	**populus,**	*people.*
māter (mātris, 3),	*mother*	**medicus,**	*physician.*
parentēs, 3,	*parents.*	**magister (magistrī),**	*teacher.*
fīlius,	*son.*	**discipulus,**	*scholar.*
fīlia,	*daughter.*	**nūntius,**	*messenger.*
līberī,	*children.*	**tabellārius,**	*postman.*
frāter (frātris, 3),	*brother.*	**faber (fabrī),**	*carpenter.*
soror, 3,	*sister.*	**rūsticus,**	*countryman.*
avus,	*grandfather.*	**pastor, 3,**	*herdsman.*
avia,	*grandmother.*	**vēnātor, 3,**	*hunter.*
avunculus,	*uncle* (mother's brother).	**mercātor, 3,**	*merchant.*
		uxor, 3,	*wife.*
mātertera,	*aunt* (mother's sister).	**scrība,**	*clerk.*
		nauta,	*sailor.*
puer,	*boy.*	**poēta,**	*poet.*
puella,	*girl.*	**agricola,**	*farmer, peasant.*
vir (virī),	*man.*		
fēmina,	*woman.*	**aurīga,**	*driver.*
senex (senis, 3),	*old man.*		
juvenis, 3,	*youth.*		**COMMON GENDER.**
virgo, 3,	*maiden.*	**convīva, m. & f.,**	*guest.*
dominus,	*master.*	**conjux, 3 (conjugis),**	*spouse* (husband, wife)
famulus,	*man-servant.*		
ancilla,	*maid-servant.*	**dux,**	*leader.*
servus,	*male slave.*	**sacerdōs, 3 (sacerdōtis),**	*priest, priestess.*
serva,	*female slave.*		
socius,	*partner.*	**custōs,**	*guardian.*
rēx (rēgis, 3),	*king.*	**cīvis,**	*citizen.*

2. Names of Animals.

bestia,	*beast.*	aquila,	*eagle.*
fera,	*wild beast.*	cicōnia,	*stork.*
gallus,	*cock.*	corvus,	*raven.*
gallīna,	*hen.*	musca,	*fly.*
pullus,	*chicken, young.*	formīca,	*ant.*
taurus,	*bull.*	rāna,	*frog.*
vacca,	*cow.*	coluber, colubra,	*snake.*
hircus,	*he-goat.*	cervus,	*stag, hart.*
capra,	*she-goat.*	cerva,	*doe, hind.*
equus,	*horse.*	lupus,	*wolf.*
asinus,	*ass.*	ursus,	*bear.*
agnus,	*lamb.*	aper, aprī,	*wild boar.*
catulus,	*whelp, puppy.*	leo, 3,	*lion.*
columba,	*pigeon.*	leaena,	*lioness.*
luscinia,	*nightingale.*	elephantus,	*elephant*
sturnus,	*starling.*	graculus,	*jackdaw.*

3. Names of Things.

a. concrete.

terra,	*earth.*	oculus,	*eye.*
caelum,	*sky.*	nāsus,	*nose.*
stella,	*star.*	barba,	*beard.*
schola,	*school.*	digitus,	*finger.*
penna,	*feather (pen).*	collum,	*neck.*
liber (librī),	*book.*	cibus,	*food.*
tabula,	*tablet, slate.*	pecūnia,	*money.*
epistola,	*letter.*	animus,	*spirit, temper.*
āra,	*altar.*	anima,	*breath, soul.*
templum,	*temple.*	mundus,	*world.*
fenestra,	*window.*	ventus,	*wind.*
porta,	*gate, door.*	culter, cultrī,	*knife.*
silva,	*wood, forest.*	vīnum,	*wine.*
campus,	*field.*	bellum,	*war.*
herba,	*herb, grass*	corōna,	*wreath.*
folium,	*leaf.*	umbra,	*shadow.*
rāmus,	*branch.*	pictūra,	*picture.*
aqua,	*water.*	viola,	*violet.*
fluvius,	*river.*	vestīgium,	*track.*
rīvus, rīvulus,	*brook.*	hōra,	*hour.*
prātum,	*meadow.*	spēlunca,	*cave.*
vīcus,	*village.*	sagitta,	*arrow*

oppidum,	*town.*
patria,	*country, native land.*
fossa.	*ditch.*
nīdus.	*nest.*
ŏvum,	*egg.*
lacrima,	*tear.*
laqueus,	*rope, snare, noose*
dorsum,	*back.*
frēnum,	*rein.*
ostium,	*door.*

b. ABSTRACT.

vīta,	*life.*
īra,	*anger.*
rixa,	*strife.*
pugna,	*fight.*
fuga,	*flight.*
forma,	*shape.*
poena,	*punishment.*
venia,	*permission, pardon.*
fortūna,	*luck.*
culpa,	*blame.*
fāma,	*fame, rumor, reputation.*
cūra,	*care.*
glōria,	*glory.*
cōpia,	*abundance.*
lūdus,	*game.*
dolus,	*craft, trick.*
morbus,	*disease, sickness.*
somnus,	*sleep.*
nûntius,	*message.*
modus,	*manner.*
odium,	*hate.*
gaudium,	*joy.*
studium,	*zeal.*
initium,	*beginning.*
vitium,	*fault.*
imperium,	*command.*
officium,	*duty.*
perīculum,	*danger.*
commŏdum,	*advantage, profit.*
damnum,	*disadvantage, loss.*
ōtium,	*ease.*
negōtium,	*business, occupation*
cônsilium,	*advice.*
auxilium,	*aid.*
praemium,	*reward.*
amor, 3,	*love.*
timor, 3,	*fear.*
labor, 3,	*toil.*
ordo, 3,	*order, rank.*
spēs, 5,	*hope.*
miseria,	*wretchedness.*
amīcitia,	*friendship.*
inimīcitia,	*enmity.*
dīligentia,	*carefulness, diligence.*
industria,	*energy, industry.*
pigritia,	*laziness.*
jûstitia,	*justice.*
modestia,	*moderation, modesty.*
stultitia,	*stupidity, folly.*
concordia,	*concord.*
audācia,	*boldness.*
invidia,	*envy.*
lībertās, 3,	*freedom.*
sapientia,	*wisdom.*
victōria,	*victory.*
custōdia,	*custody, prison.*
praeceptum,	*precept.*
valētūdo,	*health* (often *ill health*)

Exceptions in Gender.—Feminines in *us.*

alvus,	*belly.*
colus,	*distaff.*
humus,	*ground.*
atomus,	*atom.*
methodus,	*method.*
periodus,	*period.*
dialectus,	*dialect.*
diametrus,	*diameter*
paragraphus,	*paragraph.*

4. Adjectives.

bonus,	*good.*
malus,	*bad.*
magnus,	*great.*
parvus,	*small, little.*
sānus,	*sound.*
aegrōtus	*sick.*
probus,	*upright.*
improbus,	*wicked, naughty.*
vērus,	*true.*
falsus,	*false.*
cautus,	*wary, cautious.*
incautus,	*unwary, careless.*
callidus,	*sly.*
stultus,	*stupid, foolish.*
novus,	*new.*
antīquus,	*old, ancient.*
plēnus,	*full.*
vacuus,	*empty.*
jūcundus,	*agreeable.*
molestus,	*burdensome, disagreeable.*
laetus,	*glad.*
maestus,	*sad.*
mōrōsus,	*sour (-tempered).*
cārus,	*dear.*
odiōsus,	*hateful.*
superbus,	*haughty, overbearing.*
modestus,	*modest, moderate.*
grātus,	*thankful, acceptable.*
clārus,	*clear, loud, renowned.*
pius,	*pious, dutiful.*
timidus,	*fearful, timid.*
validus,	*strong.*
firmus,	*fast, firm.*
jūstus,	*just.*
generōsus,	*noble-spirited, gentlemanly.*
sevērus,	*strict.*
avārus,	*covetous.*
propinquus,	*near.*
dīversus,	*different.*
rēgius,	*royal.*
acūtus,	*sharp, pointed.*
eximius,	*distinguished.*
ferus,	*wild.*
varius,	*various.*
multus,	*much, many*
prīmus,	*first.*
optimus,	*best.*
maximus,	*greatest.*
altus,	*high.*
prŏfundus,	*deep.*
longus,	*long.*
lātus,	*broad.*
crassus,	*thick.*
beātus,	*blessed.*
albus,	*white.*
sēdulus,	*industrious.*
piger, gra, grum,	*lazy.*
niger, gra, grum,	*black.*
aeger, gra, grum,	*sick.*
pulcher, chra, chrum,	*beautiful.*
ruber, bra, brum,	*red.*
sacer, cra, crum,	*sacred.*
sinister, tra, trum,	*on the left.*
vesper, erī,	*evening.*
socer, erī,	*father-in-law*
gener, erī,	*son-in-law.*
miser, era, erum,	*wretched.*
asper, " "	*rough.*
prosper, " "	*prosperous.*
tener, " "	*tender*
līber, " "	*free.*
lacer, " "	*torn.*
adulter, erī,	*adulterer.*
dexter, tera, terum, *and* tra, trum,	*on the right.*
signifer, erī,	*standard bearer.*
armiger, erī,	*armor-bearer*
meus, mea, meum,	*mine.*
tuus, tua, tuum,	*thine.*

suus, sua, suum,	*his, her, its, their* (reflexive).	nullus, a, um,	*none.*
		sōlus, a, um,	*sole.*
nôster, tra, trum,	*our.*	tōtus, a, um,	*whole.*
vester, tra, trum,	*your.*	alius, a, ud,	*other.*
		uter, tra, trum,	*which of two.*
ūnus, a, um,	*one.*	alter, tera, terum,	*the other* (of two).
ullus, a, um,	*any.*		
		neuter, tra, trum,	*neither.*

I. First and Second Declensions.

5. The adjective attribute agrees with its substantive in gender, number, and case.

DECLINE—

barba longa,	*the long beard.*	puer piger,	*the lazy boy.*
equus albus,	*the white horse.*	poēta clārus,	*the famous poet.*
collum longum,	*the long neck.*	vir bonus,	*a good man.*

6. THE POSSESSIVE GENITIVE:

barba longa,
equus albus, domini superbi, *of the haughty master.*
collum longum,

7. The great fame of the good queen. The burdensome cares of the wretched sailors. My son's little book. The black slates of the lazy scholars. The long necks of the white storks. The beautiful beard of the black goat. The rough fingers of the strong farmer.

II. Conjugation of SUM. Gr. 112.

8. Predicate and Copula: G. 192, 193, 196.

SUBJECT. PREDICATE.	SUBJECT. PREDICATE.	SUBJECT. PREDICATE
Poēta est clārus.	Rēgina est clāra.	Bellum est clārum.
Poētae sunt clārī.	Rēgīnae sunt clārae.	Bella sunt clara.
sum lætus.	sum puer.	estis puerī.
I am glad.	*I am a boy.*	*You are boys.*
Ego sum magnus.	Nos sumus magnī.	
Ego sum magna.	Nos sumus magnae	
Piger es.	Pigrī estis.	
Pigra es.	Pigrae estis.	

9. Bonī sunt beātī, improbī sunt miserī.
Pater meus est rūsticus. Soror amīcī meī est conjux poētae.
Sumus discipulī. Tū es fīlius dominī, nōs sumus servī.
Discipulī nōn fuērunt sēdulī.
Beātī eritis, puerī! Beātae eritis, puellae!

10. The world is great, the altar is great, the temple is great. We are great, you are small. We were friends. I am a slave, you are the sons of my master. The feathers of the raven are black. The new scholars are timid. The beautiful girls have been sick. Thou wilt be thankful.

III. Active Voice of the First Conjugation. Gr. 119–120.

The Accusative is called the Direct, and the Dative the Indirect Object.

11.

SUBJECT.	PREDICATE.	OBJECT.
magister	laudat	discipulum.
magister	laudat	discipulōs.
magistrī	laudant	discipulum.
magistrī	laudant	discipulōs.
	laudo	discipulum.
	amā	amīcōs.
magister sevērus	vituperat	discipulum pigrum.

12.

SUBJECT.	PREDICATE.	DIRECT OBJECT.	INDIRECT OBJECT.
puer	dōnat	librum	amīcō.
puer grātus	dōnat	librum pulchrum	amīcō cārō.
discipulus	obtemperat (*is obedient*)		magistro.
	obtemperā		praeceptis magistrī.

13. Vocabulary:

laudāre,	to *praise.*	dīlaniāre,	to *tear in pieces.*
vituperāre,	*blame.*	dāre,	*give* (do dedī dātum)
clāmāre,	*cry* (aloud).	dōnāre,	*present.*
portāre,	*carry.*	nārrāre,	*narrate, tell.*
vocāre,	*call.*	mōnstrāre,	*point out.*
dēvorāre,	*devour.*	parāre,	*get ready, prepare.*
necāre,	*kill.*	mūtāre,	*change.*
vītāre,	*shun.*	superāre,	*overcome, surpass*
servāre,	*preserve.*	fugāre,	*put to flight.*
dēlectāre,	*delight.*	collocāre,	*set up, post.*
pugnāre,	*fight.*	līberāre,	*free.*
expugnāre,	*to take, carry (a city).*	ornāre,	*adorn, furnish.*
cūrāre,	*take care of.*	postulāre,	*demand*
corōnāre,	*crown.*	putāre,	*think.*

14. Analyze the following examples:

Lupī dēvorant agnōs. Lupī ferī dēvorāvērunt agnōs parvōs. Vocāvī amīcum meum. Portātis librum puerī aegrōtī. Portāte librum puerī aegrōtī. Parentēs piī nautae miserō dōna multa dabant. Agricola grātus fīliō magistrī agnum dōnāvit. Date pecūniam fīliō miserō nautae aegrōtī.

15. Translate the following sentences into Latin:

☞ The possessive pronoun is not expressed unless emphatic.

(1.) Direct Object: The boy is killing the fly. We are carrying a slate, a book, a pen. The girl was nursing (*cūrāre*) [her] sick grandfather. Strong men will overcome dangers. The teacher will praise the good scholar, will blame the bad [one]. You demand reward and (*et*) glory. Preserve the good reputation of the school. Why (*cūr*) have you killed the ants? O careless boy, you are devouring unwholesome [= bad] food. Call the physician, the master's daughter is sick. The naughty boys had killed the nightingale.

(2.) Indirect Object: A kind uncle has given the boy a knife and books. The herdsman had shown the peasants the tracks of the wolf. The herdsman has shown the boy a nest. Give your friend the pigeon's eggs. The boys gave [their] mothers apples. The kind teacher will tell the good scholars a pretty story (*fābula*). The messenger announces to the physician [his] master's sickness. The kind-hearted master granted (*dare*) pardon to the careless girl. The boys were not (*nōn*) obedient to [their] teacher.

(3.) Ablative as a Whence Case (Syntax, § 388): Thy help has freed the careless girl from danger. The kind teacher will free the modest scholar from punishment.

16. The teacher will call attention to the variety of position in the Latin language, and practise the beginner in varying the order of the words in the Latin examples. The following general principles may suffice at first:

I. The adjective follows its substantive, and so do the equivalents of the adjective—genitive and the like.

II. The qualifiers of the verb precede the verb; for instance, adverbs and oblique cases with or without prepositions. 1. The adverb is put near the verb. 2. The indirect object generally precedes the direct object.

III. The reversal of the above rules prod... nt miseri.
for the *verb* is at the beginning; for th... ...ror amicī meī est conjux poëtae.
jective, before the substantive; for ... ...us dominī, nōs sumus servī.
indirect object, after the direct object.
the points of emphasis. ...eritis, puellae!

IV. Th... ...ar is gr...

17. Liquid Stems in ... Gr., §§ 40, 42.

a. NAMES OF PERSONS.		*b.* NAMES OF ANIMALS.	
latro (praedo),	*robber.*	draco,	*dragon, snake.*
centūrio,	*centurion (captain).*	pāvo,	*peacock.*
agāso,	*hostler, groom.*	hirundo, inis, *f.*	*swallow.*
histrio,	*actor.*	vespertīlio, *m.*	*bat.*
caupo,	*innkeeper.*	pāpilio, *m.*	*butterfly.*

c. NAMES OF THINGS.

aquilo, ōnis, *m.*	*north wind.*	imāgo, ĭnis, *f.*	*likeness, image.*
sermo, ōnis, *m.*	*talk, conversation.*	orīgo, ĭnis, *f.*	*origin, source.*
altitūdo,	*height.*	obsidio, ōnis, *f.*	*siege.*
longitūdo,	*length.*	religio,	*religion.*
magnitūdo,	*greatness.*	regio,	*region.*
multitūdo,	*crowd.*	legio,	*legion.*
fortitūdo,	*bravery.*	nātio,	*nation.*
sōlitūdo,	*solitude.*	opīnio,	*opinion.*
pulchritūdo,	*beauty.*	occāsio,	*occasion.*
cōnsuētūdo,	*custom.*	contentio,	*exertion.*
		narrātio,	*tale, narrative.*
flūmen,	*river.*	condicio,	*condition.*
fulmen,	*lightning (stroke).*	suspīcio,	*suspicion.*
lūmen,	*light.*	reconciliātio,	*reconciliation.*
nūmen,	*divinity.*	EXCEPTIONS.	
agmen,	*line of march.*	caro, carnis, *f.*	*flesh.*
carmen,	*poem.*	ordo, ordinis, *m*	*order.*
certāmen,	*contest.*	cardo, inis, *m.*	*hinge.*
grāmen,	*grass.*	ligo, ōnis, *m.*	*mattock.*
turbo, ĭnis, *m.*	*whirlwind.*	harpago,	*grappling hook.*
sanguis, ĭnis, *m.*	*blood.*	margo,	*border.*
pollis, ĭnis, *m.*	*flour.*	pūgio,	*dagger.*
tībīcen, ĭnis,	*fluter.*		
tubicen,	*trumpeter.*		
cornicen,	*horn-blower.*		

18. Liquid Stems in *r*.

a. NAMES OF PERSONS AND ANIMALS.

E.		O.	
passer,	*sparrow.*	mercātor,	*merchant.*
anser,	*goose.*	gubernātor,	*pilot, helmsman.*
accipiter, ris,	*hawk.*	imperātor,	*general, emperor.*
mulier,	*woman*	conditor,	*founder.*
		adūlātor,	*flatterer.*
O.		adjūtor,	*helper.*
praeceptor,	*instructor*	auctor,	*author, originator*
cantor,	*singer.*	uxor,	*wife.*
victor,	*conqueror.*	U.	
viātor,	*wayfarer, traveller.*	fūr, fūris,	*thief.*
ōrātor,	*orator.*	vultur, ŭris, *m.*	*vulture.*

b. NAMES OF THINGS (CONCRETE AND ABSTRACT).

E.		O (U).	
venter,	*belly.*	rōbur, rōboris,	*strength (oak)*
imber, bris,	*rain.*	ebur, eboris,	*ivory.*
āēr, āēris,	*air.*		
carcer,	*jail.*	U.	
agger,	*mound.*	fulgur, ŭris,	*lightning (flash).*
		guttur, ŭris,	*throat.*
O.		EXCEPTIONS.	
labor,	*toil.*	arbor, ŏris, *f.*	*tree.*
color,	*colour.*	fār, farris, *n.*	*spelt.*
honor,	*honour.*	aequor, ŏris, *n.*	*sea.*
dolor,	*pain.*	iter, itineris, *n.*	*journey, route.*
furor,	*madness.*	vēr, vēris, *n.*	*spring.*
clāmor,	*cry, shouting.*	cadāver, eris, *n.*	*dead body.*
terror,	*fright.*	verber, *n.*	*blow.*
error,	*mistake.*	ūber, *n.*	*teat.*
cruor,	*gore.*	papāver, *n.*	*poppy.*

RULE OF SYNTAX:

Cause, manner, and instrument are put in the Ablative.

19. Latrōnēs sunt callidī. Audācia latrōnum est magna. Laudāmus fortitūdinem victōrum. Puer mônstrat sorōribus imāginem pāvōnis. Mulierēs modestae vītant occāsiōnem certāminis. Imperātor collocābat legiōnēs. Viātōrēs vītābant flūmen. Hominēs cautī vītābunt perīcula. Clāmōrēs mulierum fugāverant fūrem. Nūntius līberāvit uxōrem mercātōris falsā opīniōne. Vēnātōrēs necāvērunt leōnem sagittīs. Superābis frātrem dīligentiā et studiō. Avunculus est mātris frāter, mātertera est mātris soror; patris frātrem vocābant Rōmānī patruum, patris sorōrem amĭtam.

20. The sun is large, the moon [is] small. Salt is white. Gall is bitter (*amārus*), honey is pleasant. The winters are long. Avoid the occasions of contest. The centurions have saved the heedless (*incautus*) general by [their] bravery. The cautious traveller will avoid the danger. Good people (*homo*) will be thankful to the divinity. The bravery of the generals, the captains [and] the legions was distinguished (*ēgregius*). The cunning thieves had carried off (*asportāre*) the peacocks and the geese. The hawk devoured the sparrow, the great eagle tore-in-pieces the hawk. The hunter killed the sparrow, the hawk [and] the eagle. The bulls were devouring the grass. Lions do not (*nōn*) devour the dead-bodies of beasts and men (*homo*). The victory of the legions frees the people from fear. The slave procured (*parāre*) many advantages for [his] master by [his] toil.

V. Second Conjugation. Gr., 123.

(Only the Infinitive, Indicative Present, and Imperf. 2 p., sing. and pl. Imperat. Active.)

21. Vocabulary:

habēre,	*to have.*	dēbēre,	*to owe* (dēbeo. *I ought, must*).
dēlēre,	*to blot out, destroy*	nocēre,	*to do harm*
monēre,	*to remind, warn.*	respondēre,	*to make answer.*
movēre,	*to move.*	pārēre,	*to be obedient.*
vidēre,	*to see.*	praebēre,	*to afford.*
tenēre,	*to hold.*	placēre,	*to be pleasing.*
timēre,	*to fear.*	solēre,	*to be accustomed.*
terrēre,	*to frighten.*	flēre,	*to weep.*
tacēre,	*to be silent.*	nēre,	*to spin.*

Rule of Syntax:

The Indirect Object is put in the Dative with many verbs of advantage and disadvantage, yielding and resisting, pleasure and displeasure, bidding and forbidding.

22. Agricola habet equum et vaccam et capram. Habēmus sturnum et lusciniam. Improbī puerī dolent nīdōs lusciniārum. Ōrātōrēs bonī monent hominēs malōs. Movētis oculōs. Nōn vidēmus āërem et ventum. Ventus movet altās arborēs. Discipulī praeceptōrēs dēbent amāre. Discipulī praeceptōribus respondēbant. Pārēte praeceptīs mātris. Plēnus venter nōn studet libenter (*willingly*). Mulierēs terrent fūrēs clāmōribus. Nocēs valētūdinī tuae labōribus et contentiōnibus.

23. Our father has many sons and many (Synt., 286, R. 1) daughters. Thou hast a handsome and sharp knife. The sons of the merchant have pigeons, a monkey [and] a black he-goat. The timid women were screaming and weeping. Magnanimous conquerors do not destroy the temples of the gods. We were warning our brothers and our sisters. I saw the cunning thief. The strong peasant was holding the wild cow. Doves fear the falcon. The rumor of war frightens timid mothers. False opinions do harm to men (people, *hominēs*). The hawk makes answer to the sparrow: Thou hast devoured the fly, I will devour the sparrow. You lazy scholars do not answer [your] teacher. The wind is moving the water. Good (*probus*) servants are obedient to [their] masters. The harmony (*concordia*) of [their] children is-pleasing to father and mother. Rivers afford to merchants many advantages. Anger and fear do harm to the health of men. Stop (*tenēre*) the thieves! The servants were holding the mad (*ferus*) bull with a lasso (*laqueus*). Answer, boy! why (*cūr*) art thou weeping? Be silent and obey! for (*nam*) children must obey [their] parents.

VI. Stems in S. (Third Declension.)

24. NAMES OF THINGS (ABSTRACT AND CONCRETE).

MASCULINES.		NEUTERS.	
pulvis,	*dust.*	E.	
mōs,	*custom.*	genus,	*kin, kind.*
flōs,	*flower.*	onus,	*burden.*
rōs,	*dew.*	opus,	*work.*

NEUTERS.

scelus,	*crime.*	lītus,	*shore.*
sīdus,	*constellation.*	pectus,	*breast.*
foedus,	*treaty, league.*	pecus,	*cattle (sheep).*
latus,	*side.*	pignus,	*pledge.*
vellus,	*fleece.*	stercus,	*dung.*
vulnus,	*wound.*	U.	
O.		jūs,	*right.*
corpus,	*body.*	crūs,	*leg.*
tempus,	*time.*	tūs,	*frankincense.*
facinus,	*(shameful) deed.*	rūs,	*country.*
frīgus,	*cold.*		

vās, vāsis, *n.*	*vessel,* pl. vāsa, vāsōrum.	ōs, ōris, *n.*	*mouth.*
		tellūs, ūris, *f.*	*earth.*
as, assis, *m.*	*copper (coin).*	lepus, ŏris, *m.*	*hare.*
os, ossis, *n.*	*bone.*	mūs, mūris, *m.*	*mouse.*
aes, aeris, *n.*	*brass, bronze.*		

25. Vidēmus multum pulverem. Servāte bonum mōrem! Hortī habent multōs flōrēs. Asinus portat magnum onus. Laudāmus opera deī. Tempora mūtant mōrēs. Tenē jūra Aegrōtō corporī labōrēs sunt molestī. Imperātor superbus dēlēbat glōriam suam scelere et facinoribus.

26. The kinds of animals are various. The wayfarers were bearing great burdens. We blame the shameful-deed of the conqueror. The treaties of the good are firm. Strokes of lightning destroy the works of men. Cold does no harm to healthy bodies. Dew is grateful to cattle. The girls were adorning the lambs with flowers and wreaths. You must not fear a wound. Times change the customs of men.

VII. Third Conjugation.

(Only Infin., Indic. Pres. and Imperf. 2 p., sing. and pl. Imperat. Act. of *emo*, Gr., § 131, and *capio*, § 139.)

27. VOCABULARY:

emere,	*buy.*	lūdere,	*play.*
vēndere,	*sell.*	scrībere,	*write.*
dīcere,	*say.*	discere,	*learn.*
dūcere,	*lead.*	bibere,	*drink.*

cadere,	*fall.*	frangere,	*break.*
caedere,	*fell, cut.*	dēfendere,	*defend.*
pellere,	*drive.*	cingere,	*gird, surround.*
spernere,	*despise.*	sūmere,	*take.*
gerere,	*carry on.*	legere,	*read.*
quaerere,	*seek.*	relinquere,	*leave.*
cēdere,	*give way.*		——
regere,	*rule, keep right.*	capere,	*take, catch.*
claudere,	*close.*	accipere,	*receive.*
colere,	*cultivate, honour.*	rapere,	*snatch, carry off.*
canere,	*sing.*	corripere,	*seize.*
currere,	*run.*	facere,	*make.*
mittere,	*send.*	interficere,	*make away with, kill.*
alere,	*nourish.*	tribuere,	*impart.*

28. Bibimus aquam. Centurio dūcēbat agmen. Puer discit carmen. Imbrēs pellunt ventī. Sperne invidiam. Imperātōrēs gerunt bella. Mercātōrēs emēbant ebur et aes. Accipiter corripiēbat passerēs et columbās. Vēnātōrēs interficiunt ursum. Parentēs līberīs multa beneficia tribuunt. Vēnātor quaerit lupum. Nauta relinquit uxōrem miseram. Cēdite furōrī aprī. Rēgēs bonī regunt populōs cônsiliō et jûstitiā. Imperātor oppidum obsidiōne claudēbat. Deum colimus precibus. Servī portābant onera. Agricolae caedunt altās arborēs.

29. The scholars were reading various books. The robbers are carrying-off the lambs of the unfortunate farmer. The merchants are buying and selling. We are reading and writing, you are playing and singing. Run, boys, and catch the butterfly. Thou art not learning, thou art playing. The father was buying [his] son a starling. The boy would not answer (= was not answering); he was screaming and singing. The captain was receiving wounds. The robbers give-way to the strong travellers. The herdsmen are driving [off] the wolves. My father sends my uncle a letter. The sons gave their sick mother beautiful flowers. The great seize and devour the small. The herdsman shows the timid traveller the way. The traveller fears the deep river. Food nourishes the body, studies (*studium*) nourish the mind. You were breaking the back (*dorsum*) of the ass by loads. Despise crime.

VIII. Mute Stems. (Third Declension.)

30. Vocabulary.

Stems in a *P* mute. Gr., § 52.

trabs,	*beam.*	ope (*Abl.*),	*by help.*
plēbs,	*commons.*	urbs,	*city.*
stips,	*dole, contribution.*	stirps,	*stock.*
prīnceps,	*chief, prince.*		

Stems in a *K* mute. Gr., § 53.

pāx,	*peace.*	faex,	*dregs.*
rēx,	*king.*	salix,	*willow.*
lēx,	*law.*	jūdex,	*judge.*
rādīx,	*root.*	vindex,	*avenger, advocate.*
cornīx,	*crow.*	paelex (pellex),	*concubine.*
victrīx,	*conqueress.*	artifex,	*artisan.*
imperātrīx,	*empress.*	culex,	*gnat.*
vōx,	*voice.*	cortex,	*bark.*
lūx,	*light.*	frutex,	*shrub.*
nux,	*nut.*	dux,	*leader.*
crux,	*cross.*	conjux,	*spouse (husband, wife).*
fax,	*torch.*	arx,	*citadel.*
grex,	*flock (herd).*	falx,	*sickle.*
nex, necis,	*death, murder.*	faucēs (*pl.*),	*throat.*
precēs (*pl.*),	*prayers.*		

Stems in a *T* mute. Gr., §§ 55–57.

A.

aetās,	*age.*	dēformitās,	*ugliness.*
aestās,	*summer.*	taciturnitās,	*reserve.*
lībertās,	*freedom.*	tranquillitās,	*calmness.*
paupertās,	*poverty.*	sterilitas,	*barrenness.*
pietās,	*piety, dutifulness.*	anas,	*duck.*
societās,	*company.*	vas,	*surety.*
sēdulitās,	*application, industry.*		
calliditās,	*cunning.*		

E.

probitās,	*uprightness.*	quiēs,	*rest.*
auctōritās,	*authority, influence.*	pariēs, *m.*	*wall, party wall.*
calamitās,	*disaster.*	seges,	*crop.*
cīvitās,	*state.*	ariēs,	*ram.*
tempestās,	*storm.*	hērēs,	*heir.*
voluntās,	*will.*	mercēs,	*pay.*
voluptas,	*pleasure.*	pēs, *m.*	*foot.*

I.

līs,	*strife, suit at law.*
lapis, *m*	*stone.*
mīles,	*soldier, warrior.*
comes,	*companion.*
eques,	*horseman.*
pedes,	*foot-soldier.*
hospes,	*guest, host, stranger.*
cêspes,	*turf.*
obses,	*hostage.*

O.

sacerdōs,	*priest.*
nepōs,	*grandson.*
custōs,	*guard, keeper.*

U.

virtūs,	*manliness, worth.*
salūs,	*welfare*
juventūs,	*youth.*
senectūs,	*old age.*
palūs,	*bog, swamp.*
laus,	*praise.*
fraus,	*cheating.*
pecus,	*head of cattle, sheep.*

NT,

frôns,	*brow.*
înfâns,	*baby.*
adolêscêns,	*young man.*
serpêns, *com.*	*snake.*
gêns,	*race, people, tribe.*
mêns,	*mind.*
môns, *m.*	*mountain.*
pôns, *m.*	*bridge.*
fôns, *m.*	*spring.*
dêns, *m.*	*tooth.*
torrêns, *m.*	*torrent.*
rudêns, *m.*	*rope.*

ND.

frôns,	*leafy branch, foliage.*
glâns,	*acorn.*

RT.

pars,	*part.*
ars,	*art.*
mors,	*death.*

LT, RD, CT.

puls, *f.*	*porridge.*
cor, *n.*	*heart.*
nox, *f.*	*night.*
lac, *n.*	*milk.*
caput, *n.*	*head.*

31. Trabēs parietis sunt longae. Colite rēgem et rēgīnam et prīncipēs. Mīlitēs dēfendunt patriam et lībertātem. Sī vīs (*you wish*) pācem, comparā[1] bellum. Nōmina rēgum et prīncipum sunt clāra. Frīgora et tempestātēs nocent gregibus et segetibus. Senectūtem dēbēmus colere. Timēmus arietem ferum. Juventūs praebet multās voluptātēs. Custōdēs probī servābant arcem. Obsidēs miserōs imperātor dīmittēbat.[2] Avus laudat nepōtum pietātem. Jūstō jūdicī hominēs tribuunt laudem et honōrem. Cornīx cornīcī oculōs nōn effodit.[3] Imperātor cingit urbem fossā et aggere. Īnfantēs clāmant. Mūs habēbat acūtōs dentēs. Leo sūmit prīmam partem praedae. Spēs pellit corde dolōrem. [1] *prepare.* [2] *let go.* [3] *digs (picks) out.*

32. Chiefs rule the tribes. God rules the universe. A just king maintains [preserves] peace. The slave is cutting the roots of the high trees. The voices of nightingales are pleasant. The keepers (*pastor*) of the flocks are singing. Obey ye the laws of the state. The horsemen were affording aid and safety to the foot-soldiers. Legions defend cities and citadels. The soldiers were conquering and destroying the strong (*firmus*) cities. Just masters give (*praebēre*) [their] servants pay and rest. We give-way to thy will. The companions of the prince were receiving many wounds. The leaders of the cavalry and infantry [=horsemen and foot-soldiers] were timid.

The grandfather gives to [his] grandson a little ram. Industry and modesty are virtues of youth. He is throwing a stone. Shut the gates of the citadel. The peasants were surrounding the bog, and trying-to-drive-away (G. § 224.) the goddess. The master detects (*dētegere*) the fraud of the ass. The boys drive away the sparrows with stones. The [high] water [pl.] was breaking the beams of the bridge. Trees have a trunk and bark, roots, branches (*rāmus*), foliage, flowers. The sun drives-away the night. The general disbands (*dīmittere*) a great part of [his] soldiers. Good soldiers do not fear wounds and death. The inventors of arts are famous. Babies drink milk. The Furies (*Furiae*) are the avengers (fem. of *ultor*) of shameful-deeds and crimes.

IX. Parisyllabic Vowel Stems. (Third Declension.) Gr., 58.

33. VOCABULARY.

1. NAMES OF PERSONS.		2. NAMES OF ANIMALS.	
hostis,	*enemy.*	**ovis, *f.***	*ewe, sheep.*
cīvis,	*citizen.*	**avis, *f.***	*bird.*
testis,	*witness.*	**apis, *f.***	*bee.*
sodālis,	*(boon-)companion.*	**canis, *m.***	*dog* (canēs, *pl. f., hounds*)
juvenis,	*youth.*	**vulpēs, *f.***	*fox.*
vātēs,	*prophet, prophetess.*	**fēlēs, *f.***	*cat.*

3. Names of Things.

a. FEMININE.		*b.* MASCULINE.	
nāvis,	*ship.*	amnis,	*river.*
pellis,	*skin, fleece.*	axis,	*axle.*
vestis,	*raiment, clothes.*	crīnis,	*hair.*
auris,	*ear.*	fascis,	*fagot.*
clâssis,	*fleet.*	fustis,	*cudgel.*
vallis,	*valley.*	fūnis,	*rope.*
nūbēs,	*cloud.*	fīnis,	*end.*
rūpēs,	*rock.*	ignis,	*fire.*
clādēs,	*defeat, disaster.*	orbis,	*circle.*
sēdēs,	*seat.*	unguis,	*nail, talon, claw.*
famēs,	*hunger.*	ênsis (*poetic*),	*glaive (sword).*
struēs,	*heap.*	vectis,	*lever.*
		vermis,	*worm.*
vīs,	*violence.*	sentis,	*bramble.*
sitis,	*thirst.*	mênsis,	*month.*
tussis,	*cough.*	cassēs, ium,	*toils (hunter's net)*
secūris,	*axe.*	callis,	*footpath.*
febris,	*fever.*	caulis,	*stalk (cabbage).*
puppis,	*stern.*	collis,	*hill.*
turris,	*tower.*	pānis,	*bread.*
		piscis,	*fish.*
		postis,	*door post.*
		follis,	*bellows.*

c. NEUTER.

mare,	*sea.*	animal,	*animal.*
rēte,	*net.*	vectīgal,	*tax.*
bovīle,	*cowhouse.*	calcar,	*spur.*
cubīle,	*couch.*	exemplar.	*pattern.*

d. DISGUISED I-STEMS.

imber,	*m.*	*shower.*	venter,	*m.*	*belly.*
ūter,	*m.*	*skin (bottle).*	linter,	*f.*	*skiff.*

34. Pennae avis sunt rubrae. Ovēs habent pellem albam. Corpus tegimus[1] vestibus. Magnum numerum nāvium vocāmus clâssem. Canis est fēlī inimīcus.[2] Servī secūrī caedunt arborēs. Imperātor magnam clādem accipit. Terror movet juvenēs sēdibus. Hostēs dēlēbant urbem ferrō[3] et ignī. Septimum[4] mênsem vocāmus Jūlium. Vulpēs rapiunt gallīnās. Fīnis corōnat opus. [1] *cover.* [2] *enemy.* [3] *sword.* [4] *seventh.*

35. The sailors are casting off (*solvere*) the rope. The master seizes the long ears of the ass. The kinds of birds are various. High towers surround the city. The herdsmen drive-away the wolf with cudgels. We do not believe an enemy. Princes do not always (*semper*) maintain (*servāre*) the welfare of the citizens. The seas are full of fish [pl.]. The Egyptians (*Aegyptiī*) killed no animal. The virgins loosen the braids (*nōdus*) of their (*suus*) hair. The lictors carried fagots and axes. Many birds have great talons. The whole earth (*orbis terrārum*) obeyed the Roman emperor. The slaves move the beams with levers. The tops (*cacūmen*) of the hills were free from brambles. I see no end of the misfortune (*malum*).

X. Adjectives of the Third Declension.

Adjectives of one termination. Gr., 84–85.

36. Vocabulary.

LIQUID STEMS.

memor,	*mindful.*	vigil,	*watchful, alert.*
pauper,	*poor.*		
cicur,	*tame.*	pūbēs, eris,	*adult, marriageable.*
pār, pāris	*equal.*	vetus, eris,	*old.*

MUTE STEMS

	P.		T.
particeps,	*partaking.*	dīves,	*rich.*
caelebs,	*unmarried.*	dēses,	*slothful.*
inops,	*without means, poor.*	compos,	*possessed (of).*
	K.	prūdēns,	*wise.*
audāx,	*bold.*	impudēns,	*shameless.*
rapāx,	*grasping.*	potēns,	*powerful.*
mendāx,	*lying.*	vehemēns,	*impetuous.*
fallāx,	*treacherous*	ingēns,	*huge, big.*
fēlīx,	*lucky.*	patiēns,	*enduring.*
duplex,	*double.*	petulāns,	*saucy.*
supplex,	*suppliant.*	nocēns,	*hurtful.*
ferōx,	*fierce, uncontrollable.*	innocēns	*innocent, harmless.*
atrōx,	*atrocious.*	absēns,	*absent.*
vēlōx,	*fleet.*	concors,	*harmonious.*
trux,	*wild, savage.*	expers,	*without share of.*

XI. Adjectives of the Third Declension.

Adjectives of two terminations—Vowel stems.

brevis, e,	*short.*	**hostīlis,**	*hostile.*
omnis,	*all, every.*	**mortālis,**	*mortal.*
fortis,	*brave.*	**laudābilis,**	*praiseworthy.*
nōbilis,	*noble.*	**fertilis,**	*productive.*
ūtilis,	*useful.*	**mīrābilis,**	*wonderful.*
inūtilis,	*useless.*	**facilis,**	*easy.*
tristis,	*sad.*	**difficilis,**	*hard to do.*
dulcis,	*sweet.*	**similis,**	*like.*
crūdēlis,	*cruel.*	**dissimilis,**	*unlike.*
fīdēlis,	*faithful.*	**gracilis,**	*slender.*
incolumis,	*unhurt, unscathed.*	**humilis,**	*low, grovelling.*
suāvis,	*sweet.*	**tenuis,**	*thin.*
turpis,	*base, shameful.*	**pinguis,**	*fat.*
levis,	*light, slight.*	**ācer, ācris, ācre,**	*keen, violent, eager.*
gravis,	*heavy, oppressive.*	**celeber, bris, bre,**	*celebrated, populous.*
commūnis,	*common.*	**salūber, bris, bre,**	*healthy, wholesome.*
īnsignis,	*distinguished.*	**celer, celeris, celere,**	*swift.*

39. Servī dominī pauperis sunt fidēlēs. Pauperum cenae[1] nōn sunt grātae dīvitibus. Memorēs estōte officiōrum vestrōrum. Spernimus pānem veterem, dīligimus[2] vīnum vetus. Participēs estis omnium perīculōrum et praemiōrum. Dominus dīligentī famulō duplicem mercēdem tribuit. Nēmo crēdit[3] juvenī mendācī. Suāvēs odōrēs[4] flōrum placent hospitibus. Praecepta magistrī puerō dīligentī[5] sunt ūtilia. Vēnātor interficit cervum vēlōcem sagittā. Luxuria omnī aetātī turpis est. Mīlitēs turpī fugā perdunt[6] glōriam. [1] *dinners.* [2] *love.* [3] *believes.* [4] *odors.* [5] *diligent.* [6] *lose.*

40. The shepherds' dogs are watchful. The virtues of men are not equal, but (*sed*) the rights of the citizens ought to be equal. The brave Germans used-to-conquer the old soldiers of the Romans. The peasants had old wine. The pains of my wounds were keen. The life of the rich has many pleasures. Avoid unwholesome (*nocēns*) food. Laws are useful to the citizens. Many animals are useful to men. The wound of the youth is slight.

The time of our life is short. Sleep is like [to] death. Every beginning is difficult. The boy's anger is violent. The boy's hate is violent. The boy's temper (*animus*) is violent. Thou hast keen eyes and a keen intellect. The eager dogs seize the fleet doe. All seas have fish [pl.]. Send me all the works of the celebrated poets. The authors of laws are not always (*semper*) men of foresight and wisdom—(*adjectives*).

XII. Comparison of Adjectives, G. 86.

41. VOCABULARY:

POSITIVE.	COMPARATIVE.	SUPERLATIVE.
longus,	long-ior, ius,	long-issimus, a, um.
piger,	pigr-ior, ius,	piger-rimus.
miser,	miser-ior, ius,	miser-rimus.
vetus,		veter-rimus.
audāx,	audāc-ior, ius,	audāc-issimus.
fēlix,	fēlic-ior, ius,	fēlic-issimus.
vehemēns,	vehement-ior, ius,	vehement-issimus.
brevis,	brev-ior, ius,	brev-issimus.
ācer,	ācr-ior, ius,	ācer-rimus.
celer,	celer-ior, ius,	celer-rimus.
facilis,	facil-ior, ius,	facil-limus.
benevolus, *kindly*,	benevolent-ior, ius,	benevolent-issimus.
idōneus, *fit, adapted*,	magis idōneus,	maximē idōneus.
	IRREGULAR COMPARISON.	
bonus,	melior, melius,	optimus.
malus,	pejor, pejus,	pessimus.
magnus,	mājor, mājus,	maximus.
parvus,	minor, minus,	minimus.
multus,	plūs,	plūrimus.
nēquam, *worthless*,	nēquior, nēquius,	nēquissimus.

RULES OF SYNTAX:

Comparison is made by the particle QUAM, *than*.

Adjectives of likeness take the Dative; SIMILIS and DISSIMILIS have also the Genitive.

42. Negōtium est longius quam putābam. Māter tua est beātissima omnium mulierum: habet enim (Synt., § 500) līberōs sānissimōs et probissimōs. Oculōrum sēnsus est ācerrimus. Puellae sunt dīligentiōrēs quam puerī. Sōcratēs erat sapientissimus[1] omnium Graecōrum. Praemium dulcius est quam labor. Tigrēs[2] sunt crūdēlissimī. Rhēnus[3] est flūmen lātissimum et altissimum.[4] [1] *wise.* [2] *tiger.* [3] *Rhine.* [4] *deep.*

43. The liar is the most unprincipled (*improbus*) of all men. The names of great poets are more celebrated than the names of kings. My business is more burdensome than thine. The horsemen were shrewder and braver than the foot-soldiers. The monkey is an animal very like man. I am holding the shorter rope: do you hold the longer rope. Envy is a very disgraceful fault. Faithful friends delivered the heedless youth from the gravest danger. Of all pains tooth-ache (*dolor dentium*) is the most acute (*ācer*). Sparrows are larger than gnats; hawks are swifter than sparrows; the eagle is the swiftest of all birds. Man is wiser than the wisest animals. Augustus is more like his father than his mother. Thy brother is very like thee. The inhabitants of the village were very wretched. Thou art wont to write very short letters. Thou hast given (*parāre*) thy parents great joy.

XIII. Fourth Declension. Gr., 67.

44. Vocabulary:

sēnsus,	*sense.*	reditus,	*return.*
cantus,	*song.*	exitus,	*issue.*
impetus,	*attack, charge.*	nūtus,	*beck, nod, wink.*
magistrātus,	*magistracy, civil authorities.*	vultus,	*countenance.*
metus,	*fear.*	ūsus,	*use, practice.*
mōtus,	*movement, commotion.*	fremitus,	*roar.*
adventus,	*arrival.*	aspectus,	*aspect.*
cāsus,	*fall, chance.*	portus,	*harbor.*
currus,	*chariot.*	ornātus,	*ornament, attire.*
cursus,	*course.*	passus,	*step, pace.*
morsus,	*bite (teeth).*	arcus,	*bow.*
exercitus,	*army.*	quercus,	*oak.*
equitātus,	*cavalry.*	lacus,	*lake*

REMARKS.

artus, *joint.*	partus, *birth.*	sinus, *fold, bosom.*

EXCEPTIONS.

īdūs, -uum, *f.*	*15th (13th) day of the month.*	acus, *f.*	*needle.*
tribus, *f.*	*tribe, ward.*	manus, *f.*	*hand.*
porticus, *f.*	*piazza, porch.*	domus, *f.*	*house.*

45. Cynaegīrus Athēniênsis nāvem Persārum morsū tenēbat. Senātūs cônsultum[1] terrēbat improbōs cīvēs. Luscinia nōs dēlectat suāvī cantū. Hostis habet magnōs exercitūs. Persae bella gerēbant ingentibus exercitibus. Imperātor superābat hostēs audācī impetū. Metus nocet exercituī. Lavā[2] manūs tuās. Omnium sênsuum sēdēs est caput. [1] *decree.* [2] *wash.*

The king has a brave army. The leaders of our army are brave and wise. The movements of the hands are various and wonderful. The elephants are frightening the cavalry. The enemy is closing the harbors with a fleet. The victory of the army frees [our] country from [its] fear. A white dress was the attire of the authorities. The messenger delivers (*reddere*) the letter to the magistracy. We write with the hand. The soldiers were making a very-bold attack. Frogs live in swamps and lakes. The roots of literature (*literae*) are bitter, the fruits sweet.

XIV. Fifth Declension.

46. VOCABULARY:

aciēs,	*line of battle.*	fidēs, fidĕī,	*faithfulness, confidence.*
faciēs,	*face.*	spēs,	*hope.*
speciēs,	*appearance.*	rēs,	*thing.*
perniciēs,	*ruin.*	rēs pûblica,	*commonwealth.*
plānitiēs,	*level, flat.*	rēs familiāris,	*estate, property.*

47. Deus est dominus omnium rērum. Hieme diēs sunt breviōrēs quam noctēs. Pater mortis memor trādit[1] rem familiārem fīliō dīligentī. Crêbrī[2] mōtūs rēbus pûblicīs nōn sunt ūtilēs. Mendācēs hominēs saepe fallunt[3] nōs vēritatis speciē. Occāsus[4] sōlis fīnem facet diēī. [1] *hands over.* [2] *frequent.* [3] *deceive.* [4] *setting.*

48. You are disappointing my hope. The soldiers of the right line of battle were making the first attack. All the hopes of the poor mother were vain (*vānus*). The welfare of the state is dear to all citizens. The eyes are the noblest part of the human face. Thou showest the appearance of faithfulness, but thou hast no faithfulness. We learn many things by practice. Preserve [your] property! Examples of true faithfulness are rare.

XV. Fourth Conjugation. Gr., 135

(Only Infin., Indic., Pres., and Imperf., Imperat. Active, 2 Pers. s. and pl.)

49. Vocabulary:

pūnīre,	*punish.*	lēnīre,	*soften, mitigate.*
venīre,	*come.*	scīre,	*know.*
invenīre,	*find.*	nēscīre,	*not know.*
pervenīre,	*arrive.*	sentīre,	*feel, perceive.*
dormīre,	*sleep.*	vincīre,	*bind.*
fīnīre,	*finish.*	reperīre,	*find, discover.*
servīre,	*be a slave, have regard to, serve.*	sitīre,	*thirst.*
mūnīre,	*fortify.*	saevīre,	*rage.*
obēdīre,	*be obedient.*	condīre,	*spice, preserve, embalm.*
impedīre,	*hinder.*	ērudīre,	*instruct.*
custōdīre,	*guard.*		

50. Adventus tuus fīnit labōrēs nôstrōs. Causās multārum rērum nêscīmus. Obēdīte parentibus et praeceptōribus! Sērō[1] venītis in scholam. Servī valētūdinī tuae! Nêsciēbam voluntātem tuam. Gaudia lēniunt dolōrēs vehementissimōs. [1] *late.*

51. Animals feel pain. Be obedient to the authorities. We are slaves to a fierce master. The soldiers are conquering and binding the highwaymen. The soldiers were guarding the gates. You do not know the charming story. We perceive (*percipio*) earthly things with the senses; we see, we hear, we taste (*gustāre*), we smell (*olfacere*), we touch (*tangere*).

PART II.

XVI. Remarks on the First and Second Declensions. Gr., §§ 27–35.

52. The parents have given [their] sons and [their] daughters new clothes. Unhappy slave! thou art bearing a heavy burden. Cruel boy! you will kill the little gnat. Cornelius! call Peter (*Petrus*). O Gâjus Jūlius Cæsar, thou hast saved the state, but thou hast destroyed freedom. My son, fear the danger of pleasures. The ancient nations used to give presents to the gods and goddesses.

53. No man's soul is free from care. Augustus was emperor of the whole world. Thy shameful-deed is ruinous (*perniciōsus*) to the whole country. To which boy [of the two] will you give the book? To neither. The advantages of another excite (*commovēre*) the envy of the avaricious man. The bravery of one soldier saved the whole army. Both consuls lead the army out of (ex *with abl.*) the camp. The soldiers of both fought bravely.

REMARK.—*Both* (viewed separately) = either, UTERQUE. *Both* (together) = AMBO.

XVII. Conjugation of ESSE. Gr., § 112. First Conjugation. Gr., 119–122.

SYNTAX.—Forms of the Subject, § 194–5;
Forms of the Predicate, § 192;
Concord of the Predicate, § 202;
The direct object, § 327.
The indirect object, §§ 343, 344.
The Passive, Ablative of the Agent, Ablative of the Instrument, } § 205.

53. VOCABULARY:

vocāre,	*call.*	peccāre,	*sin.*
mūtāre,	*change.*	habitāre,	*dwell, inhabit.*
postulāre,	*demand.*	volāre,	*fly.*
invītāre,	*invite.*	intrāre,	*enter.*
ēducāre,	*educate*	natāre,	*swim.*
vulnerāre,	*wound.*	nāvigāre,	*sail.*
aedificāre,	*build.*	migrāre,	*migrate.*

54. Magister laudat discipulum.
Discipulus laudātur ā magistrō.

Magistrī laudant discipulum.
Discipulus laudātur ā magistrīs.

Corōna ornat puellam.
Puella ornātur corōnā.

Corōnae ornant puellās.
Puellae ornantur corōnīs.

Rêx parat bellum.
Bellum parātur ā rēge.

Rēgēs parant bella.
Bella parantur ā rēgibus.

Put the above sentences into all the tenses of the Passive. The tenses of the Passive must be fully illustrated by the teacher, as the temporal relations are not clearly marked in English. Distinguish between: puella ornātur, *the girl is adorned* (for instance *daily*), and: puella ornāta est, *the girl is adorned* (her adornment is completed). Parāmur, *we are getting ready*: Parātī sumus, *we are ready*: Parābāmur, *we were getting ready*: Parātī erāmus, *we were ready.*

Parentēs ēducanto līberōs.

Līberī ēducantor ā parentibus.

55. The hunter killed the fleet deer. The soldiers have set the captive (*captus*) virgins free. The great-hearted lion is set free by the little mouse. Flowers and wreaths were adorning the gate of the city. The vigorous (*ācer*) attack of the enemy [*pl.*] had put to flight our legions; but (*sed*) the arrival of the cavalry (*eques*) saved the army. The master will scold the lazy slaves. Call the faithful[1] servants. If (*sī*) thou shalt have observed [his] precepts, the teacher will praise thy industry. The grandfather has given [his] grandson a book. [1] *fidēlis.*

56. The scholars are questioned by the teacher. The books of the sick poet were carried off by [his] enemies (*inimīcus*). The sea is swallowing up the ship. The sea has swallowed up the ship. The ship is swallowed up by the sea. By the arrival of [thy] friend thou art delivered from the punishment. We were saved by the bravery of [our] companions. All danger will be overcome by exertions. The letters will be given to the teacher by the messenger. The city will be carried (*expugnāre*) by the enemy. The city is carried. The city is, has been, carried by the enemy. The belly of the elephant is pierced (*perforāre*). The belly of the elephant has been pierced by the horn of the rhinoceros (Gen. *rhīnocerōtis*). The teacher will blame the scholar. We will save [our] sister. Teachers will praise industrious scholars. We are saved. The scholars are praised. Thou wilt kill the lion. Thou wilt be killed by the lion. The thieves are put to flight by the keepers.

57. The general will carry the city. The city will be carried by the general. We shall invite all our friends. All our friends will be invited. You have changed your plan. I will invite your brother, but you [*sing.*] will not be invited. I am educated by my uncle. The hunter had wounded the bird, but it flew away (*āvolāre*). The bird is wounded, but it will fly away.

58. Thou art called. The enemy had built a large tower and besieged the city, but the brave citizens put to flight (*Perf.*) the army of the enemy [*pl.*] You will be blamed by [your] parents. You were carried. You are adorned with flowers, for you overcome all danger by your bravery. Servants, cleanse (*purgāre*) the stalls! Judges must [*Imperat.*] always be just. Let men be always mindful of death. You must be attentive[1] and obey your teacher. The clothes shall be changed. Let good morals be maintained. Thou shalt love father and mother.[1] *attentus.*

XVIII. Optative Subjunctive.—WISHES.—Syntax, 253.

59.

DECISION IN SUSPENSE.	DECISION ADVERSE.
(Utinam) magister discipulōs laudet,	Utinam magister discipulōs laudāret,
May the teacher praise the scholars.	*Would that the teacher praised the scholars.*
(Utinam) nē discipulōs vituperet,	Utinam magister discipulōs laudāvisset
May he not chide the scholars.	*Would that the teacher had praised the scholars.*

60. May the good old man tell [us] a story! Would that I had changed [my] dress (*vestītus*)! May the brave soldier put to flight the army of the enemy! Would that he invited (*vocāre*) the good boy, and not (*nōn*) the lazy girl! May the enemy [*pl.*] not carry the city! Would that we had preserved [our] liberty! Would that the master were setting up the statue (*signum*) in (in *with abl.*) our garden! Would that the wolves were not devouring the timid lambs! Would that you had overcome the boastful (*glōriōsus*) soldier.

61. Rules of Syntax:

1. Ut, that, in order that—**Nē,** in order that not, lest, **take the Present Subjunctive after the Present or Future; the Imperfect Subjunctive after the Imperfect, Pluperfect, or (Historical) Perfect. In English the translation is often** to, **with the Infinitive.**

2. Quum, when, as, since **(in past relations) takes the Imperfect and the Pluperfect Subjunctive.**

3. Si, if, **is used with the Imperfect Subjunctive when the supposed case** is **not so.**

Si, if, **is used with the Pluperfect Subjunctive when the supposed case** was **not so.**

62. Discipulī ōrant magistrum, ut historiam nārret.
Discipulī ōrābant (ōrāvērunt) magistrum, ut historiam nārrāret.

Amīcus rogat (*asks*) puerum, nē rānam necet.
Amīcus rogābat (rogāvit) puerum, nē rānam necāret.
Quum magister historiam nārrāret, discipulī attentī erant.
Quum magister historiam nārrāvisset, discipulī clāmāvērunt.

Discipulī ōrant magistrum, ut poenā līberentur.
Discipulī ōrābant magistrum, ut poenā līberārentur.

Puerī dīligentēs sunt, nē ā magistro vituperentur.
Puerī dīligentēs erant (fuērunt), nē ā magistro vituperārentur.

Quum mulierēs vulnerārentur, clāmābant.
Quum mulierēs vulnerātae essent, clāmāvērunt.

Sī mē rogārēs, veniam tibi dārem.
Sī mē rogāvissēs, veniam tibi dedissem.

(Learn the declension of ego and tū.)

63. The teacher demands that we be industrious. The teacher demanded that we should be industrious. We begged the hunter to kill the bears. We begged the hunter not to kill the cat. The wayfarers called the herdsmen to show the way. Work that ye may be happy and contented. Fight bravely (*fortiter*) to save [your] country. We will call the servant to carry the burden. The boys had carried the bundles (*fasciculus*) in order to relieve the girls from the burden. The herdsmen killed the wolves lest they should devour the lambs. When the sparrow had devoured the gnat, the hawk tore-in-pieces the sparrow. When the vulture was-tearing-in-pieces the hawk, the hunter killed the vulture. As you had begged me, I told you the story. The scholar exerts himself (*dare operam*) to be praised. The good scholars begged to be questioned. We avoid faults lest we be blamed. The general demanded that rewards should be given to the soldiers. The army fought bravely, but when the general was [= had been] wounded, the soldiers were put to flight. If you were industrious, you would be praised. If you had called the physician, you would have been delivered from the disease.

XIX. Second Conjugation. Gr., 123–130.

64. VOCABULARY:

impleo, ēre, ēvī, ētum,	*fill.*
habeo, ēre, uī, ĭtum,	*have.*
adhibēre,	*apply, use.*
prohibēre,	*hinder.*
praebēre,	*afford, grant.*
dēbēre,	*owe.*
terrēre,	*frighten.*
exercēre,	*practise.*
nocēre,	*hurt.*
pārēre,	*obey.*
appārēre,	*appear.*
placēre,	*please.*
displicēre,	*displease.*
jacēre,	*lie.*
tacēre,	*be silent.*
valēre,	*be well.*

NO SUPINE.

timēre,	*fear.*
ēminēre,	*stand out.*
latēre,	*lie hid.*
silēre,	*be still.*
flōrēre,	*flourish.*
doceo, ēre, uī, doctum,	*teach.*
teneo, ēre, uī (ntum),	*hold, keep.*

retineo, ēre, uī, retentum,	*retain, keep back*
cēnseo, ēre, uī, cēnsum,	*appraise, think.*

---

misceo, ēre, miscuī, mixtum,	*mix.*
torreo, ēre, torruī, tostum,	*parch, toast, dry.*

WITH CHANGE OF CONJUGATION.

video, ēre, vīdī, vīsum,	*see.*
respondeo, ēre, dī, sum,	*answer.*
sĕdeo, ēre, sēdī, sessum,	*sit.*
pendeo, ēre, pependī, ——	*hang.*
rīdeo, ēre, rīsī, rīsum,	*laugh.*
suādeo, ēre, suāsī, suāsum,	*persuade, advise.*
mŏveo, ēre, mōvī, mōtum,	*move.*
voveo, ēre, vōvī, vōtum,	*vow.*
caveo, ēre, cāvī, cautum,	*beware.*
augeo, ēre, auxī, auctum,	*increase* (trans.)
măneo, ēre, mānsī, mānsum,	*remain.*
jubeo, ēre, jussī, jussum,	*order, bid.*

65. The violent wind moves the leaves of the trees. The slaves will move the great beam with levers. You see the constellations of heaven. Fright hurts the body. The long wars had hurt the state. Parents will grant [their] children many pleasures. The rich father-in-law will give the poor son-in-law a field. The coldness of the evening and of the night has hurt the tender plants. The cities are destroyed. The cities have been destroyed by the enemy [*plur.*].

The thick beam was moved by the slaves with levers. The book is held by the boy with the hand. Ye shall be silent. I will warn the boy. I am warned. I must (*dēbeo*) warn lazy scholars. Fables are incredible, and-yet' (*tamen*) they excite the feelings of men. All ancient nations once obeyed kings. Let the citizens obey the magistrates.

66. Magister monet discipulōs, ut praecepta memoriā (*in mind*) teneant.
Magister monēbat (monuit) discipulōs, ut praecepta tenērent.

Suādeo tibi, nē noceās valētūdinī tuae.
Saepe tibi suādēbam, nē valētūdinī tuae nocērēs

Quum puerum monērem, pārēbat.
Quum puerum monuissem, pāruit.

Fūgimus, nē teneāmur.
Fugiebāmus, nē tenērēmur.

Quum urbs dēlērētur, mātrēs īnfantēs servābant.
Quum mūrus urbis dēlētus esset, cīvēs obsidēs dedērunt.

67. Children ought to be good that they may please their parents. Father is calling us to see the elephant. I advise thee not to frighten the bull. I advised thee not to frighten the bull. The strong farmers were holding the mad (*ferus*) bull that he might not destroy the garden. Drive away the sparrows that they may not hurt the crops. When our father appeared, the naughty boys feared punishment. Our mother (*quum, with Subj.*) having furnished us with (*praebēre, with Dat.*) many apples, we filled our bags (*pēra*). When you were holding me, my companions tried-to-set me free (224). When the armies were [= had been] overcome, the citizens begged the conqueror that [their] city might not be destroyed. Obey the precepts of your parents, that ye may not be taught by loss.

XX. Rules of Gender of the Stems in l, n, r, and s, with the Exceptions. Gr., §§ 40–49.

APPOSITION.—SYNTAX, § 318.

68. *l.* The sun is obscured (*obscūrāre*) by clouds. The moon is obscured by the shadow of the earth. Bees prepare sweet honey. The sun, the regulator of the other (*cēterī*) lights, occupies (*obtineo*) the centre (*centrum*) of the universe. To the oldest nations the moon was the regulator of the year and of the months.

(*Regulator*, moderātor, moderātrīx.)

69. *n.* I am entertained by your conversation. The boldest soldiers swam across (*trānāre*) the broad river. The vain actor had a false suspicion. Many great cities have an humble [= small] origin. Butterflies are adorned with many colors. Many animals devour raw (*crūdus*) flesh; human-beings eat cooked (*coctus*) or dried meat. The order of the words is

changed The borders of the lakes are sandy (*arēnōsus*). The heedless captain gave the boy a sharp dagger. Birds have very warm blood. The little likeness of the celebrated poet is very dear to me. A fixed (*certus*) order is necessary. Thy opinion we do not approve.

70. *r.* We see the long line of wild geese. The ancient nations used to burn (*cremāre*) the dead-bodies of men. We had great and constant (*assiduus*) rains. The spring was short. Thou wilt procure for thyself great honor by great toil. Lightnings (*fulmen*) strike[1] the high tree. The whole surface-of-the-sea is disturbed by winds. Parian (*Parius*) marble was the best. Lightnings (*fulgur*) purify the air. The lion surpasses most animals by [his] strength. The branching (*rāmōsus*) oaks of the royal garden please us greatly (*valdē*). Tall cedars (*cedrus*) adorn Mount Lebanon (*Libănus*). [1] *feriunt.*

71. *s.* The good morals of the scholars delight [their] teachers. Much dust has been raised (*moveo*) by the violent wind. Cold is not disagreeable to a sound body. Angry-passion (*īrācundia*) has been the cause of many crimes. Modesty is the greatest ornament of youth. I will give you a great pledge. The frog has long and soft legs.

XXI. Prepositions with the Accusative. (Partial view.)

Learn the whole list. Syntax, § 417.

72. Erat fluvius ante urbem, palūs post urbem.
Pugnāvimus ante lūcem, superāvimus hostēs post merīdiem.
Avēs volant ad silvam. Dūcimus amīcum ad patrem.
Pugnāvimus ad (usque ad) vesperum. Stābam ad portam.
Coenāvī apud amīcum. Inter Alpēs et Āpennīnōs est Padus (*Po*).
Puer currit per hortum. Servāmus pōma (*fruit*) per hiemem.
Germānī pugnāvērunt contrā Rōmānōs.
Superāvistis hostēs contrā omnium opīniōnem.

73. The soldiers were standing before the bridge. The general posted (*collocāre*) the line of battle behind the river. Storks migrate before winter to the south (*merīdiēs*). The maid-servant is calling the children to dinner. I shall stay with my parents. Concord is preserved among friends. The sailors sail through the vast sea. You are killing the bees and the ants against my will. Thou art set free contrary to my expectation. Against the power of death there is no remedy (*remedium*).

XXII. Prepositions with the Ablative. § 418. (Partial view.)

74. Ambulāmus[1] ab urbe ad montēs. Ambulāvimus ab ortū sōlis ad occāsum. Laudāris ā patre. Puerī ē scholā currunt in viam. Puerī lūdunt in viā. Eques dēcidit[2] ex equō. Fontēs fluunt dē montibus. Ōrātor dīcit de sceleribus latrōnis. Aenēās ex patriā migrāvit cum patre et fīliō. Sine pennīs nōn volābis.

[1] *walk.* [2] *falls.*

REM.—CUM, *in company with*; APUD, *at the house, apartment of*; *within, in the eyes of.*

75. The hens have been killed by the fox. The hunter was killed by the boar. The imprudent sailors were sailing out of the harbor. Sweat (*sūdor*) was flowing (*fluere*) from the body. He draws (*trahere*) the ring (*ānulus*) from [his] finger (*digitus*). I will walk with my brother through the wood. We will obey without fear. We are walking into the garden. We are walking in the garden. Rivers flow into the sea. Fish live (*vīvere*) in the sea.

XXIII. Time, when (§ 392). Time, how long (§ 387).

76. Hieme (*winter*) quiēscit terra. Scholae initium est hōrā octāvā (*eighth*). Dormīmus septem (*seven*) hōrās (per septem hōrās).

77. In the autumn (*autumnus*) the fruits of the trees are gathered; at that season of the year the leaves fall from the trees. In former (*superior*) times you used-to-send letters to me. Augustus died (*mortuus est*) in the fourteenth year after the-birth-of-Christ (= *Christum nātum*). Troy was besieged by the Greeks ten years. The hunter remained the whole night [long] in the woods.

XXIV. Third Conjugation. Gr., 157–176.

78. VOCABULARY.

I. Stems in a *P* mute.

1. *With a short stem-syllable.* Gr., 157–8.

capio,	cap-ere,	cēp-ī,	cap-tum,	*to take, catch.*
accipio,	accipere,	accepī,	accep-tum,	*to receive.*
rumpo (rup),	rump-ere,	rūp-ī,	rup-tum,	*to break, burst*

2. *With a long stem-syllable.*

rēpo,	rēp-ere,	rêp-sī,	rêp-tum,	*creep.*
carpo,	carp-ere,	carp-sī,	carp-tum,	*to pluck.*
scrībo,	scrīb-ere,	scrīp-si,	scrīp-tum,	*to write*

II. Stems in a *K* mute.

1. *With a short stem-syllable.* Gr., 159.

lego,	leg-ere,	lēg-ī,	lec-tum,	*to read.*
colligo,	collig-ere,	collēgī,	collec-tum,	*to gather.*
ago,	ag-ere,	ēg-ī,	ac-tum,	*to do, act, drive, lead*
redigo,	redig-ere,	redēgī,	redactum,	*to bring back, reduce.*
cōgo (co + ago)	cōg-ere,	coēgī,	coactum,	*to compel.*
fugio,	fug-ere,	fūg-ī,	fug-i-tum,	*to flee.*
facio,	fac-ere,	fec-ī,	fac-tum,	*to make.*
perficio,	perfic-ere,	perfēcī,	perfectum,	*to achieve, finish.*
interficio,	interfic-ere,	interfēcī,	interfectum,	*to make away with, kill*
patefacio,	patefac-ere,	patefēcī,	patefactum,	*to disclose, reveal.*
jacio,	jac-ere,	jēcī,	jactum,	*to throw.*
injicio,	injic-ere,	injēcī,	injectum,	*to throw in.*
vinco (vīc),	vinc-ere,	vīc-ī,	vic-tum,	*to conquer.*
frango (frăg)	frang-ere,	frēg-ī,	frac-tum,	*to break.*
relinquo,	relinqu-ere,	relīqu-ī,	relic-tum,	*to leave.*

2. *With a long stem-syllable.* Gr., 160.

dīco,	dic-ere,	dīxī,	dic-tum,	*to say.*
dūco,	dūc-ere,	dūxī,	duc-tum,	*to lead.*
cōnflīgo,	cōnflīg-ere,	cōnflīxī,	cōnflīc-tum,	*to strike together, clash.*
fīgo,	fīg-ere,	fīxi,	fīxum,	*to fix, fasten.*
jungo,	jung-ere,	junxī,	junc-tum,	*to join.*
cingo,	cing-ere,	cinxī,	cinc-tum,	*to gird, surround.*
tingo (tinguo),	ting-ere,	tinxī,	tinc-tum,	*to dip, dye.*

exstinguo,	exstingu-ere,	exstinxī,	exstinc-tum,	*to extinguish*
pingo,	ping-ere,	pinxī,	pic-tum,	*to paint.*
mergo,	merg-ere,	mersī,	mer-sum,	*to plunge.*
flecto,	flect-ere,	flexī,	flexum,	*to bend.*
necto,	nect-ere,	nexī (nexuī),	nexum,	*to knot, tie.*

EXCEPTIONS. Gr., 165.

rego,	reg-ere,	rexī,	rec-tum,	*to keep right*
dīrigo,	dīrig-ere,	dīrexī,	dīrec-tum,	*to direct.*
surgo,	surg-ere,	surrexī,	surrec-tum,	*to rise.*
tego,	teg-ere,	texī,	tec-tum,	*to cover.*
coquo,	coqu-ere,	coxī,	coc-tum,	*to cook.*
cônspicio,	cônspic-ere,	cônspexī,	cônspec-tum,	*to behold.*
dīligo,	dīlig-ere,	dīlexī,	dīlec-tum,	*to love.*
intelligo,	intellig-ere,	intellexī,	intellec-tum,	*to understand*
negligo,	neglig-ere,	neglexī,	neglec-tum,	*to neglect.*

III. Stems in a *T* mute. Gr., 164–168.

1. *With a short stem-syllable and* nd *stems.*

edo,	ed-ere,	ēd-ī,	ē-sum,	*to eat.*
fodio,	fod-ere,	fōd-ī,	fos-sum,	*to dig.*
dēfendo,	dēfend-ere,	dēfend-ī,	defên-sum,	*to strike off.*
ascendo,	ascend-ere,	ascend-ī,	ascên-sum,	*to mount.*
reprehendo,	reprehend-ere,	reprehend-ī,	reprehên-sum,	*to chide.*
comprehendo,	comprehend-ere,	comprehend-ī,	comprehên-sum,	*to arrest.*

2. *With a long stem-syllable.*

lūdo,	lūd-ere,	lū-sī,	lū-sum,	*to play.*
rōdo,	rōd-ere,	rō-sī,	rō-sum,	*to gnaw.*
claudo,	claud-ere,	clau-sī,	clau-sum,	*to shut.*
exclūdo,	exclūd-ere,	exclū-sī,	exclū-sum,	*to shut out.*
invādo,	invād-ere,	invā-sī,	invā-sum,	*to invade.*
mitto,	mitt-ere,	mī-sī,	misŝum,	*to send.*
dīmitto,	dīmittere,	dīmīsī,	dīmissum,	*to dismiss.*
permitto,	permittere,	permīsī,	permissum,	*to allow.*
cēdo,	cēd-ere,	cês-sī,	cêssum,	*to give way*

EXCEPTIONS.

dīvīdo,	dīvid-ere,	dīvī-sī,	dīvī-sum,	*to divide.*
percutio,	percut-ere,	percus-sī,	percussum,	*to smite.*
cônsīdo,	cônsīd-ere,	consēdī,	consêssum,	*to settle down*
verto,	vert-ere,	vert-ī,	versum,	*to turn.*

IV. Stems in Liquids. Gr., 169.

emo,	em-ere,	ēm-ī,	em(p)-tum,	*to buy.*
interimo,	interimere,	interēmī,	interem(p)tum,	*to kill.*
sūmo,	sūm-ere,	sūm(p)-sī,	sūm(p)-tum,	*to take.*
vello,	vell-ere,	vell-ī, vulsī,	vulsum,	*to pluck.*

V. Stems in *U*.

tribuo,	tribu-ere,	tribu-ī,	tribū-tum,	*to allot.*
induo,	indu-ere,	indu-ī,	indū-tum,	*to put on.*
statuo,	statu-ere,	statu-ī,	statū-tum,	*to settle.*
cônstituo,	cônstitu-ere,	cônstitu-ī,	cônstitū-tum,	*to establish.*
dīruo,	dīru-ere,	dīru-ī,	dīrū-tum,	*to tear down.*
metuo,	metu-ere,	metu-ī,	——	*to fear.*
solvo,	solv-ere,	solv-ī,	solū-tum,	*to loosen.*

VI. Reduplicated forms.

cado,	cad-ere,	cecĭd-ī,	cāsum,	*to fall.*
occido,	occidere,	occĭdī,	occā-sum,	" "
caedo,	caed-ere,	cecīd-ī,	cae-sum,	*to fell.*
occīdo,	occīdere,	occīdī,	occī-sum,	*to kill.*
cano,	can-ere,	cecin-ī,	can-tum,	*to sing.*
pello,	pell-ere,	pepul-ī,	pul-sum,	*to drive.*
curro,	curr-ere,	cucurr-ī,	cur-sum,	*to run.*
disco,	disc-ere,	didic-ī,	——	*to learn.*
tango,	tang-ere,	tetig-ī,	tac-tum,	*to touch.*
attingo,	attingere,	attigī,	attactum,	*to attain.*
fallo,	fall-ere,	fefell-ī,	fal-sum,	*to cheat.*
pendo,	pend-ere,	pepend-ī,	pên-sum,	*to hang.*
pario,	par-ere,	peper-ī,	par-tum,	*to bring forth*
parco,	parc-ere,	peperc-ī,	par-sum,	*to spare.*
bibo,	bib-ere,	bibī,	(bib-i-tum),	*to drink.*
do,	dăre,	dedī,	dătum,	*to give.*
reddo,	reddere,	reddidī,	reddĭtum,	*to give back.*
trādo,	trādere,	trādidī,	trāditum,	*to hand over*
vêndo,	vêndere,	vêndidī,	vênditum,	*to sell.*
prōdo,	prōdere,	prōdidī,	prōditum,	*to betray.*
addo,	addere,	addidī,	additum,	*to add.*
condo,	condere	condidī,	conditum,	*to found.*
perdo,	perdere,	perdidī,	perditum,	*to ruin.*
crēdo,	crēdere,	crēdidī,	crēditum,	*to believe*
sto,	stāre,	stetī,	stătum,	*to stand.*
resisto,	resistere,	restitī,	restĭtum,	*to resist.*

VII. Change of Conjugation.

veto,	vetā-re,	vet-uī,	vetitum,	*to forbid.*
alo,	al-ere,	al-uī,	altum,	*to nourish, foster*
colo,	col-ere,	col-ui,	cultum,	*to cultivate, honor*
rapio,	rap-ere,	rap-uī,	rap-tum,	*to carry off.*
corripio,	corripere,	corripuī,	correp-tum,	*to seize.*
fremo,	frem-ere,	frem-uī,	fremītum,	*to roar, growl.*
recumbo,	recumb-ere,	recub-uī,	recub-itum,	*to recline.*
peto,	pet-ere,	pet-īvī,	petī-tum,	*to seek.*
cupio,	cup-ere,	cupī-vī,	cupī-tum,	*to desire.*
quaero,	quaer-ere,	quaesī-vī,	quaesī-tum,	*to seek.*
requīro,	requīrere,	requīsīvī,	requīsī-tum,	" "

VIII. Various Peculiarities.

pōno,	pōnere,	posuī,	positum,	*to place.*
sero,	serere,	sēvī,	sătum,	*to sow.*
dēcerno,	dēcernere,	dēcrēvī,	dēcrētum,	*to determine.*
sperno,	spernere,	sprēvī,	sprētum,	*to despise.*
crēsco,	crēscere,	crēvī,	crētum,	*to grow.*
quiēsco,	quiēscere,	quiēvī,	quiētum,	*to rest.*
cognōsco,	cognōscere,	cognōvī,	cognitum,	*to find out.*
gero,	gerere,	gessī,	gestum,	*to carry on.*
ūro,	ūrere,	ūssī,	ūstum,	*to burn.*
premo,	premere,	pressī,	pressum,	*to press.*
opprimo,	opprimere,	oppressī,	oppressum,	*to oppress*
fero,	ferre,	tulī,	lātum,	*to bear.*
tollo,	tollere,	sustulī,	sublātum,	*to lift, raise.*

79. A. 1. Folia dē arboribus cadunt in terram. Passerēs corripiunt parvōs culicēs. Fūrēs metuunt canēs. Viātōrēs dulcēs ūvās[1] ab agricolīs accipiēbant. Puerī discēbant multōs versūs. Legimus librum. Lēgimus librum. Puer scrībet epistolam. Puerī nōmina sua in prīmā pāginā librī scrīpsērunt. Hostēs rumpunt pontem lapideum.[2] Fidem rūpistī. Pastor caprās in altōs montēs aget. Malam vītam ēgistī. Cīvēs timidī portās clauserant. Mīlitēs patriam dēfendērunt. Leo praedam in partēs quātuor dīvīsit. Rōmānī multa bella gessērunt. Dārīus ingentem exercitum in Graeciam nāvibus trānsmīserat.[3] Xerxēs ingentem exercitum cum clāsse in Graeciam dūxit. Imperātor prōditōrem interfēcit. Dōnum accipiēs ā mātre. [1] *grapes.* [2] *of stone.* [3] *send over.*

2. Rich citizens buy images and rings. The maids have bought meat. The merchants will buy ivory. I will dismiss the second section (*ordo*) of the scholars. The brave captain led the first company (*ordo*) of the second legion. The boys wrote short letters. The enemy [*pl.*] had surrounded the city with an intrenchment (*vallum et fossa*). Ye have broken this treaty. We honor the old friendship. You are drinking old wine. The fierce Germans[1] conquered the old soldiers of the Romans. He has broken the iron (*ferreus*) hinges. The stupid peasants have felled the beautiful trees. Old wines are good for [= useful to] the sick. Orestes killed his mother, for she (*illa*), said he (*inquit*), had killed my father. [1] *Germāni.*

80. B. 1. Puerī in scholam veniunt ut legant et scrībant. Puerī in scholam veniēbant ut legerent et scrīberent. Athamās mīsit Iāsŏnem ad Aeētam rēgem ut vellus aureum[1] peteret. Mīlitēs arma cēpērunt ut impetum facerent. Quum imperātor exercitum ex urbe dūxisset, monuit mīlites, nē multitūdinem hostium timērent sed patriam fortiter dēfenderent. [1] *golden.*

2. My father gives me money to buy books. Parents send children to school that they may learn. The timid drivers urged on (*incitāre*) the horses in order to finish the journey. The soldiers finished the long marches (*iter*) with great exertion, in order that the enemy [*pl.*] might not escape. When I had received your letter, I answered at once (*statim*). When Nero and Phylax had joined (*committere*) battle, another dog carried off the bone. [1] *aurīga.*

81. C. 1. Petunt puerī ut ē scholā dīmittantur. Imperātor redūxit exercitum nē hostium multitūdine cingerētur. Quum oppidum captum esset, imperātor praedam mīlitibus permīsit.

2. The bridge having (§ 586. R.) been cut (*rumpere*), the general led the cavalry through the river. The cautious farmer shut the gate before night, in order that the hens might not be carried off by the fox. The hunter sets the dog on [set on = *incitāre*] to catch the fleet hare. If the general had sent help, the citizens would have defended the city.

XXV. Fourth Conjugation.

82. Vocabulary.

Change of Conjugation. Gr., 176, 3.

venio,	venī-re,	vēn-ī,	ven-tum,	*to come.*
invenio,	invenīre,	invēnī,	inventum,	*to find out.*
pervenio,	pervenīre,	pervēnī,	perventum,	*to arrive.*
sentio,	sentī-re,	sēn-sī,	sēn-sum,	*to feel, perceive.*
vincio,	vincī-re,	vinxī,	vinctum,	*to bind.*
haurio,	haurī-re,	hau-sī,	haus-tum,	*to draw, drain.*
reperio,	reperī-re,	reper-ī,	reper-tum,	*to find.*
aperio,	aperī-re,	aper-uī,	aper-tum,	*to open.*
īnsilio,	īnsilī-re,	īnsil-uī,	īnsul-tum,	*to leap in.*
sepelio,	sepelī-re,	sepelī-vī,	sepultum,	*to bury.*
eo,	ī-re,	ī-vī,	ītum,	*to go*—Gr. 185.

83. 1. Pūnīmus peccāta et scelera. Scelus pūnītur ā magistrātibus. Improbī hominēs corripiuntur. Custōdēs arcem custōdiēbant nē hostēs aditum[1] invenīrent. Cantum lusciniae in hortō audiētis. Dormīvimus usque ad hōram sextam. Quum puerī voluntātī parentum nōn obēdīvissent, punītī sunt. Mīlitēs castra (*camp*) mūnīverint, antequam (*before*) hostēs advēnerint (*arrive*). [1] *approach.*

2. We are slaves (*servīre*) to cruel masters. If we feel pains, we cry out. If you are obedient to your teacher, you are not punished. If you are [shall be] obedient to your teachers, you will not be punished. The enemy conquers; the conquerors bind the captives (*captīvus*). The soldiers fought so bravely (*tam fortiter*) in order to conquer the great number of the enemy [*pl.*]. The general gave-orders (*imperāre*, with Dat.) to the soldiers that they should bind the captives. Ye do not know the plans of the shrewd general. We come to soothe thy pains. We came to soothe thy pains. If we had known thy will, we should have obeyed.

XXVI. Pronouns. Gr., 97 foll.

84. 1. We praise these poets. We praise those youths. We praise these poems. That journey does not please me. I am moving the globe (*globus terrae*) that you may see it from (*ab*) this side (*pars*) too (*quoque*). This country is called (*dīcere*) Asia; that is named Africa. This sea is called the Atlantic, that the Pacific; between them lies (*est*) America (*America*). Answer him who asks you. Those will be praised who have [= shall have] learned well (*bene*). Those legions will receive a great reward which shall have stood (*sustinēre*) this attack.

2. I will always honor that friend (*hospes*); for through him I was delivered from the danger which threatened me (*imminēre*, with Dat.). The thief whose garment (*vestis*) was left behind, was arrested. I will present to you this book. Keep it (*retinēre*). [It is] the same [that] we are reading in school. We are all fearing the same danger. The brilliancy of the same stars delights the country-people (*rūsticus*) and the city-people (*urbānus*). I gave my second letter to the same messenger. My father praised the clerk who wrote this letter. I have already (*jam*) given this woman bread; give thy money to that poor man. I do not approve that opinion (of yours). The horses were frightened by the screaming (*clāmor*) of these boys. The Lydians (*Lȳdī*), whose king Croesus was, were subjugated (*subigo*) by Cyrus. The Amazons (*Amazones*), whose queen Hercules overcame, lived [= dwelt] by (*ad*) the sea of Azov (*palūs Maeōtis*, Gen. *idis*).

3. What did your father say to you? Which of you has lost this book? I lost it. Who will save us? Who will give us advice? Which place is the first? Which place have (*obtinēre*) you? When (*quando*) will the teacher dismiss you? When did your mother send you those apples?

4. Most of you know this thing. If you will always remember [= be mindful of] us, you will always be loved by us. Who did this? He who has done this will suffer for it (*poenam dare*). What dost thou say? What thou sayest is incredible. What have you seen? What have you heard? I have seen nothing. What I have heard I will repeat (*referre*) [Abl.] in the same words in which it was said. What is honorable?

Answer. I ask you, what is honorable? (§ 469, R.) What is good is honorable. I expect some one of my-family (*meī*). You did this with somebody's help. Some bold leader [or other] is chosen. Some part of the work you will undertake yourself. I fear something. I fear some evil. I blame this deed (*facinus*); another it will, perhaps (*fortasse*), please. I do not approve that judgment (*sententia*) of yours; mine is different. The consuls drew lots for (*sortīrī*, with Acc.) the provinces (*prōvincia*): Gaul (*Gallia*) fell (*obvenīre*) to the one, Spain (*Hispānia*) to the other. Both managed (*gerere*) matters (*rēs*) ill. Neither triumphed (*triumphāre*). When the Greeks were fighting with the Persians in Asia, the rumor of the victory at Plataeae (*Plataeēnsis*, Adj., 360, R.) came to both armies [either army].

XXVII. Adsum, absum, prōsum, possum. Gr., 113, 114.

85. The messengers, whose arrival we had expected, are here. Those who have been away will learn those poems (*carmen*), which the rest of the scholars [the remaining (= *reliquī*) scholars] have learned. The traitor profited (§ 345) those whom he betrayed. The plan of the deserter was to (*ut*) betray the legion, but an accident (*cāsus*) brought it about (*efficere*) that (*ut*) he profited it. Thou hast profited me very much (*plūrimum*) by thy faithfulness. The hounds could not surpass the fleet hare in running (*cursus*). The herdsman led his flocks to the river that they might be able to drink. We shall be able to defend the city. The city can be [*fut.*] defended by us, when reinforcements (*auxilia*) shall have arrived. You could not hear the voice of the judge. The slave could not carry the heavy stones. This man might have been liberated. (246, R. 1.)

XXVIII. Imperative. (Syntax, §§ 259–69.)

86. With the Imperative, *not* is NĒ; but in the ordinary forms of the second person, singular and plural, NŌLĪ and NŌLĪTE, be unwilling, with the Infinitive, are used instead, or NĒ with the Perfect Subjunctive.

Nōlī, nōlīte mē tangere,	*touch me not.*
(nē tetigeris, nē tetigeritis),	*do not touch me.*
Nē tangito mē,	*thou shalt not, he shall not touch me.*
Nē tangitōte mē,	*ye shall not touch me.*
Nē tangunto mē,	*they shall not touch me.*

87. The slaves shall carry heavy burdens. Thou shalt avoid bad company. Ye shall keep the laws. Men [= people] shall worship (*colere*) God. Yield not to misfortunes (*malum*). Boys are not to read bad books. The keepers are to guard the gates; they are not to sleep. The lazy scholar shall be blamed. The feet are not to be moved. Let the book be bought. Let not the bridge be cut (*rumpere*). Let traitors be punished with the bitterest death (*acerbus*). Thou shalt not kill. It is a sacred law: Animals are not to be killed wantonly (*temerē*).

88. VOCABULARY:

PLURALIA TANTUM. Gr., § 75.

dīvitiae,	*riches.*	**arma, ōrum,**	*arms.*
tenebrae,	*darkness.*	**faucēs, ium,**	*gullet, jaws.*
īnsidiae,	*ambush.*	**nārēs, ium,**	*nose.*
indutiae,	*armistice.*	**cassēs, ium,**	*toils (snare).*
nūptiae,	*wedding.*	**moenia, ium,**	*town-wall.*
angustiae,	*straits, pass.*	**viscera, um,**	*entrails.*

Different signification in singular and plural.

SINGULAR.		PLURAL.	
lītera,	*letter of the alphabet.*	**līterae,**	*a letter (epistle).*
opera,	*trouble, work.*	**operae,**	*workmen.*
cōpia,	*abundance.*	**cōpiae,**	*forces, troops.*
auxilium,	*help.*	**auxilia,**	*auxiliaries, reinforcements*
castrum,	*fort.*	**castra,**	*camp.*
fīnis,	*end, limit.*	**fīnēs,**	*territory (borders).*
aedēs, is,	*temple.*	**aedēs, ium,**	*house, palace.*

89. Avārus magnās dīvitiās collēgit. Imperātor auxilia mīsit in castra. Accēpī līterās tuās, quibus nūptiās fīliae nūntiāverās Fīnēs hostium vastātī sunt.

90. The enemy [*pl.*] has made a truce in order to prepare an ambush for us. The soldiers seize [their] arms, rush out (*ērumpere*) of (*ex*) the camp [and] make a charge on (*in*) the advancing (*accēdere*) forces of the enemy. The general shut the gates of the camp that the enemy might not rush (*irrumpere*) into the camp with the fleeing recruits (*tīro*). The king has extended (*propāgāre*) the borders of his kingdom. The general has led [his] troops (*intrōdūcere*) into the territory of the enemy. Hercules went to the (*usque ad*) extreme limit of Europe (*Eurōpa*). The darkness was frightening the children. The avaricious merchant collected great wealth. The door of the temple was open. The king has built a splendid palace. I am very much (*valdē*) delighted with your letter.

XXIX. Deponent Verbs.

91. Vocabulary:

I. hortor,	hortārī,	hortātus sum,	*exhort, encourage.*
lāmentārī,	*lament.*	lūdificārī,	*to make sport of*
contemplārī,	*regard.*	luctārī,	*to wrestle.*
cōnspicārī,	*behold.*	precārī,	*to beg, pray.*
rixārī,	*squabble.*	imitārī,	*to imitate.*
admīrārī,	*admire.*	glōriārī,	*to boast.*
cunctārī,	*linger.*	augurārī,	*to prophesy.*
comitārī,	*attend.*	populārī,	*to lay waste.*
cōnsōlārī,	*comfort.*	vagārī,	*to roam about.*
laetārī,	*be glad.*	versārī,	*to be engaged, be.*
minārī,	*threaten.*	īnsidiārī,	*to lie in wait, in ambush.*
morārī,	*delay.*	ōsculārī,	*to kiss.*
II. vereor,	verērī,	veritus sum,	*to fear, stand in awe of*
polliceor	pollicērī,	pollicitus sum,	*to promise.*
tueor,	tuērī,	tuitus sum (tūtātus),	*to protect.*
(videor,	vidērī,	vīsus sum,	*to appear*).
fateor,	fatērī,	fassus sum,	*to acknowledge.*
III. loquor,	loquī,	locūtus sum,	*to speak.*
sequor,	sequī,	secūtus sum,	*to follow.*
lābor,	lābī,	lāpsus sum,	*to glide, slip.*
vehor,	vehī,	vectus sum,	*to ride (be borne).*
patior,	patī,	passus sum,	*to suffer.*
aggredior,	aggredī,	aggressus sum,	*to attack.*
ūtor,	ūtī.	ūsus sum,	*to use.*

	revertor,	revertī,	revertī (*act.* Gr. 182),	*to turn back.*
	īrâscor,	īrâscī,	(īrātus sum),	*to be angry.*
	nâscor,	nâscī,	nātus sum,	*to be born.*
	nanciscor,	nanciscī,	nactus sum,	*to get.*
	prŏficiscor,	prŏficiscī,	prŏfectus sum,	*to set out, march.*
	adipiscor,	adipiscī,	adeptus sum,	*to attain*
	expergiscor,	expergiscī,	experrectus sum,	*to awake, get up.*
	ulciscor,	ulciscī,	ultus sum,	*to avenge.*
	morior,	morī,	mortuus sum,	*to die.*
	ŏblīviscor,	oblīviscī,	oblītus sum,	*to be forgetful of* [*Gen.*]
	vescor,	vescī,		*to feed* [*Abl.*].
IV.	mentior,	mentīrī,	mentītus sum,	*to tell a lie.*
	blandior,	blandīrī,	blandītus sum,	*to flatter* [*with Dat.*].
	partior,	partīrī,	partītus sum,	*to divide.*
	potior,	potīrī,	potītus sum,	*to possess one's self of.*
	experior,	experīrī,	expertus sum,	*to try.*
	orior,	orīrī,	ortus sum,	*to arise.*

92. Admīrâmur splendōrem sīderum. Vulpēs leporibus īnsidiātur. Cīvēs tōtam regiōnem populātī sunt, nē hostēs in eā versārentur. Fatēbor omnia peccāta,[1] ut veniam nanciscar. Quum exercitus hostem aggressus esset, auxilia advēnērunt. Patiminī fămem et sitim! Pater fīlium vagantem epistolā hortatus est, ut reverterētur. Cônsōlāre miserōs, tuēre vexātōs, nōlī oblīviscī pauperum (§ 375). Nēmo mentītor. "Morere, Diagorā, nōn enim in caelum ascênsūrus es." [1] *sins.* [2] *harassed.*

93. The brother lamented long (*diū*) the bitter death of [his] sister. We admired thy strength and speed. The soldiers were angry with [*Dat.*] the lingering general. The troops marched day and night, in order to get an advantageous (*opportūnus*) position for [*Gen.*] the camp. The messengers have told a lie. Try [your] luck. We have tried it. My friend has a raven, which imitates human speech (*sermo*). When two sons of Diagoras had received wreaths on one day, a Lacedaemonian spoke to this effect (*ita ferē*): Why dost thou linger in life, Diagoras? Greater glory and greater joy thou wilt not attain. I shall breathe again (*respīrāre*) when I behold thee (236, R. 2). No one who has obtained (*cônsequī*) the reputation of bravery by treachery (*insidiae*) and malice (*malitia*) has obtained honor.

94. MISCELLANEOUS EXAMPLES.

1. Mothers like to talk [= talk willingly (*libenter*)] about [their] sons and daughters. We had caught a very beautiful butterfly, but it flew away out of our (*nōbīs*) hands. One row of trees was felled in order that the approach to the house might be broader. Some (*nōnnullī*) mice are white. I see thy shameless face (*ōs*). These flowers have a beautiful color and an agreeable smell (*odor*). The legs of the fleet stags are slender (*gracilis*). The fleet hounds catch the timid hare.

2. The walls of the cities were destroyed by the enemy. The decision of the judges was not just. Just judges guard good laws. In our garden there are many bushes. The nut has a hard shell (*cortex*). Ye shall avoid the dangers of bad company. The feet of ducks are broad. The wall [= of the house] had been broken through (*perrumpere*) by the thieves. Thou wilt receive no reward, for thou hast been very lazy. Let the rich man aid (*juvāre*) the poor man. Let man be always mindful of death. The elephant has a big head, long ears, thick legs, two long tusks (*dēns*), a thin tail. His whole body is huge, but his eyes are small and his throat is narrow. He is a very sagacious (*prūdēns*) animal. The members of the body are the head, the shoulders, the hands, the legs, the feet [and] so forth (*cētera*).

3. The birds which in summer delight thine ears, in winter migrate to (*in*) other regions. The city was betrayed by a traitorous (*perfidus*) citizen. The rider urges his horse on (*incitāre*) with the spur. The Romans laid heavy taxes on the provinces (*impōnere* with *Dat.*). The ship was held by one slender (*tenuis*) rope. An end has been put to the war [= of the war an end has been made]. Ye have caught many fish. The elephant is carrying a wooden (*ligneus*) tower on [his] back (*dorsum*). The city [of] Rome is situated (*situs*) on the Tiber, which empties (*effundī*, 209) into the Tyrrhenian (*Tyrrhēnum*)

sea. The pilot sits on the stern (*puppis*) of the ship and holds the rudder (*clāvus* or *gubernāculum*). Let the traitors be cut down with the axe. The wisdom of the old (*senex*) is not less profitable (*minus prōdesse*) than the bravery of the young (*juvenis*).

4. The head is the seat of all the senses. The cavalry had come at a gallop (*cursus citātus*) to defend the entrances to (= of) the harbor. The nightingale delights men [= people] by sweet song. Ye shall obey the senate and the authorities. The Scythians (*Scytha*) were armed with bows and arrows. I wrote these letters with [my] left hand. We admire the lofty porticoes of the royal palace. The issues of all wars are uncertain. In winter the nights are long, the days short; in summer the days are long, the nights short.

5. I have marked me (Syntax, § 351) the places (*passages*) which we have read in school. The general occupied[1] the places (*positions*) which the enemy had left. The youths presented to the old-man a silver vessel; the rim (*margo*) of the vessel was of gold (*aureus*). [*Same sentence in the plural.*] The dog was holding a bone in [his] mouth. The dogs were holding bones in [their] mouths. Oxen have a large head. The slaves are putting the yoke[2] (*impōnere*, with *Dat.*, or *in* and *Acc.*) on the oxen. The bear surpasses the man in [= by] strength; the man surpasses the bear in [= by] cunning. Violence is warded off (*dēfendo*) by violence. The lightning of Jove smote (*percutere*) the lofty towers. [1] *capere.* [2] *jugum.*

II.

1. The Greeks built many temples to their gods and goddesses. When will you come to me with your distaff and wool (*lāna*)? The cherry-tree (*cerăsus*) was brought by (*translātus*) Lucullus, the richest of the Romans, from (*ex*) Asia to Italy. The emperor Augustus exclaimed: O Quintilius Varus, give me back my legions.

2. The villainous (*improbus*) robber stabbed (*percutere*) the

old man's heart. Trees of various-sorts (*varius*) and beautiful flowers adorn the gardens of the rich princes. The timid bat will be caught by the cat. The heads of the beams project from (*ēminēre ex*) the wall [= of the house]. Large flocks of little birds fly in autumn from Europe across the sea to Africa; in the beginning of spring (287 R.) they return (*reverti*). The little gnats creep under the dry (*āridus*) bark of the trunk. The shady (*umbrifer*) plane-tree (*platanus*) sends forth (*agere*) very long roots. Nut shells [the shells (*cortex*) of nuts] are hard. The towers of old citadels adorn the tops (*cacūmen*) of the mountains. The fine (*laetus*) crops promise (*prōmittere*) the farmers a great reward (*mercēs*). The sods (*caespes*) have been put on the mound. The feet of geese are broad. On the land they move them clumsily (*tardē*). The walls of the temples have been broken through by the fierce soldiers; the stones of them have been scattered (*disjicere*). Little mice have sharp teeth, with which they can gnaw-through (*rōdere*) thick walls. True honor consists (*positus est*) in virtue. Mothers and teachers are wont to chastise (*castīgāre*) boys, and-not (*nec*) with-words only (*sōlum*), but with blows. No animal that has blood can be without a head. The sons of rich parents are often poor; for, corrupted by-luxury, they squander (*dissipāre*) the greatest riches.

3. Even the greatest birds fear the sly fox, which lies-in-wait for them. The city was saved (*Perf.*) by one brave citizen. The fire is quenched. We have thrown the ashes into the neighboring river. The Cheruscans (*Chĕruscī*), a people of Germany, used-to-dwell between the Weser (*Visurgis*) and the Elbe (*Albis*). If you quench (*sēdāre—Fut. Perf.*) [your] thirst with-much water while-in-a-sweat (*sūdāns*), you will suffer (*labōrāre*) to-morrow (*crās*) from-a-cough. Swiftness of foot [*pl.*] snatched the hare from (*ēripere*, with *Dat.*) the jaws (*faux*) of the dogs. The fettered captives stood naked in the open-air (*āër*), in the rain, in the cold.

4. By-thy-arrival thou hast averted (*āvertere*) the ruin of the whole army. The entrances to [= of] the harbors were fortified.

The city is protected by lakes and swamps. The doors of the royal palace were closed in order that the hostages might not escape (*effugio*) from the house. The maidens have embroidered (*acū pingere*) a coverlet (*strāgulum*). The prisoners have had their hands cut off (§ 344) (*abscīdere*).

5. The fowlers have caught many birds. The first day of the week (L. *hebdomas, ădis, f.*) is called Sunday [= day of the sun]; the second, Monday [the day of the moon]; the third, the day of Mars; the fourth, the day of Mercury (*Mercŭrius*); the fifth, the day of Jupiter; the sixth, the day of Venus; the seventh, the day of Saturn (*Sāturnus*). Farmers keep (*alo*) many herds (*armentum*) of oxen; they plough with-oxen. The soldiers fought with fresh (*integer*) strength. Men have greater strĕngth than women. We made a long journey on that day. The Greeks used to sacrifice (*sacra facere*) not to Jupiter alone (*Dat.* of *sōlus*), but also to Apollo, to Venus, to Ceres, [and] to many other gods and goddesses.

95. *Miscellaneous Examples, especially in Comparison and Pronouns.*

1. The most learned and wisest men have always been the most modest. The song of the nightingale is very-sweet. Cicero was the most celebrated orator of the Romans. The name of Homer is more celebrated than the names of many kings. The ass is carrying a very heavy load. This food is nicer than that. This business is lighter than that. The Alps are the highest mountains in [= of] Europe, but the mountains of Asia are higher. When (*quando*) is the longest day and the shortest night? What is more difficult than this business? This garden is larger than the one (*is, ea, id*) which my father bought; but the trees, which are in it, are very-low (*humilis*). The burden, which *we* are carrying, is heavier than yours. Achilles killed Hector (*Acc. Hectŏra*), the son of King Priam [and] the bravest of the Trojans. The brave soldiers did not fear the most violent (*ācer*) charges of the enemy [*pl.*]. No vice is more shameful than avarice. The easiest work is not

always most pleasant; the most difficult not always the most disagreeable. Thou art the most beneficent of all my friends. Xanthippe, the wife of Socrates, was very-abusive (*maledicus*). Times will be better if men are [= shall be] better. We admire the bold (*superl.*) sailors. Farmers ought to be the most energetic (*industrius*) of all men. The hog is very-fat; its flesh is very tender. Your brother is smaller than you. The greatest blessing (*bonum*) is friendship; for in friendship there are most enjoyments (*dēlectātio*). You returned more than you had received. The fierce soldier plunged (*īnfīgo*) [his] sword into the enemy's [*Dat.*] breast. The best poets are heard, read, learned-by-heart (*ēdiscere*), and fix-themselves (*inhaerēscere*) in the mind [*pl.*]. By this hatred you are doing harm not to me but to yourself (§ 298). This apple-tree (*mālus*) I planted myself. We desire (*optāre*) rest; to us also is perpetual unrest (*inquiēs*) disagreeable (*molestus*).

XXX. Formation of Adverbs. Gr., § 90.

96. The sparrow, which had cruelly devoured the little gnat, screamed affrightedly (*Adv.*, fr. *anxius*) when the hawk seized it suddenly. That boy acted foolishly who judged of (*dē*) the song of the birds by (*ex*) the finery (*ornātus*) of [their] feathers. Write this letter carefully; those who write it [= shall have written it] most carefully will be praised most. The Lacedæmonians (*Laco*) were wont to answer briefly and pointedly (*acūtus*). The lark sings more sweetly than the goldfinch (*acanthis*). Of all birds the nightingale sings most sweetly. The war has been conducted (*gerere*) successfully (*fēlīx*). The soldiers made a charge on the enemy boldly. In the Alps you can travel safely. The (*quō*) more concealed (*occultus*) the dangers are, the (*eō*) greater the difficulty of avoiding them [= with the greater difficulty are they avoided]. This business can very easily be settled (*absolvere*).

XXXI. Numerals. Gr., § 92.

97. Three beasts made a treaty with the lion that the booty (*praeda*) should be divided into four shares (*pars*); but when they had caught a stag, the lion took not only his own (*suus*) share, but also the shares of his three partners. Two birds were hanging before the window; the one was a goldfinch (*acanthis*), the other a nightingale. Two travellers met (*occurro* with *Dat.*) a bear in the wood. The feelings (*animus*) of the two carpenters were different (*dīversus*); therefore the god gave one three axes, to the other he did not even (*nē-quidem*) give the one which he had thrown into the river. The hydra had nine heads; Cerberus had three heads. The poor farmer has two cows[1]; his rich neighbor has twenty-one oxen. The Athenians had two hundred ships. Priam had fifty sons and fifty daughters. Priam had one hundred children. Nature gave us two ears and one mouth, in order that we should hear more than we speak [*Subj.*]. The year is a space (*spatium*) of three hundred and sixty-five days.

[1] *vacca*.

XXXII. Irregular Verbs. Gr., 184.

8. VOCABULARY:

abeo,	abīre,	abiī,	abĭtum,	*to go away.*

adīre,	*to approach.*	obīre,	*to take on one's self, to die*
exīre,	*to go out.*	prōdīre,	*to go forth.*
inīre,	*to go into.*	redīre,	*to return.*
interīre,	*to go down to ruin.*	trānsīre,	*to go beyond, to pass over, by.*
perīre,	*to perish.*	vēnīre,	*to be for sale.*

dēferre,	*to bring down.*	trānsferre,	*to bear across, to transfer*
perferre,	*to bring through, to bear.*	praeferre,	*to prefer.*
prōferre,	*to bring forth.*	sē cōnferre,	*to betake one's self.*

refero,	referre,	retulī,	relātum,	*to bring back, report.*
affero,	afferre,	attulī,	allātum,	*to bring to.*
aufero,	auferre,	abstulī,	ablātum,	*to bring away, to carry off.*
cōnfero,	cōnferre,	contulī,	collātum,	*to bring together, compare.*
īnfero	īnferre	intulī,	illātum,	*to bring into.*
effero,	efferre,	extulī,	ēlātum,	*to bring out, to extol, to bury.*
offero,	offerre,	obtulī,	oblātum,	*to offer.*
differo,	differre,	distulī,	dīlātum,	*to delay, to differ.*
tollo,	tollere,	sustulī,	sublātum,	*to lift.*

99. 1. The soldiers are passing over the river. A bridge is building that (*quō*) the armies may cross the rivers more quickly

The dog is barking-at (*allatrāre*) the passers-by. The eyes of all passers-by turn (*convertī*, 209) to (*in, ad*) the beautiful flowers which adorn the windows of your house.

2. Bring me aid. If you do not (*nisi*, with *Fut.*) bring me aid, I shall perish. Frequent (*crēber*) raids (*incursio*) were made by the enemy into the province. The inhabitants of the province asked the general to bring them (*sibi*) aid. As the general would not bring them aid, they applied-to (*adīre*, with *Acc.*, Syntax, § 330, R. 2) the king to have aid brought them, *i. e.*, that aid should be brought them (*sibi*).

3. No one becomes good by accident. What is done cannot be undone [*i. e.*, be made undone (*infectus*)]. Whatever King Midas touched (*Pluperf. Ind.*, § 625) became gold. King Midas asked that whatever he touched (*Pluperf. Subj.*) should be made gold (§ 630).

4. We would rather (*mālle*) be unhappy than bad. If thou wishest to be loved, love. Sometimes it happens that (*ut*) he who wishes to profit us, injures us. Everybody prefers (*mālle —quam*) blaming other people's (*aliēna*) faults to correcting (*corrigere* or *ēmendāre*) his own. If you want peace, prepare [for] war. Do not put off (*differo*) to (*in*) the morrow (*crāstinus diēs*) what you can do to-day (*hodiē*). I will do what you wish. When I would, he would not; when I would not, he would. He will not be willing to set out. I do not know whether he will [*Subj.* of *volo*] or (*an*) will not (*nōlo*). (§ 463 469.)

5. The boys have begun to play. Good men remember the benefits (§ 375) which they have received. I shall remember thy precepts. The bad hate the good. Remember death and the infirmity of man (*hūmānus*). The bad are wont to hate the good.

XXXIII. Neuter Adjectives and Pronouns.

☞ These when used as substantives are often put in the plural.

100. Hear much, speak little. We often lose the certain (*certus*) while (*dum*) we are striving after (*petere*) the uncertain (*incertus*). All this seemed to him new and wonderful (*mīrificus*). Everything that happens (*accidere*) to us we ought to bear bravely. The past (*praeteritus*) cannot be changed. We can distinguish (*discernere*) white [and, § 483] black, good [and] bad, fair [and] unfair, the honorable [and] the disgraceful, the useful [and] the useless, the great [and] the small. We do not always think the same about the same things on the same day. Everything that you have said is true. Repeat, (*repetere*) what you began. What we wish, we readily (*libenter*) believe.

XXXIV. Numerals.

101. 1. Enumerate the seven kings of Rome. The captain who reconnoitred (*explōrāre*) the roads (*iter*) had forty-eight foot-soldiers and twenty horsemen with him (*sēcum*); therefore (*itaque*), when five hundred horsemen of the enemy [*pl.*] advanced (*accēdere*), he withdrew (*sē recipere*) quickly into camp. In that war one thousand soldiers were killed, two thousand soldiers wounded (§ 308). The 15th day of this month the Romans called the Ides (*Īdūs*). Draco made [his] laws (*lēgēs ferre*) in the year 620; Solon, in the year 594; Lycūrgus, about (*circiter*) the year 888. Rome was founded in the year 754 before the birth of Christ (*ante Christum nātum*, § 357, R. 2). Charlemagne (*Carolus Magnus*) was emperor in the year 800 after the birth of Christ. The Emperor Augustus reigned from (*inde ab*) the year 30 before Christ to (*usque ad*) 14 after Christ.

2. Six scholars sit on each (*singulī*) bench (*subsēllium*). Twelve scholars sit on two benches.

3. In Athens there reigned seven kings before the Trojan war; the eighth was Demophon (*Dēmophōn*), the son of Theseus (*Thēseus*). In his time [*pl.*] Troy was destroyed 1184 before Christ. From that year on (*inde ab*) Athens was 116 years under kings. The last of them, Codrus, offered himself [up] to death in the year 1068 for the salvation (*salūs*) of his country. After Codrus there were Archons (*Archontes*) at

Athens, at first for life [while (*dum*) they lived], then (*deinde*) for (*in*) ten years each; finally (*dēnique*) from the year 752 on, nine were chosen yearly (*quotānnīs*).

4. Agamemnon led on (*Abl.*, § 387) 1180 ships 100,000 soldiers before Troy (*ad T.*, § 410 R. 3). Therefore there were in each ship about (*ferē*) eighty-three men. In the oldest times ships had fore and aft (*ab utrāque parte*) two thwarts (*trānstrum*), on which ten or fifteen rowers (*rēmex, rēmigis*) used to sit. After the battle of Salamis (*Adj.*, *Salamīnius*, § 157), large ships were built. Those which had three thwarts were called triremes (*trirēmis*). The Carthaginians and Romans built ships of four, or as many as (*vel*) five thwarts, so that (*ut*) there were (*Subj.*) on one ship three hundred rowers.

5. Hercules was sent twelve-times by Eurystheus to undertake (*suscipere*) enormous (*ingēns*) labors. The god of the river emerged thrice from (*ex*) the water; the first time he brought up a golden axe; the second time (*iterum*), a silver one; the third time, the iron one. How many are twice-two? Twenty-five times 241 make [= become] 6025. I have said that a hundred times [merely exaggeration: the Romans say, six hundred times].

REMARK.—The beginner is called on to notice particularly the use of the distributives, which are employed with an exactness which is foreign to our idiom, whenever repetition is involved, as, for example, in the multiplication table. When singulī, *each*, is expressed, the cardinal may be used.

SECOND COURSE.

XXXV. Whither? G. 410; A. 55, 3, *b*; A. & S. 237; B. 938; H. 421, II
Whence? G. 411; A. 55, 3, *a*; A. & S. 255; B. 941; H. 379.
Where? G. 412; A. 55, 3, *c*; A. & S. 254; B. 932–3; H. 421.

102. VOCABULARY:

NAMES OF CITIES.

Rōma,	*Rome.*	Leuctra, ōrum,	*Leuctra.*
Athēnae,	*Athens.*	Carthāgo, inis,	*Carthage.*
Corinthus,	*Corinth.*	Aulis, idis,	*Aulis.*
Tarentum,	*Tarentum.*	Neāpolis, is,	*Naples.*
Delphī, ōrum,	*Delphi.*	Sardēs, ium,	*Sardis.*

103. Cadmus came from Phoenicia to Thebes (*Thēbae*); Cecrops from Egypt (*Aegyptus*) to Athens; Danaüs sailed (*advehī*) from Egypt to Argos (*Argos, n,* or *Argī ōrum, m*); Pelops from Phrygia to the Peloponnēsus. Menelāüs returning home from Troy was driven out-of-his-course (*dēfero*) to Egypt; from Egypt he returned to Sparta. [It was] from Aulis [that] the Greeks set out for Troy. Ambassadors were sent to Delphi; in Delphi there was a very celebrated oracle (*ōrāculum*) of Apollo. The ambassadors returned from Delphi to Sparta. A slave ran away (*aufugere*) from Rome to Athens; thence (*inde*) he came to Asia; afterwards (*posteā*) he [was] arrested (*comprehendere*) at Ephesus [and] was sent back to Rome.

104. 1. Aeneas (*Aenēās*) fled from Ilium (*Ī*) with twenty ships to Thrace (*Thrācia*), thence to Delus and Crete (*Crēta*); after touching at [= when he had already touched] Sicily he [was] driven by a storm to Africa, [and] came to Carthage, which city Dido was at that time building. Setting-out (*profectus*) from Carthage he made-for (*petere*) Italy. First he came to Cūmae, thence he landed on (*appellere nāvēs ad*) the coast of

Latium. He reigned at Lānŭvium, his (*ējus*) son Ascănius at Alba Longa.

2. Hippias fled (*cōnfugere*) to Darius (*Dārēus*) at Susa [= to Susa (*Sūsa, ōrum*) to Darius]. The Persian king [= king of the Persians] resided (*sēdem habēre*) at Susa. Solon betook himself (*sē cōnferre*) to Sardis. In Sardis he conversed (*colloquī*) with Darius. Regulus (*ē*) died at Carthage.

3. My master (*herus*) is not at home; he went from home early in the morning (*māne*); he will return home in the evening (*vesperī*). My friend came straight (*rectā*) to my house. My guest (*hospes*), who lived (*vīvere*) with me, died lately (*nūper*) at my house. My guest, who dwelt (*habitāre*) with (*apud*) me, departed lately from my house. When the war had been brought to an end (*cōnficere*), the army was disbanded (*dīmittere*); the soldiers returned [to their respective] homes. The father has taken (*ēdūcere*) [his] son with him (*sēcum*) to the country; they will remain several (*aliquot*) months in the country. When my son returns (236, R. 2) from the country, I will send him to (*ad*) thee. Aristīdes conducted public affairs (*rem pūblicam gerere*) excellently in peace and in war. Yesterday (*herī*) evening Hirtius was at my lodgings (*apud mē*).

XXXVI. Accusative and Infinitive.

G. 530; A. 70, 2; A. & S. 272; B. 1152; H. 551.

105. 1. We perceive (*sentīre*) that snow is white. Anaxagoras said that snow was black. I believe that the souls (*animus*) of men are immortal. Thou knowest that [thy] father is angry with (*Dat.*) thee. Report says (*fāma fert*) that you are in Syria. Democritus said that there are worlds without number (*innumerābilis*). I believe the violets (*viola*) are blooming (*flōrēre*) already. The sentinel (*vigil*) announces that the enemy is approaching. We have read that the little mouse delivered the lion. We have read that the lion was delivered by the little mouse. I have learned (*comperīre*) that the enemy is cutting (*rumpere*) the bridge.—(*The same, passive.*) I have learned that the enemy has cut the bridge. I have learned that the bridge is already cut. I suspect (*suspicor*) that the enemy will cut the bridge; that the bridge will be cut by the enemy. Word-has-been-brought (*nūntiāre*) to me that you have suddenly fallen-sick-of (*incidere in*) a fever. Nobody will deny (*negāre*) that the world is kept-together (*cōnservāre*) by God; that the world was created by God. There is a tradition (*memoriae trādere*) that Socrates was a wise man. I hope that the teacher will praise thee. I hope that the boy will be praised. I hope to be in Athens shortly (*brevī*). I suppose that the slave will have finished* the business before the return of my father. I suppose that the business will be finished (*cōnfectum fore*) before the return of my father.

2. The starling (*sturnus*) informed the cuckoo (*cucūlus*) that people (*hominēs*) praised the song of the nightingale (*luscinia*) in-the-highest-terms (*maximopere*); that others praised the song of the lark (*alauda*); that some (*nōnnullī*) were delighted with the song of the quail (*coturnix*); but (*autem*—Syntax, § 486) of the cuckoo mention was made nowhere (*nusquam*).

3. The fox announced (*nūntiāre*) to the cock that all enmities between (*Gen.*) the animals were extinguished; that peace was made; that the deer were walking (*ambulāre*) with the lions, the sheep with the wolves, the mice with the cats. But when he heard [*Plpf.*] that the dog was running up, he fled. I suspect you-must-know (*enim*, 500, R. 2), said he (*inquit*), that the peace has not been announced to the dogs yet (*nōndum*).

4. A lying (*mendāx*) boy deceived (*dēcipere*) the shepherds twice [by] crying out that the wolf was there (*adesse*). When the wolf was really (*rēvērā*) there, and the boy cried out, the shepherds did not run to [him] (*accurrere*). For they supposed

* *Fut. Inf.* FORE UT with Perf. or Plpf. Subj. is rare

that the lying [fellow] would deceive [his] friends a-third-time (*tertium*).

5. LEWIS (*Lūdovīcus*): I hear that the postman (*tabellārius*) has brought you a letter; I suspect that your brother sent it. Give me the letter to read (§ 431), for you know that I love your brother very-much (*magnopere*). WILLIAM (*Guilielmus*): I am well aware (*probē scio*) that you are the most faithful friend of my brother, but I have not yet read the letter through (*perlego*) myself. I promise to communicate the contents [= the letter] to you (*tēcum*, § 346, R. 1).

6. The mythologists (*fābulārum scrīptōrēs*) inform [us] (*trādere*) that Phrixus and Hellē were the children of Athamās (*Gen., Athamantis*) and Nephelē (*Gen., ēs*); that after the death of the mother Athamas married (*dūcere*) Īnō (*Accus., ō*) the daughter of Cadmus; that the bad (*improbus*) stepmother (*noverca*) persuaded (§ 345, R. 2) him to (*ut*) sacrifice (*immolāre*) the children to Jupiter, and that on that account (*quam ob rem*, § 612) they fled from home; that when they had arrived at (*ad*) the sea, Jupiter, [their] grandfather, gave them a ram adorned with a golden fleece (*pellis*), but timid Hellē fell (*dēcidere*) from the ram; that Phrixus was borne (*dēferre*) by the ram to King Aeētēs in Colchis (*Colchī, ōrum*) [= to Colchis to King Aeētēs]; that he sacrificed the ram there and suspended the skin of it (*ējus*) from (*ē*) an oak in the grove of Mars; that a sleepless (*īnsomnis*) dragon guarded the fleece, [and] that afterward Jason sailed (*vehī*) to Colchis to fetch (*petere*) the golden fleece.

XXXVII. Dependent Interrogatives.

G. 469; A. 67, 2; A. & S. 265; B. 1182; H. 525.

106. Who were the parents of Phrixus and Helle? Do you know who were the parents of Phrixus and Helle? Phrixus asked [his] father why he wished to sacrifice him (*sē*). Aeētēs asked Phrixus why he had fled to Colchis. Did not the stepmother of Phrixus act (*facere*) unjustly (*injustē*)? Aeētēs asked Jason when he would return home. "I will tell you," said Jason, "at the right time (*in tempore*), when I shall return."

XXXVIII. Determinative and Reflexive.

G. 294, 521; A. 19, 3; A. & S. 208; B. 1018; H. 448

107. 1. The lion was lying in *his* cave (*spēlunca*); the fox went to *his* cave. 2. The carpenter had lost *his* axe (*secūris*); the god of the river brought back *his* axe. 3. The birds tore-out (*ēripere*) *their* feathers from the (*Dat.*) jackdaw (*graculus*); for the jackdaw had adorned himself with *their* feathers. 4. A certain lady (*mātrōna*) showed Cornelia *her* jewels (*ornāmenta*); then (*tum*) she wished (*cupere*) to see *her* jewels too; Cornelia said that [her] sons were *her* jewels. 5. Hippólyta was queen of the Amazons (*Amazones*). Hercules was sent by Eurystheus to bring *her* belt (*balteus*) to Mycēnae. The warlike (*bellicōsus*) Amazons defended *their* queen. Hercules captured *their* queen and gave her to Theseus, *his* companion. 6. Hercules gave (*trādo*) Philoctētēs *his* arms. When Hercules mounted (*cōnscendere*) the funeral-pile (*rogus*), Philoctetes received *his* arms. 7. Bias said that he carried everything [that was] his with him. 8. The bat, [when] caught (*comprehendere*) by the cat, said that he was a bird. But the cat maintained (*disputāre*) that he was a mouse. 9. The young man hopes to live long; the young man is healthy (*validus*), therefore we hope that he will live long. 10. Androclus said that he had entered a (*quīdam*) cave; that not long afterwards (*multō post*) a lion came to the same cave with a disabled (*dēbilis*) and bloody (*cruentus*) paw (*pēs*): at the first sight (*cōnspectus*) he was frightened (*terrēre*), but that he had come up [with] mild and gentle [mien] (*mānsuētus*), and raised up [his] paw [and] held [it] out (*porrigo*, § 667, R. 1); that he plucked out (*revello*) a huge splinter (*stirps*) and wiped off (*dētergere*) the blood (*cruor*); and that from that day he and the lion had lived three whole years (*triennium*) in the same cave.

XXXIX Sentences of Design.

G. 545 foll.; A. 64; A. & S. 262; B. 1205; H. 497.

108 Mūs cito accurrit ut leōnem līberāret,
The mouse ran up quickly that he might, in order to, set the lion free.
Cervus fūgit nē ā canibus corriperētur,
The stag fled that he might not, lest he should, in order not to be caught to keep from being caught by the hounds.

The lion feigned sickness to deceive the beasts. The ass put on the lion's skin to frighten the beasts. Phrixus and Helle fled from home in order not to be sacrificed (*immolāre*) by [their] father. The birds flew away to keep from being seized by the vulture. Parents send [their] children to school in order that they may learn. Many praise others in order to be praised by them (*ille*).

Eris threw a golden apple among the guests (*convīva*) in order to excite discord. Agamemnon was-about-to-sacrifice his daughter to appease (*plācāre*) the anger of Diana. The wolf put on a sheep's skin to keep from being recognized. The soldier rent the coat (*tunica*) apart (*discindere*) in order to show (*ostendere*) his scars (*cicātrīx*) on the breast.

109. Rogo tē ut proficīscāris, *I beg you to set out.*
Rogo tē nē proficīscāris, *I beg you not to set out.*

The mouse exerted itself (*operam dare*) to set the lion free. We beg you to show us the way. The father exhorts [his] sons to be harmonious (*concors, rdis*). The generals gave instructions (*praecipere*) that the gates of the town should be shut. The father reminded (*admonēre*) the son to get up early (*māne*). Menēnius Agrippa induced (*commovēre*) the commons to return to (*in*) the city.

The priest Lāōcoōn exhorted the Trojans not to draw the wooden horse into the city. Beware (*cavēre*) of falling (*incidere*) into the snare [*pl.*]. Be sure (*cūrāre*) to be at Rome in the month [of] January. I beg of you to dine (*coenāre*) with me. You bring me (*addūcere*) to agree (*assentīrī, Dat.*) with you. The general admonishes [his] lieutenant (*lēgātus*) to beware of getting into an engagement (*proelium inīre*).

XL. Sentences of Tendency and Result.

G. 553 foll.; A. 65; A. & S. 262; B. 1218; H. 494.

110. Jūppiter furōrem taurō injēcit ut flammās vomeret,
Jupiter enraged the bull so that he vomited flames.

Tanta tranquillitās exstitit ut nāvēs ex locō movērī nōn possent,
There came so great a calm that the ships could not (be) move(d) from the spot.

1. The lion divided the booty (*praeda*) in such a way that he himself received all the shares (*pars*), his partners (*sociī*) nothing. The roar of the lion was such [= so great] that it could be heard from a great distance (*ē longinquō*). The teeth of mice are so (*tam*) sharp that they easily gnaw through cords (*laqueus*). The ass, which had put on the lion's skin, frightened the animals to-such-a-degree* that they sought safety in [= by] flight. The storm was so violent (*tantus*) that the ships were carried (*dēferre*) out of (*dē*) [their] course. Seneca's memory was so strong (*tantus*) that he repeated (*recitāre*) two thousand verses (*versus, ūs*). The doves which Zeuxis had painted were so-well-done (*tālis*) that the birds were deceived.

2. The faithfulness of the dog was such that he did not go away (*discēdere*) from the corpse of [his] master. The infant Hercules was so strong (*validus*) that he killed two snakes with [his] two hands. A huge rock was hanging over (*impendēre with Dat.*) Tantalus, so that he was always in fear. Oenomăus had very-swift horses, so that he easily outstripped (*superāre*) the suitors (*procus*) of [his] daughter in [*Abl.*] the race (*cursus*). The Trojans kept (*sē continēre*) within the walls (*moenia*), so that a pitched battle was not fought (*aciē pugnātur*) until the tenth year [= in the tenth year at length, *dēmum*]. Poets are so (*ita*) charming (*dulcis*) that they are not only (*modo*) read but even (*etiam*) learned by heart (*ēdiscere*).

XLI. Miscellaneous Examples.

Accusative and Infinitive.—Sentences of Design and Result.

111. 1. The grapes were hanging so high that the fox could not reach them: and so he said that the grapes were sour

* *adeō*

(*amārus*). I do not agree with (*assentīrī, with Dat.*) those who set forth (*disserere*) that the soul [*pl.*] perishes at the same time (*simul*) with the body [*pl.*], and that everything is annihilated (*dēlēre*) by death. I beg that you do not let-your-courage-fail (*animum dēmittere*). Pylădes said that he was Orestes that he might die for his friend. We see that the moon is occasionally (*interdum*) eclipsed (*obscūrāre*) by the sun. We have heard that the fields were laid waste (*vastāre*) by the enemy. So great was the bravery of the enemy [*pl.*] that none ran, but all were killed fighting. Many undergo (*subīre*) all dangers that they may attain (*assequī*) fame.

2. The shamelessness (*impudentia*) of the fellow (*homo*) is so great that he would rather beg (*mendīcāre*) than work. We perceive by the touch (*tactus*) that ice (*glaciēs, ēī*) is cold (*gelidus*); that stones are hard. Return home that you may not lose your property (*rēs familiāris*). Write distinctly (*distinctē*) that I may be able to read thy letter.

XLII. Ablative Absolute.

G. 408 foll. 668 foll.; A. 54, 10, *b*; A. & S. 257; B. 965; H. 431.

112. Xerxe regnante = Quum Xerxēs regnāret,
Xerxes reigning. When Xerxes was reigning. In the reign of Xerxes.

Xerxe victō = Quum Xerxēs victus esset,
Xerxes being, having been, defeated. When Xerxes had been defeated. After the defeat of Xerxes.

Xerxe rēge = Quum Xerxēs rêx esset,
Xerxes [being] *king. When Xerxes was king.*

Mīlitēs trânseunt, rēge sedente in soliō,
The soldiers pass by [while] *the king* [is] *sitting on* [his] *throne.*

Urbe expugnātā imperātor rediit,

Passive Form: *The city* [being] *taken, after the city was taken, the general returned.*

Active Form: *Having taken the city, after he had taken the city, the general returned.*

Abstract Form: *After the taking of the city. After taking the city.*

113. 1. Tantalus stood in the midst of the water (287, R.), while apples were hanging over (*super*) his head. Those who are afraid turn pale (*pallēscere*), because the blood goes down (*dēscendere*) from the face (*ōs*). After the kings were banished consuls were chosen at Rome. Demosthenes told a story (*fābula*) in court (*jūdicium*) to make the judges [= that they might be] attentive. When all were listening (*auscultāre*), he went off suddenly. Once-upon-a-time (*ōlim*), although the rest of the city had been taken by the Gauls (*Gallus*), nevertheless (*tamen*) the Romans kept possession of (*retinēre*) the citadel. As the murderers (*percussōrēs*) of [his] master were passing by, the dog rushed forth (*prōcurrere*) in a rage (*furēns*).

2. After Hercules had killed the lion, he took off (*dētrahere*) the skin. After I had read thy letter, I at once had a talk (*colloquī*) with thy brother. The mouse, having heard the roar (*fremitus*) of the lion, ran up. Loosening [= having loosened] the snares (*laqueus*), it set the lion free. After Darius had got up (*parāre*) great forces, he waged war on (*bellum īnferre, with Dat.*) the Scythians (*Scytha*). Phrixus having sacrificed the ram, hanged up (*suspendere*) the fleece on (*dē*) an oak in the sanctuary (*fānum*) of Mars. After Jason had taken (*tollere*) the fleece from the sanctuary, he fled back (*refugere*) to [his] native-land.

3. At the arrival (*advenīre*) of the Persians, the Greeks occupied Thermopylae. After overcoming the Persians, the Athenians restored (*restituere*) the walls. After losing (*āmittere*) [their] camp, the Persians fled to [their] ships. After the expulsion (*pello*) of the royal family [= kings], Brutus and Collatinus were made consuls. Immediately after receiving (*accipere*) thy letter I set out. After murdering his mother, Orestes fled, driven (*agitāre*) by the Furies. We set out from Rome at sunrise (*orīrī*), and hastened (*accelerāre*) our journey so that we came to Circēji at sunset (*occidere*). Jason, with the help of (*adjuvāre* or *adjūtrīx*) Medea, accomplished

everything that Aeētēs had imposed on him (*imperāre aliquid alicui*). Paris carried Helen off at the instigation (*instīgāre*) of Venus.

XLIII. Double Accusative.

G. 333; A. 52, 2; A. & S. 230 foll.; B. 734; H. 374.

114. Orāre (rogāre) aliquem aliquid, *to beg a man for a thing.*
interrogāre aliquem aliquid, *to ask a man a question.*
dē aliquā rē, *to ask about a thing.*
poscere (flāgitāre) aliquem aliquid,
ab aliquō aliquid, } *to demand a thing of a man.*
postulare (petere) ab aliquō aliquid, *to ask a man for a thing.*
quaerere ex (ab, dē) aliquō aliquid, *to ask a man about a thing.*

115. Many men beg the gods for riches. We ought (*dēbēre*) not to beg [our] friends for shameful things. I ask this benefit of you with perfect (*meus*, § 299 R.) right. The father asked [his] son [his] opinion. What? If I ask (236 R. 2) a question of you, will you not (§ 457) answer? The proconsul demanded money of the authorities (*magistrātus*) of the city. Darius demanded earth and water of the Scythians. They sent [him] a bird, a frog, [and] a mouse. Imitate these little animals (*bestiola*), said the ambassadors, if you wish to escape (*effugere*) destruction (*interitus*). Beg thy mother ['s] pardon. Before the battle of Marathon (*Marathōnius*) the Athenians asked the Lacedaemonians for help. The boy asked [his] teacher about the contents (*argūmentum*) of the book. I ask your advice as (*ut*) I usually do (*soleo*).

Accusative of Extent: G. 335–8; A. 55; A. & S. 236; B. 958, 950; H. 370.

116. The wall is five hundred feet long. The tower is one hundred and eighty-nine feet high. We were (*Perf.*) two hours together (*ūnā*). The soldiers were kept back (*retinēre*) in the harbor by storms [for] many months. I am with him whole days and often (*saepe*) a part of the night. Appius Claudius was blind for many years. The Greeks besieged Troy ten years. The Spartans preserved their customs and laws seven hundred years. Cato [was] ninety-five years old [when he] departed (*excēdere*) [this] life (*Abl.*). Alexander [was] twenty-one years old [when he] became king. There was a certain Arganthonius at Cadiz (*Gādēs, ium*) who reigned eighty and lived one hundred and twenty years. He has been teaching (§ 221) by this time (*jam*) above seven years [= the eighth year]. He has been reigning going on thirty-one years.

XLIV. Prepositions with the Accusative.

G. 417 ; A. 56 ; A. & S. 235 ; B. 981 ; H. 433.

117. With the Greeks geometry (*-tria*) was in the highest honor. The river Eurōtās flows (*fluere*) past Sparta. Nothing delays (*morārī*) our journey except the storm. Besides thee no one feels my pain. This happens contrary to my wish and contrary to [= aside from] expectation (*opīnio*). The command in chief (*summum imperium*) was in the hands of (*penes*) Agamemnon (*Gen., ŏnis*). The earth revolves (*sē convertere*) around its axis with the greatest speed. Naevius sent (*dīmittere*) the boys round-among (*circum*) [his] friends. There were temples round about the forum. The armies are marching towards (*ad—versus*) the ocean. We sailed southward [south = *meridiēs*]. We have love and kindly feeling (*benivolentia*) towards friends. The soldiers fought bravely against the enemy. The Romans called the land this side the Alps Cisalpine Gaul (*Gallia*), the land beyond the Alps, Transalpine [Gaul]. The timid proconsul did not set (*efferre*) [his] foot out of (§ 388) the gate so long as (§ 571) the enemy was this side of the Euphrates. There is a sanctuary (*fānum*) in the field hard by (*propter*) the town. On account of the snow Mount Taurus can not be passed before the month of June (*Jūnius*). The dangers of navigation were so great that death often stared us in the face (*versārī ob oculōs*) ; therefore I will return by land (*pedibus*). The Greeks had their camp along (*secundum*) the sea [shore]. The legion marched (*iter facere*) along the river. Hold what [*pl.*] is according to nature ; reject what is contrary to nature. Enemies are within the walls and without the walls. Without [= outside of] the gate there is a temple. We are talking with one another (212). The boys love one another. I dictated this letter to my clerk [while] at (*inter*) dinner. In the midst of arms laws are silent. Between the Lydians and the Persians (*Persa*) ran (*esse*) the Halys. The general pitched (*pōnere*) [his] camp hard by (*juxtā*) the wall. The Athenians brought the Ionians (*Iōnes*) help against the Persians. Sardanapālus sat among the women, and distributed the wool[1] among them. There is a great difference (*discrīmen*) between a bold and a rash (*temerārius*) man. I cannot believe that you will go across the sea. [1] *lana*

XLV. Dative.

G. 343 foll.; A. 51; A. & S. 222; B. 814; H. 382.

118. This business is too (*nimis*) difficult for thee. We are not on earth to live merely (*tantum*) for ourselves (*nōs*). To the husbandmen peace (*ōtium*) is very desirable (*optātus*). To the unhappy man, time is very long; to the happy man, very short. In the lower world (*apud inferōs*) punishments are in readiness (*parātus*) for the impious. That cry (*vōx*), "I am a Roman citizen," has brought to many, in the most distant (*ultimus*) lands, help (*ops*) and salvation. I beg you to care for (*servīre*) your health. Nothing is difficult for a man in-love (*amāns*). Perseus cut off (*abscīdere*) the dragon's head for him. The girl snatched (*ēripere*) the apples from the boy [= the boy's apples from him]. The tailor (*sartor*) will get his head broken (*comminuere*). I will send you a letter. I will send a letter to you. It is honorable (*decōrum*) to undergo death for [one's] parents.

G. 345; A. 51, 2; A. & S. 223, R. 2; B. 831; H. 385.

119. Your friends favor (*favēre*) you. The king will not favor the flatterer (*assentātor*). My brother has not favored my interests (*rēs*). The prince favored the arts. I study literature (*literae*). My brother devotes himself to (*studēre*) agriculture. Be zealous for virtue. The Athenians are fond of (*studēre*) revolution (*rēs novae*). I have long (*diū*) devoted myself to this art. The bad are wont to depreciate (*obtrectāre*) the praise of the good. The good man (*probus*) envies nobody. Men are most (*maximē*) envious of [their] equals (*pār*) or [their] inferiors. The bad are envious-of the praise of the good. I will supplicate the king for thee. You will not persuade me. Ino persuaded Athamas (*Gen. Athamantis*) to sacrifice the children. Themistocles persuaded Xerxes to return home quickly. Spare me! I beg you on my knees (*supplicāre*). Codrus spared not his life that he might provide for (*cōnsulere*) his native-land. The bad are often spared by the good (208). When the enemy had carried (*expugnāre*) the city, they spared neither old men nor women nor little children [= not old men, not women, not little children]. Clytaemnēstra had married Aegisthus. The physician (*medicus*) heals diseases. I beg you to cure me. Cicero wished (*cupere*) to heal civil discord.

120. Thou art acting as becomes thee. It is becoming to a youth to be unassuming (*verēcundus*). It is unbecoming (*dēdecet*) to a philosopher to do anything (§ 304) for (*Gen.*) which he can (*Subj.*, § 633) give no reason. Philip the Fifth of Macedon (*Adj.*) was more satirical (*dicāx*) than is seemly for a king. Credit usually fails men, when money fails [them]. (*Abl. Abs.*) Peace has-its-charms (*juvāre*) for some (*aliī*), war for others (*aliī*). No one has ever come up to (*aequāre*) Dionysius in cruelty [= the cruelty of Dionysius].

G. 346; A. 51, 2; A. & S. 224; B. 826; H. 386.

121. I have always stood by (*adesse*) the king in his absence (§ 324, R. 6). The infant crept up (*adrēpere ad*) the breast (*mamma*) of [his] mother [as she was] dying. Cicero excelled (*antecēdo*) [his] contemporaries (*aequālis*) in (*Abl.*) eloquence. The virgin dares (*audēre*) to come into conflict with (*concurrere*) men. The countenance of Domitius did not tally (*cōnsentīre*, § 346, R. 1) with his talk (*ōrātio*). The whole discourse is consistent with (*cōnstāre*) itself, and tallies with itself (§ 298) in (*ex*) every part. The patricians were compelled (*cōgere ut*) to share (*commūnicāre*) [their] honors with the plebeians. The orator pressed the accuser (*accūsātor*) hard (*īnstare*, press hard). It is a bad thing to fall into (*incidere*) the hands of wicked (*improbus*) men. Sulla said that there were (*inesse*) many Mariuses in Caesar. The ploughman bends (*incumbere*) over [his] plough. Great [is the] danger [that] threatens (*imminēre*) us. Night interrupted (*intervenīre*) the engagement. What is the use (*quid juvat*) of running to meet (*occurrere*) suffering (*dolor*) [half-way]? He said that [his] modesty (*pudor*) interfered with (*obesse*) [his] flow-of-language (*ōrātio*). It is hard to preserve fairness (*aequitās*) when you desire (*Perf. Subj.*) to excel (*praestāre*) all. Dolabella succeeded (*succēdere*) you so soon (*tam cito*) that many people abused (*vituperāre*) him soundly (*valdē*). The general exhorted the soldiers to move up (*succēdere*) into the fight. If you hasten (234, R. 1), you will surprise (*supervenīre*) the enemy.

G. 349; A. 51, 8; A. & S. 226; B. 821; H. 387.

122. My father has many sons and [only] one daughter. I have this book always in hand [*pl.*]. Men have a certain likeness to (*cum*) God. An obliging (*officiōsus*) man has many friends. You will have the first place in the school (*lūdus*). Socrates had great wisdom. Themistocles had extraordinary (*incrēdibilis*) readiness of invention (*sollertia ingeniī*). My name is Lucius. Her name is Tulliola.

G. 350; A. 51, 5; A. & S. 227; B. 848; H. 390.

123. Avarice is of great harm to men. Thy state-of-health (*valētūdo*) is a source of great anxiety (*sollicitūdo*) to me. Your recommendation (*commendātio*) will be of great use to me. This thing is a great pleasure to me. Thy interests (*rēs*) are very near (*cūrae*) to me. I have this duty at heart (*cordī*). We beg you to come to our help. The Plataeans (*Plataeēnsēs*) sent the Athenians a thousand men as reinforcement[s] (*auxilium*). Thy rescue is not [a matter] of greater concern to you than [it is] to me. In many things the faithfulness and foresight of slaves have been of great use.

XLVI. Construction of Sundry Adjectives.

G 356, 373; A. 51, 6, 54, 5; A. & S. 222, R. 2, 213, R. 5 (3), 244; B. 863. 867, 919; H. 391, 399, 419.

124.

idōneus,	*suitable.*	refertus,	*filled.*
aequālis,	*contemporary.*	vacuus,	*empty.*
contrārius,	*opposite.*	frētus,	*trusting.*
proprius,	*own, peculiar.*	praeditus,	*endowed.*
commūnis,	*common.*	contentus,	*content.*
dignus, indignus,	*worthy, unworthy.*	aliēnus,	*foreign, averse.*

125. Horses are useful for war. The general picked out (*dēligere*) a suitable place for the camp. As (*ut*) a shore without a harbor cannot be safe (*tūtus*) for ships, so (*sīc*) a heart (*animus*) without fidelity cannot be stable (*stabilis*) for friends.

126. Wolves are like dogs. Monkeys (*sīmia*) are like men. Death is very like sleep. Charles the Twelfth wished (*velle*) to be like Alexander. I am of the same age (*aequālis*) as thy brother. Vice is the opposite of virtue. Bravery is especially (*maximē*) peculiar to men. In a proverb of the Greeks it is said (*est*) that all things are common to friends.

127. Only (*tantum*) few are deserving of praise. The city was surrendered to Caesar empty of [its] garrison (*praesidium*), [but] filled with stores (*cōpiae*). Thou art free (*vacuus*) from faults. We are free (*līber*) from all mental excitement (*animī perturbātio*). The deeds (*rēs gestae*) of the general deserve a triumph (*triumphus*). To wail (*lāmentārī*) is unworthy of a man. Thou hast (*esse*), Marcus Tullius, children and relations worthy of thee. Relying (*frētus*) on thy help, we have undertaken (*suscipere*) this business. A bad man is never free (*vacuus*) from fear. Fraud is foreign to a good man.

XLVII. Genitive with Substantives.

G. 357; A. 50; A. & S. 211; B. 751; H. 393.

(In English, other prepositions besides *of* are often used to express the Genitive relation.)

128. Many sought participation (*societās*) *in* the emigration (*dēmigrātio*). Sleep is a refuge (*perfugium*) *from* all toils and cares (*sollicitūdo*). You cannot escape punishment *for* this fault (*culpa*). We will have consideration (*ratio*) *for* thee and thine. Know that thy grandmother is almost dead of (*Abl.*) longing (*dēsīderium*) *for* thee.

G. 366 foll.; A. 50, 2; A. & S. 212; B. 748; H. 396, III.

129. The number of the enemy and the great quantity (*vis*) of missiles (*tēlum*) did not frighten off (*absterrēre*) Alexander [not the number . . . not the great quantity]. The conquered paid (*pendere*) a great amount (*pondus*) of gold and silver. In the provinces of the Roman Empire there was a great number of Roman citizens.

130. Five hundred soldiers were in the city. But two hundred of the soldiers were wounded. Only (*tantum*) a few of the scholars are lazy. Many Romans had one thousand slaves; some had three thousand slaves; the richest as many as [= even] thirty thousand slaves. Many of those trees were set out (*sero, sēvī, satum*) by my hand. Tarquinius Superbus was the seventh and (*atque*) last of the kings of Rome (*Adj.*). Forty of us are bound (*astringere*) by an oath (*jūs jūrandum*). Which of us will bell the cat (*annectere tintinnābulum*, with *Dat.*)? To which of these boys did you give the letter? Two boys spoke at the same time (*simul*). Which of them answered correctly (*rectē*)? Which of you will help the unfortunate man? No mortal is happy at all hours. Which of (*inter*) all the orators was more eloquent than Demosthenes? Does not another example occur to each one (*ūnus quisque*) of you? Tarquin had two sons, one of whom was like [his] father; the other was of a milder disposition (*ingenium*). The soul (*animus*) is divided (*distribuere*) into two parts, one of which partakes of (*participem esse*) reason, the other does not (*expertem esse*).

131. Alexander sent his older (*senior*) soldiers back to their country. Of all the Greeks the bravest were the Lacedaemonians. Athens had many orators, of whom the most eminent (*praestans*) was Demosthenes. We believe that our better part is immortal.

132. Of those who have held absolute-authority (*dominātus*) the most prominent (*excellēns*) have been among the Persians, Cyrus and Darius, the son of Hystaspes, each (*uterque*) of whom obtained the throne (*regnum*) by merit (*virtūs*). The first of them fell in the land of (*apud*) the Massagetae in an engagement; Darius died (*suprēmum diem obīre*) of (*Abl.*) old age. There are three besides of the same family (*genus*), Xerxes and two Artaxerxes. Of the people (*gēns*) of the Macedonians two distinguished themselves (*excellere*) by [their] achievements in war (*rēs gestae*), Philip,[1] the son of Amyntas, and Alexander the Great; of these one was carried off (*cōnsūmere*) by sickness at Babylon; the other, Philip, was murdered by one[2] Pausanias near the theatre at Aegae. [1] *Philippus.* [2] *quīdam.*

G. 372; A. 50, 1, 4; A. & S. 247, R. 2; H. 414, 2, 3.

133. The avaricious do everything for the sake of money. The universe was made for the sake of gods and men. Sailors are wont to hasten (*festīnāre*) for the sake of gain (*quaestus, ūs*).

XLVIII. Genitive with Adjectives and Verbs.

A. *Genitive with Adjectives:* G. 373; A. 50, 3, *b*; A. & S. 213; B. 765. H. 399.

134. Vocabulary:

plēnus,	*full.*	memor,	*mindful.*
cupidus,	*eager.*	immemor,	*unmindful.*
avidus,	*greedy.*	particeps, ipis,	*sharing in.*
studiōsus,	*zealous of, devoted to.*	expers, tis,	*without share in.*
īnscius,	*ignorant.*	compos, otis,	*in possession of.*
perītus,	*skilled.*	inops, opis,	*needy.*
imperītus,	*unskilled.*	tenāx,	*tenacious.*
amāns,	*loving.*	appetēns,	*desirous.*

135. The houses of the Greeks and Romans were full of the most beautiful statues (*signum*) and paintings. The letter which you wrote [*Ppf.*] on your birthday (*diēs nātālis*) was full of good promise (*spēs*). The proconsul was eager for gold.

Cicero was always very greedy of fame (*laus*). Boys are devoted to ball (*pila*). Cato was very fond (*perstudiōsus*) of Greek literature in [his] old age. I am conscious of my guilt (*culpa*). Histiaeus was privy to the conspiracy. I have made all my friends partakers of my pleasure. Thou hast been a partaker of all my toils and dangers. The beasts have no share in reason (*ratio*) and speech. A drunken (*ēbrius*) man is not in possession of his mind. Miltiades was highly skilled in war. I will be mindful of thy commission (*mandātum*). A life without friends is full of treachery (*īnsidiae*) and fear. You are greedier of fame than is enough. Cicero was very much devoted to (*amāns*) Pompey.[1] All who are in possession of virtue are happy. I envy [those-who-are] tenacious of purpose (*prōpositum*). I know that you are not poor in words. All hate the-man-that-is-unmindful of benefits [1] *Pompējus*

B. *Genitive with Verbs:* G. 375 foll.; A. 50, 4; A. & S. 214 foll.; B. 780; H. 291 foll.

136. The father reminded his son of [his] duty. Remember thy promise. Croesus remembered Solon when he was placed (*impōnere, Ppf. Subj.*) by Cyrus on the pile (*rogus*). Recollect (*reminiscī*) the ancient (*pristinus*) virtue of [thy] forefathers (*majōrēs*). I have not forgotten thy advice. Men usually forget benefits more readily than insults. Do not forget my sufferings.

137. I am ashamed of my folly. I pity you. I am disgusted (*piget*) with flatterers (*assentātor*). I am sorry for my angry temper (*īrācundia*). Who is not weary of the long journey? There are [people] who are neither ashamed of their faults (*vitium*), nor sorry [for them].

138. Roscius of Ameria (*Amerīnus*) [was] accused of parricide (*parricīdium*) [but he] was acquitted of this charge (*crīmen*) by the exertion [s] (*opera*) of Cicero. Socrates was accused of impiety and condemned to death. Many of the judges wished to acquit him of the capital charge (*caput*) and mulct (*multāre*) him in a [sum of] money.

XLIX. Ablative (Separative).

G. 388; A. 54, 1; A & S. 251: B. 916: H. 425.

139. VOCABULARY:

prīvāre,	*rob.*	abundāre,	*abound.*
spoliāre,	*despoil.*	redundāre,	*overflow.*
solvere,	*loosen, free.*	flōrēre,	*flourish.*
nūdāre,	*strip.*	vacāre,	*be empty, free.*
implēre,	*fill.*	carēre,	*do, be, without.*
orbāre,	*bereave.*	egēre,	*need.*

140. A heart-ache (*aegritūdo*) has robbed me of sleep. I beg you to free me from this annoyance (*molestia*). The soldier despoiled the prisoner of [his] clothes (*vestītus*) in order that he might not himself be starved (*cōnficere*) with the cold. Tomyris filled a skin (*ūter, tris*) with human blood, into which she threw the head of Cyrus.

The cellar (*cella*) of a good and energetic master is always chokeful of wine and oil (*oleum*), and his house (*vīlla*) abounds in milk, cheese [and § 483] honey. The bad are unhappy even if (*etsī*) they abound (*Subj.*) in pleasures. It is a great consolation (*sōlātium*) to be free from fault. Nothing can be honorable (*honestus*) that lacks (*vacāre*) justice. I can no longer (*diū*) do without thy counsel and thy help. Thou dost not need exhortation.

Thou hast freed the city from danger and the citizens (*cīvitās*) from fear. Old age is free from those services (*mūnus*) which cannot be assumed (*sustinēre*) without strength. I was accused of negligence, but I was free from blame. Very unfortunate are [those] who lack (*carēre*) the sense [*pl.*] of sight (*oculī*) and of hearing (*aurēs*). Your friend does not need any [re]commendation to (*apud*) me. Some are poor (*inops*) in words; some abound in words. If souls do not continue-to-live (*remanēre*), we are robbed of the hope of a more blessed life. Priam is bereft of his whole progeny (*prōgeniēs*). Wisdom heals souls, frees from desires, banishes (*pellere*) fears. The wise man does not need consolation; for he will always be free from heaviness-of-heart (*aegritūdo*).

L. Ablative with sundry Verbs.

Ūtor, fruor, potior, vescor; G. 405; A. 54, 6, *d*; A. & S. 245; B. 880; H. 419. [H. 419.
Laetor, glōrior, confīdo; G. 407; A. 54, 3; A. & S. 247, 1 (2); B. 878;
Dignor; G. 398, R. 2; A. 54, 3, *a*; A. & S. 244, R. 1; H. 419.
Nitor; G. 408, R. 3; A. 54, 6; A. & S. 245, II.; B. 880; H. 419.

141. The old painters used but few (*paucī*) colors. Thy brother has persuaded me to follow (*ūtī*) thy advice. Pausanias wore (*ūtī*) Median[1] costume (*vestis*). Navigation was very difficult, for we had (*ūtī*) head (*adversus*) winds. Not for this alone [= this one thing] hath man been born to (*ut*) enjoy pleasures. *That* is each man's (*quisque*) property (*proprium*) that he (*quisque*) enjoys and uses. The Helots (*Hēlōtae*) performed the offices (*mūnus*) of slaves. The citizens filled the offices of state for nothing (*grātīs*). Men in the earliest times [= the most ancient men] lived on acorns. The wayfarer threw himself flat (*sē prōsternere*) on the ground (*humī*), remembering (*quum*) that bears did not feed on corpses. In the cities of Ionia tyrants had made themselves masters of the supreme-authority (*imperium*). Many rejoiced at the death of Caesar. We rejoice in the recollection (*recordātio*) of past (*praeteritus*) pleasures. Who can (*Fut.*) confide in strength (*firmitās*) of body? Who can boast of stability of fortune? The insolent fellow did not deign to speak to me or to look at me (*use: sermo, vīsus*). The rule (*dominātio*) of the Greek tyrants rested on (*nītī*) the royal-power (*regnum*) of Darius. The shepherd feeds (*pascere*) the sheep leaning (278, R.) on [his] staff. [1]*Mēdus, a, um.*

I accept the excuse (*excūsātio*) which you have proffered (*ūtī*). The laws which the Athenians obeyed (*ūtī*), were given by Solon. I have been on very intimate terms (*familiārissimē ūtī*) with thy brother. We shall avail ourselves (*ūtī*) of thy help (*operā*) and thy advice. The Stoics said that all were rich who could (*Impf. Subj.*) enjoy sky and earth. Camels (*camēlus*) perform the services (*ministerium*) of beasts-of-draught (*jūmentum*). Alexander made himself master of the empire of the whole of Asia. The Pythagoreans (*Pȳtha-*

gorēus) were forbidden (*interdīcere*, 208) to (*nē*) eat beans (195, R. 8). There is nothing at which [= at nothing] I am wont to rejoice so much (*tam*) as (*quam*) at the consciousness (*cōnscientia*) of the discharge-of-my-duties (*officia*). We stay ourselves on thy advice and thy influence (*auctōritās*). The Athenians boasted of their origin. We do not deem thee worthy of such honor.

LI. Prepositions with the Ablative. 152-

G. 418; A. 56, *a*; A. & S. 195, 5; B. 982; H. 434.

142. The coldest (*frīgidus*) winds are those which blow (*spīrāre*) from the north (*septentrio*). I come from [my] mother. The fear (*metus*) of divine punishment (*supplicium*) has recalled many from crime. Philoctetes received the arrows from Hercules. You have devoted yourselves (*studēre*) from boyhood (*pueritia*) to the best branches of learning (*disciplīna*) and to the best accomplishments (*ars*). From [my] earliest youth (*iniēns aetās*) I have been on very intimate terms with Gâjus Curtius. Rome was founded by Romulus. Greece was saved by Themistocles. The souls of dying [men] fly (*ēvolāre*) from the bonds (*vinculum*) of the body, as if (*tamquam*) from a prison (*carcer*). The water runs down (*dēlābī*) from either side (*pars*) of the roof. In [= out of] all the ages (*saeculum*) there are scarcely (*vix*) three or four pairs (*pār*, *Neut.*) of friends mentioned-by-name (*nōmināre*). From this day on (*ex*) I will be good. The conquered enemies sent a commissioner (*lēgātus*) to treat (*agere*) for [concerning] peace. The sailor has leaped down from the ship, and is standing up to [his] neck in water. What do you think of this piece-of-writing (*scrīptum*)? The exiles (*exsul*) wandered about (*vagārī*) with [their] wives and children. He came from the harbor with a lantern (*lāterna*). We will speak (*colloquī*) with your father about this matter. Cyrus carried on war with the Scythians. The Greeks had (*esse*) a struggle (*certāmen*) with the Persians for [their] altars and hearth[stone]s (*focus*) and for the temples of the gods. Pylades wished to die for Orestes

The herdsman drives (*agere*) the herd (*armenta, pl.*) before (*prae*) him. My (*Dat.*) tears start forth (*praesilīre*) for (*prae*) gladness (*laetitia*). He could not speak for sorrow (*maeror*). The Scythians make use of wagons (*plaustrum*) instead of houses. I cannot write the rest (*neut. pl.*) for tears. Soon you will swim without a cork (*cortex.*)

LII. Prepositions with Accusative and Ablative.

G. 419; A. 56, 1, *c*, *d*; A. & S. 195–6; B. 987; H. 485.

143. I have not changed my plan, and will not change [it] if you are of (*in*) the same opinion. Tears dry (*ārescere*) soon, especially (*praesertim*) in-the-case-of (*in*) others' (*Adj.*) sufferings (*malum*). A certain kind of hares, which we call (*Pass.*) coneys (*cunīculus*), burrow [= make passages, *cunīculus*] under the earth in order to lie hid (*latēre*). Often there is wisdom under a dirty (*sordidus*) cloak (*palliolum*). Miltiades proceeded (*proficiscī*) with a picked (*dēligere*) force (*manus*) to Lemnos (*Lēmnus*) in order to reduce (*redigere*) that island under the rule of the Athenians. Over the funeral-mound (*tumulus*) they set up (*statuere*) a little-column (*columella*). To him who has hanging over his neck [= over the neck to whom] a drawn (*dēstrictus*) sword, the songs of birds and [the music] of the cithern (*cithara*) will not bring back sleep.

LIII. Miscellaneous Prepositions.

144. We are walking between very tall poplars (*pōpulus*) on a green (*viridis*) and shady (*opācus*) bank. We have taken a seat (*cōnsīdere*) on the little meadow (*prātulum*) by the statue of Plato. Man (*pl.*) can make use of the animals for his service (*ūtilitās*) without injustice. A fight had been started (*orīrī*) between the two dogs over a bone which they had found.

The skin (*cutis*) is drawn (*indūcere*) over the bone and the flesh. The innocent man can live even within the door (*ōstium*) and the threshold (*līmen*) of the prison without pain and torture (*cruciātus*). I am accused by thee, without ground, of sending (*missio*) letters. Hast thou never observed (*animadvertere*) in the clouds the form of a lion or a Hippocentaur? He had one wreath on [his] head, another on [his] neck. The race of man was in the beginning scattered in mountains and woods, afterwards (*posteā*) they surrounded (*sēpīre*) themselves with cities and walls (*moenia*). Nothing can be done against force (*vīs*) without force. Before the door of the royal palace there was seized (*dēprehendere*) a man with a dagger. The hunter has pierced (*percutere*) the huge boar with a spear (*vēnābulum*).

Some (*alius*) of the members seem to have been given by nature on account of their use, as (*ut*) the hands, the legs, the feet; but (*autem*, § 486) others for (*propter*) no use [but] as it were, (*quasi*) for (*ad*) a certain ornament (*ornātus*), as [for instance] the tail (*cauda*) to the peacock, the changeable (*versicolor*) feathers (*plūma*) to the doves, to men the beard.

Frightened by the greatness of the storm, all forsook the ship; they embarked (*cōnscendere*) on a skiff (*scapha*) except one sick man, who on account (*propter*) of [his] sickness could not come out (*exīre*) and flee. By an accident (*cāsus*) the vessel was driven (*dēferre*) uninjured (*incolumis*) into a harbor.

LIV. Infinitive and Gerund.

G. 420–6; A. 57, 8, 73; A. & S. 275; B. 1147 ff. 1319 ff.; H. 548 ff., 559 ff.

145. To be free (*vacāre*) from blame (*culpa*) is a great comfort. It is a virtue to flee from vice. We often wished to see this day. Leonidas (*Leōnidās*) determined (*cōnstituere*) to resist the Persians at Thermopylae. The king made the resolution (*cōnsilium capere*) to flee. Many do harm without the wish to do harm. Avaricious men are tortured (*cruciāre*) not only by the desire of making (*parāre*) but also by the fear of losing (*āmittere*). Wisdom is the art of living well and happily. To read there is always an opportunity (*occāsio*), to hear not always. It is very (*per*) useful to be skilful in swimming (*natāre*). Man is by nature inclined (*prōpēnsus*) to learn. As (*ut*) the horse [is made] for running, the ox for ploughing, the dog for tracking (*indāgāre*), so man is made (*nātus*) for two things: perceiving (*intelligere*) and acting (*agere*). The mind of man is nourished by learning and thinking. This is not the place for jesting (*jocārī*). We made an end of walking.

LV. Gerundive.

G. 243; A. 73, 2; A. & S. 275; B. 1304; H. 562.

146. Some device (*artificium*) or other must be got up (*excōgitāre*). One must die bravely for [one's] country. We must pray (*optāre*) that there be a healthy mind in a healthy body. These vocabularies (*vocābulum*) are to be learned. Not many [books] but good books are to be read. Thou art to read a good book. Often (*saepius*) lesser pains are to be undergone (*suscipere*) in order that we may escape a greater. You are to undergo this pain in order to escape a greater one. We must all die. Hidden (*occultus*) enmities are more to be feared than open (*apertus*). Each one (*quisque*) has his own burden to bear (*ferre*). In playing, a certain limit (*modus*) is to be observed (*retinēre*). We ought not to do anything without reflection (*ratio*). You must not listen to[1] a flatterer (*assentātor*). If you wish to do away with (*tollere*) avarice, you must do away with its mother, luxury. In all things diligence must be used (*adhibēre*). I perceive (*sentīre*) that I have to fight with a brave and steadfast man. Regard must be had (*ratiōnem habēre*) for (*Gen.*) [one's] health.

[1] *audīre*

LVI. Copulative Verbs.

G. 197; A. 46, 2; A. & S. 210, R. 3; B. 667; H. 362, 2.

147. The thing is useful. The thing seems useful. You are timid. You seem timid. You have seemed to be deserving of praise. Everything (*plural*) sudden (*repentīnus*) seems more important (*gravis*). All their plans seem to me full of foresight. The stars appear (*appārēre*) smaller than they are. The army remained uninjured. The Scythians always remained unconquered. Nobody became good by chance (*cāsus*). By habit labors become easier. The slave when (*quum, Ind.*) he is man manumitted (*manū mittere*) becomes a freedman (*lībertīnus*). My brother has bought a farm (*praedium*) and become a countryman. Some dreams (*somnium*) turn out true. Brutus became (*exsistere*) a champion (*vindex*) of freedom.

Tyrants are made more insolent by the long duration (*diūturnitās*) of their power (*potestās*). Darius was made king of the Persians by the neighing (*hinnītus*) of a horse. After Romulus, Numa Pompilius was chosen king. Servius Tullius was declared king with great unanimity (*cōnsēnsus*).

148. The primitive (*prīscus*) Romans were considered (*habēre*) robbers and semi-barbarians (*sēmibarbarī*). The rose is considered the most beautiful flower. The Dalmatians (*Dalmata*) have always been considered warlike (*bellicōsus*). He is to be deemed (*exīstimāre*) free, who is a slave to (*servīre*) no disgraceful vice (*turpitūdo*). Socrates is deservedly (*jūre*) called (*dīcere*) the father (*parēns*) of philosophy. No one can be called happy before death. Cicero was called (*appellāre*) father of [his] country. Romulus was called (*vocāre*) after death Quirīnus. Jason collected an army of heroes (*vir fortissimus*) who have been named (*nōmināre*) Argonauts (*Argonauta*). Among the renowned (*ille*) seven, who were considered wise and called wise, were Thales of Miletus (*Mīlēsius*) and Solon of Athens (*Athēniēnsis*). Among (*apud*) the Spartans those who filled (*gerere*) the most dignified (*amplus*) office of state (*magistrātus*) were called, as they were (*ut erant sīc etiam*), old men.

LVII. Two Accusatives.

G. 334; A. 46; A. & S. 230; B. 715; H. 373.

149. Old age makes you morose. This circumstance (*rēs*) makes the master daily (*quotīdiē*) milder. The Euphrates makes (*efficere*) Mesopotamia fruitful. Familiarity with (*cōnsuētūdo*) labor makes the endurance (*perpessio*) of labor easier. Desire makes (*reddere*) people blind. After Romulus the Romans chose Numa Pompilius king. The boys had selected (*dēligere*) Cyrus as [their] king. Many thought

Croesus the most fortunate. I considered thee safe (*salvus*). I cannot call (*dīcere*) myself restored (*recreātus*). The Romans called Cicero father of [his] country. The oracle of Apollo declared Socrates the wisest of men (*omnēs*). Solon called no one happy before death. Croesus thought (*arbitrārī*) himself the happiest man on account of his riches.

A mind (*animus*) free (*vacuus*) from excitements (*perturbātio*) will make you happy. Attalus, king of Pergamum, made by will (*testāmentum*) the Roman people [his] heir. The enemy (*pl.*) made the province insecure (*īnfestus*) by incursions (*excursio*) and raids (*latrōcinium*). The best mode (*ratio*) of life should [= is to] be chosen (*ēligere*): habit (*cōnsuētūdo*) will make it agreeable. The Persians thought the sun the only god. He who is always in want (*egēre*) we may consider (*exīstimāre*) avaricious. We call Socrates justly the father of philosophy. The timid [man] calls (*vocāre*) himself prudent, the mean [man] (*sordidus*) [calls himself] economical (*parcus*). When the supreme power of the State (*summa omnium rērum*) is in the hands (*penes*) of one [man], we call that one a king, and the condition (*status*) of such a (*is, ea, id*) state, a kingdom. He who has usurped power (*potestās*) by violence is called tyrant.

LVIII. Predicative Attribution and Apposition.

G. 324; A. 46, 2; 47, 6; A. & S. 210; B. 663; H. 441.

150. No one is born rich. The sailors escaped (*effugere*) the violence (*vīs*) of the storm and arrived in harbor unscathed (*incolumis*, or *salvus*). From those bloody (*cruentus*, or *atrōx*) engagements scarcely (*vix*) the generals escaped alive (*vīvus*). In India, when the husband dies (*perf.*) the wife (*plural*) is put on the funeral pile alive. If you love me (*dīligere*), my sister, do (*efficere ut*) get [= be] well, and come to us as soon as possible (*quam prīmum*) well and strong. Leaving (*quum*, § 586) Ephesus, he fell (*incidere*) into a sickness, from (*ex*) which he did not recover (*convalēscere*): he came to Corcyra sick; [and] there he died. Antaeus took fresh strength (*vīrēs resūmere*) from his mother earth and rose again (*resurgere*) stronger. You will be dear and welcome to all when you come [= you will come to all dear and welcome] (*exspectātus*). See to it (*cūrāre*), dear mother, that you come as soon as possible; you will be welcome to all. Cato [was] eighty-five years old [when he] departed (*excēdere*) [this] life. [My] daughter [was] twenty years old [when she] departed [this] life (*Abl.*).

151. In our boyhood [= as boys] we read the lives of Cornelius Nepos. Cato learned Greek (*Graecae līterae*) in his old age. I came to school first of all. Aeneas was the only one that escaped the dangers of war (*Abl.*).

The augury (*augurium*) is said (*ferre*) to have come to Remus first [= of the two]. Hannibal was the first-man (*princeps*) to go into a fight, the last to leave (*excēdere*) it, when it was joined (*cōnserere*). Few receive (*excipere*) death in cheerful-mood (*hilaris*). I received you into my house (*tectum*) when you were a little boy (*parvulus*).

152. You alone have we believed and are going to believe. I left Tiro sick at Patrae. To [your] enemies you show (*praebēre*) yourself placable, to your friends inexorable. The choleric (*īrācundus*) man is not always angry; but tease (*lacesso*) him, forthwith (*jam*) you will see him in-a-rage (*furēns*).

I have Hirtius and Dolabella as pupils (*discipulus*) in speaking (*dīcere*). You will certainly (*certē*) have [in] me a partner and companion in all your affairs. The inconstant man has the good for enemies, [and] not even the bad for friends. I give you my friend as surety (*vas, vadis*). To Romulus and Remus a she-wolf (*lupa*) offered (*praebēre*) herself as nurse.

The pilot (*gubernātor*) sits quiet[ly] on the stern (*puppis*) holding the tiller (*clāvus*). Themistocles, a distinguished citizen, exiled by the injustice (*injūria*) of [his] ungrateful people, betook himself to the enemy (*pl.*). Medea, inflamed (*incēnsus*) by love helped Jason, and forgetting (278) her father followed her lover (= *ille*). [As we were] disembarking (*ē nāvī dēscendere*) we received your letter. I caught the bird alive.

The general left the ship made fast (*dēligāre*) to (*ad*) the shore. [As I was] dining your letter was given to me. I will defend you in your absence [= the absent one]. The Persians deserted [their] camp filled (*replēre*) with treasures (*thēsaurus*)

LIX. Accusative and Infinitive.

G. 527 foll.; A. 70, 2; A. & S. 272; B. 1152; H. 551.

153. We learn (*accipere*) that Ulysses and Nestor were considered wise. There-is-a-tradition[1] that Darius was made king by the neighing (*hinnītus*) of a horse. We know that Socrates was declared the wisest man by the oracle of Apollo. I remember that he returned sick (277, R.). I know that you will be welcome to all [= you will come welcome, *exspectātus*]. Cicero says (*nārrāre*) that Cato [was] eighty-five years old [when he] died, and that [he was] an old man [when he] learned Greek. I knew that [when you were] boys you read the lives of Cornelius Nepos. I have learned (*comperīre*) that you were the first to come to school. We have read that Agamemnon and Menelaus [when] exiled by Aegisthus fled to Sparta. Hercules wondered (*mīrārī*) that he could not overcome Antaeus, the son of the Earth; but he perceived that he took fresh strength from [his] mother Earth, and rose again stronger. After [his] departure (*excēssus*) Romulus said to Proculus Julius that he was a god, and was called Quirinus. We think that in the beginning men lived scattered in mountains and woods, and not until (*dēmum* = *at length*) forced by necessity, built cities. Homer informs [us] (*trādere*) that the Greeks, when they came [had come] to Aulis, brought[2] sacrifice[2] to Jupiter; then (*tunc*) they saw a dragon creeping up upon (*in*) a plane tree (*platanus*); that in the top (*cacūmen*) of the tree there was a nest; that the dragon seized the eight young ones and the dam (*māter*) [for] the ninth; that the Greeks stood there affrighted (*timidus*), looking (*spectāre*) at the prodigy (*portentum*); but the augur Calchas prophesied (*augurārī*) from the number of the sparrows the years of the Trojan war. [1] *trāditum est.* [2] *sacra, ōrum.*

LX. Relative Clauses.

G. 509, 630; A. 67, 1, *b;* A. & S. 266, 2; B. 1296 E.; H. 529.

154. Ino, whom Athamas has married, is persuading him to sacrifice [his] children to Jupiter. He says that Ino, whom Athamas has married, is persuading him to sacrifice his children. They said that the ram which the children mounted (*ascendere in*) had a golden fleece. They thought that the Argonauts, who were (*Plpf.*) the first to enter the Euxine Sea, would never return by the same way by which they came. He said that the matter in question (*dē quā agitur*) was of no importance (*mōmentum*). The father promised [his] son that he would give him all (*quotquot*) the apples he should gather. They know that they are losing the only blessing (*quod ūnicum bonum*) they have. He says that he is not desirous of giving up to another the rule which he has held so long. They say that Simonides sang a poem which he had written on (*in*) Scopas; that Scopas said that he would only give him half of what he had bargained (*pacīscī*); that he must ask (*petere*, § 655) Castor and Pollux, whom he had praised as much (*aequē*) for the rest; shortly after (*paullō post*) it was announced to Simonides that two youths were standing at (*ad*) the gate, who were calling him out with great earnestness (*magnō opere*); that he got up, went out (*prōdīre*), saw no one, [and that] meanwhile (*interim*) the room (*conclāve*) where Scopas was banqueting (*epulārī*) fell in a heap (*concidere*), and Scopas and those who were with him perished.

THIRD COURSE.

PART I.

LXI. Accusative.

G. 327–341; A. 52; A. & S. 229–239; B. 711–743; H. 371–381.

155. 1. Honey smells of (*redolēre*) the flowers from which it has been gathered. No (*nēmo*) brave man shudders at the sight[1] of arms. Let any one (§ 623) laugh at me who will, I despair of freedom. Happy is he who has never thirsted for pleasures. The younger of the brothers leaped across (*trānsilīre*) the ditch and carried his brother across (*trānsportāre*) the wall. Innumerable times (*sexcentiēs*) have I applied to him, but to my petitions [= to me begging] he gave no answer. Every day the stupid creature (*homo*) makes the same blunders (*errāre*). I give you this warning [= I warn you of this] not to trust complexion (*color*). The physicians concealed the death of the king from all who were outside of the royal palace (*rēgia*). Why do you conceal your opinion from us? Who explained (*docēre*) the case of Sīlius to you? Zama is five days' journey (*iter*) from (*distāre*) Carthage. The Carthaginians built out (*porrigere*) from the land into the river a raft (*ratis*) [that was] two hundred feet long [and] fifty broad. Oh! the poor (*miser*) fellows (*homo*). What good did they do (*prōficere*)? All their toil did not help them (*juvāre*) a whit (*nihil*). [1] *conspectus, ūs.*

2. Verres demanded (*poscere*) of the parents a price (*pretium*) for (*prō*) the burial (195, R. 5) of [their] children. A friend will ask of another [= a friend] nothing except (*nisi*) what-is-hon-

orable. Antony begged (*petere*) the soldiers to follow him (§ 521) across the Alps. Euripides began (*adorīrī*) [when he was] eighteen years old to write tragedies (*tragoedia*). I lack (*dēficere*) strength [= strength fails me]. I lack time. Assuredly you are concealing from me a great misfortune. The deserters (*trānsfuga*) acquainted (*docēre*) Caesar with all the plans of the enemy (*pl.*). Misfortune teaches even the conquered the art of war (*mīlitāris*). Some endure (*sustinēre*) fasting (*inedia*) two or three days (*bīduum, trīduum*). The Saguntines [when] besieged by Hannibal made (*dūcere*) a rampart (*agger*) three hundred feet long [and] twenty feet high. The conflagration (*incendium*) lasted (*tenēre*) two nights through. Thirty days have I been on shipboard (*in nāvī*). Lost that I am [= O me lost]; ruined (*afflictus*) that I am, who will help me now? Eight and thirty years was Dionysius tyrant of Syracuse (*ae ārum*), having (§ 586) usurped (*occupāre*) the absolute-authority (*dominātus*) [when] twenty-five years old.

LXII. Dative.

G. 343–356; A. 51; A. & S. 222–228; B. 814–817; H. 382–398.

156. 1. Mucius Scaevola had his hand consumed by fire. The usurper (*tyrannus*) had his skull broken to pieces (*comminuere*) by a millstone (*lapis molāris*). The pine[tree] furnishes (*praebēre*) wood [that is] good (*ūtilis*) for ships (*nāvigium*). The bad (*improbus*) envy the good (*probus*) [their] fame (*dē* with *Abl.*). Demosthenes could not say the first letter of the very art (*ea ipsa ars*) to which he devoted-himself (*studēre*). I will make supplication to [your] angry father for you. Who was present (*interesse*) at your conversation (*sermo*)? Agesilaus presented rewards to those who had distinguished themselves above (*praestāre*) others (*cēterī*) by energy (*industria*). Caesar surrounded the camp with a rampart and a fosse (*fossa*). You write that Caesar consults you[r opinion], but I had rather (*māllem*) he consulted (*Acc.* and *Inf.*) your interest. Excessive (*nimius*) confidence is usually [= is wont to be] a disaster (*calamitās*). To many distinguished (*ēgregius*) men the fortune of war has proved (*esse*) a reproach (*opprobrium*), the envy of the people a disaster. This action (*factum*) was counted to him as cowardice. You, your people (*tuī*), [and] all that is yours, will always be very near my heart (*maximē, cūra*). He is rich [= rich is he] whose possessions are so great [= who has so great possessions] that he wishes for nothing more (*amplius*). Sensual-pleasure (*voluptās*) can have no connection (*conjunctio*) with morality (*honestās*). Publius Cornelius Scipio, who overcame Hannibal and destroyed Carthage, was surnamed [had the surname, *cognōmen*] Africanus. In Syracuse there is a fountain of sweet water, which is called Arethusa. Sicily was at first (§ 324, R. 7) called Trīnacria.

2. Epicurus reviled (*maledīcere*) Phaedo (*ōnis*) in the most shameful manner. Once the same physician treated (*medērī*) both wounds and diseases. The daughters of Servius had married Lucius and Aruns Tarquinius (286, R. 2). Alexander did not spare even (*nē—quidem*, § 444) his own relations (*cognātus*) who seemed (*vidērī*) qualified (*aptus*) for the throne Youth is not only not envied, but even favored. The Lacedaemonians were reproached (*objicere*) with (*quod*) having seized (*occupāre*, *Plpf. Subj.*, § 542) the citadel of Thebes at the time of a truce (*indutiae*). On these points (*rēs*) you are far ahead (*praestāre*) of all others (*cēterī*). In a state, those who have no (*nihil*) means (*opēs*) always envy the better-classes (*bonī*). Laelius was surnamed the Wise. To Tarquin was given (*indere*) the surname "Overbearing" (*superbus*).

LXIII. Genitive.

G. 357; A. 47, 8; A. & S. 205, R. 17; B. 662; H. 441, 5.

157. At the peep *of* day (*prīma lūx*) Titus Labienus occupied (*tenēre*) the top *of* the mountain. The ancients believed that the earth was situated (*positum esse*) in the midst *of* the universe. Darius had come to Arbēla (*ōrum*) about the middle *of* the night. Amphinomus and Anapus carried [their] father and mother on [their] shoulders through the midst *of* the flames (*ignēs*) of Aetna. Against the Tarentines, who live (*esse*) in the lowest part (*ultimus*) *of* Italy, war was declared (*indīcere*). From the foot (*infimus*) *of* the altar there issued (*ēmergere*) suddenly a snake.

2. Superstition seizes on (*occupāre*) weak (*imbēcillitās*) men. With this fellow the matter [= it] is to be settled by war (*bellō dēcertāre*); slow (*tarditās*) envoys (*lēgātus*) are to be discarded (*repudiāre*). Mathematicians (*mathēmaticī*) are engaged on (*versārī in*) obscure[1] matters. The short day is spent (*consūmere*) in feasts. [1] *obscūritās*

G. 364–5; A. 50, 1; A. & S. 211–212; B. 757, 748; H. 396, 4. III.

158. You are undertaking a great work, and one that will last many days [= of many days]. Your neighbor (*fem.*) has a dress (*vestis*) of greater value (*pretium*) than yours. The sea produces (*prōcreāre*) animals of extraordinary (*inūsitātus*) size.

Among the Greeks the oldest class (*genus*) of scholars (*doctī*) was that (293, R. 3) of the poets. Cato was [a man] of almost (*prope*) iron body and mind. When a city is taken (§ 408), everything belongs to the conqueror. The general ought to conquer by [his] head (*cōnsilium*) no less than by [his] sword. It is the duty of a judge in trials (*causa*) always to follow the truth (*vērum*). Barbarians live for the present (*in diem*); *our* thoughts (*cōnsilium*) ought (*Imper.*) to be fixed on (*spectāre*) eternity. Thoughtlessness (*temeritās*) is peculiar to the bloom of youth (*flōrēns aetās*); foresight to more-advanced (*senescēns*) age. It (*id*) is especially (*maximē*) the peculiarity of a sly (*astūtus*) man to make his own advantage the standard of everything [= to refer everything to (*ad*) his own advantage (*ūtilitās*)]. Nothing shows so narrow and little a spirit as to love riches. To desert a post (*praesidium*) from (*propter*) fear is cowardice; not to return a deposit (*dēpositum*) is injustice. It seemed to be folly (*insipiēns*) to attend to (*cūrāre*) other people's business (*aliēna rēs*) at (*cum*) one's own risk (*perīculum*). It is our duty to make a moderate use (*modicē ūtī*) of [our] victory This cape (*prōmontōrium*) is called [the cape] of Good Hope

[He] who denies that there is a God, him I deem scarcely of sound mind. The fleet of the enemy consisted (*esse*) of eighty-nine ships.

G. 366–371; A. 50, 2; A. & S. 212; B. 748; H. 396, III.

159. Caesar had left a little corn at Ilerda. I expect longer letters from you, as you have (*esse*) so much leisure. I will write more (*plūra*) when I have (§ 236) more leisure. We have time enough for (*ad*) reflection (*cōgitāre*, § 426). Caesar showed his soldiers how much good there was (§ 469) in firmness (*cōnstantia*) [= firmness had in itself]. Catiline had (§ 349, R. 4) eloquence enough, [but] too little wisdom. The consul took the city by storm (*vī*); in it (*ibi*) were taken three thousand men and some (*aliquantum*) other (*cēterus*) booty. From that side (*inde*) is the least danger. That is of no use [= has nothing of usefulness]. It is so long since I received any letter from you [= so long (*tam diū*) have I received no letter from you]. What life is left I will spend (*dēgo*) at my ease in Rhodes. What (*quid*) plan have you determined on (*capere*)? Daily something bitter (*acerbus*) and disastrous (*incommodus*) was announced.

G. 376; A. 50, 4, *e*; A. & S. 215; B. 783, 805; H. 406, 2.

160. [He] doubles (*gemināre*) [his] sin who is not ashamed of [his] misdeeds (*dēlictum*). I am tired of this undertaking. No one will repent of industry. Flattery disgusts (*piget*) a good man. Unhappy people are often disgusted with life. We feel more pity for those who do not ask for (*requīrere*) our compassion than for those who claim it loudly (*efflāgitāre*). Socrates was not ashamed to acknowledge that [there were] many things [that] he did not know. I am tired of asking again-and-again (*identidem*). I am disgusted with hearing the same thing a thousand times (*say, sexcentiēs*). There is really (*sānē*) nothing for us to repent of [= of which . . *Comp.* § 634].

G. 378 foll.; A. 54, 8; A. & S. 214; B. 884; H. 410.

161. Your help (*opera*) and your authority I value highly. I value your attentions (*officium*) to (*ergā*) me more highly than any [= all] money. My [good] conscience is worth more to me than all the world's (*hominēs*) talk. I have always loved (*dīligere*) this friend, as you know, and I prize (*facere*) him daily (*in diēs*) more [and more]. The favor of a bad (*improbus* or *nēquam indecl.*) fellow I value (*pendere*) little. Riches are very little prized (*putāre*) by me. How high do you rate (*aestimāre*) this picture (*tabula picta*)? How much did you give for (*emere*) the little-book (*libellus*)? Six pence (3 *nummī*). Verres bought a statue (*signum*) by (§ 360, R. 2) Praxiteles for 1600 sesterces (*sēstertius*). Darius wished to buy a-man-to-assassinate (*interfector*) Alexander for 1000 talents. You bought the tithes (*decumae*) of that district (*ager*) very dear. Caelius rented (*condūcere*) a house on the Palatine hill (*Palatium*) very low [= not dear; *comp.* 448, R. 2]. Dumnorix had farmed (*redimere*) all the revenues (*vectīgal*) of the Haedui for a small amount (*pretium*). A pound of violet (*violāceus*) purple (*purpura*) was sold for a hundred denarii. The victory cost (*stāre*) the lives [= the death] of many brave men. This book cost eighteen pence (9 *nummī*).

G. 357–380; A. 50; A. & S. 211 foll.; B. 744 foll.; H. 393 foll.

162. 1. The word "friendship" is derived (*Perf.*) from "friend." The opportunity for a victory has been allowed to pass by (*dīmittere*). All evils are lighter than anguish for sin. I am under the thrall of [= I am held by] an extraordinary (*incrēdibilis*) longing (*dēsīderium*) for my family (*meī*) and especially (*atque imprīmīs*) for thee. L. Quinctius Cincinnatus cultivated a piece of land (*ager*) of four jugera beyond the Tiber. Xenophanes says that there are people (*habitātur*, 199) in the moon, and that it is an earth with many cities and mountains. Superstition betrays a weak mind. Strong (*fortis*) men ought to bear pain steadfastly (*toleranter*). It is the duty of humanity to care for the welfare (*cōnsulere*) of the weak. The state (*cīvitās*) of the Sēnōnes was [one] of great authority among the Gauls. It is your duty to care for your life and your preservation (*incolumitās*). Julius adapted (*accommodāre*) the year to (*ad*) the course of the sun, so that it consisted [= was] of 365 days. The Emperor Titus was a man of such (*tantus*) good nature (*facilitās*) and generosity (*līberālitās*) that he never denied (*negāre*) anybody anything (§ 445).

2. There are two approaches (*aditus*) to Cilicia, either of which can be barred (*interclūdere*) by a small body of men (*praesidium*). Sulla lost 124 of his [men]. Saguntum was by far (*longē*) the most opulent city of Spain, situated (*situs*) about a mile [= 1000 paces] from the sea. The soldiers attacked (*adorīrī*) the rear (*novissimum agmen*) of the enemy and followed them up (*prōsequī*) many miles. Alexander marched from India into the territory of the Malli, where 80,000 infantry and 60,000 cavalry were expecting him (*opperīrī*). Of the Greek orators the foremost (*praestāns*) are those who lived [= were] at Athens. Of these, however (*autem*, § 486), by all odds (*facile*) the first (*prīnceps*) was Demosthenes. You have so many (*tantum*) books yourself; what [books] in-the-name-of-common-sense (*tandem*) are you looking for (*requīrere*) in the library (*bibliothēca*)? How much profit (*lucrum*) have you made? You wish to have more money. This thing does (*afferre*) most good (*ūtilitās*). There was less booty than they had expected. We despise those who have (§ 349, R. 4) not a trace (*nihil*) of worth, no genius, no vigor (*vīs*, or *nervus*, *pl.*). All the country [= what of country there is] between Rome and Fīdēnae is laid waste. All the gold, all the silver, [and] all the valuable articles (*ornāmenta*) that were (*Pf.*) in Sicily, have been carried off (*auferre*) by Verres.

163. When Caesar had crossed the Rubicon, everything was full of fear and confusion (*error*). Many were eager for (*avidus*) a revolution (*mūtātio rērum*). It is his habit to bear in mind (*memorem esse*) benefit and injury. Man, in that (*quod*) he is endowed with (*particeps*) reason sees the causes of things. Do (*agere*) what is suitable to your time of life. The Roman state has produced (*ferre*) [but] few equal to Metellus. He is like his father. The servant is usually like his master. Tullus Hostīlius was unlike his immediate predecessor (*proximus rēx*). The ape (*sīmia*), how like is the hideous (*turpis*) beast to us! Of (*ex*) the twins, one is like the father, the other like the mother. Peculiar to man (*homo*) is the careful search (*inquīsītio atque investīgātio*) after truth (*vērum*). The island Delos was sacred to Lātōna, Apollo, and Dïāna. It was (*Pf.*) once (*quondam*) the peculiar [fortune] of the Roman people to carry on war far from (*longē ā*) home, [and] to defend the fortunes of [their] allies, not their own roofs. When (*quum*, with *Ind.*) we are free (*vacuus*) from necessary engagements (*negōtium*) and cares, then we desire to see and hear something. The soldiers scaled (*scālīs capere*) the walls, [which were] stripped (*vacuus*) of defenders (*dēfēnsor*). I am free from all agitation (*perturbātio*) of mind. In reliance on your bravery, soldiers, I will go to meet (*obviam īre*) the superior-numbers (*multitūdo*) of the enemy. The city was surrendered (*trādere*) to Caesar, bare (*nūdus*) of [its] garrison and chokeful of provisions (*cōpiae*).

164. Misfortune (*rēs adversae*) reminds [us] of religious-duties (*religiōnēs*). He reminded me of our old friendship. The bad (*improbus*) man will some day with anguish (*dolor*) recall his crimes (*facinus*). Good citizens think of the benefits of [their] country. So strong (*tantus*) was the memory of Hortensius, the orator, that he recollected all the words of his opponents (*adversārius*). Old men remember everything they care about (*cūrāre aliquid*).

165. 1. Orestes, accused of matricide (*-cīdium*) before (*ad*) the Arēopagus, was acquitted by the vote (*suffrāgium*) of Minerva. Cicero convicted Verres of excessive (*nimius*) avarice. The jury (*jūdicēs*) condemned Socrates to death. He declared his own son-in-law guilty of the crime (*scelus*). The senate neither acquitted the king of blame (*culpa*) nor accused [him]. Catiline was indicted (*reum fierī*) for extortion (*rēs repetundae*). Camillus in his absence (§ 324, R. 6) was fined fifteen thousand ases heavy money (*gravis aeris*). The exiles are punished in money and in property. Tiberius made an interdict (*interdīcere*) that the relations [of] those [who were] condemned to death should not (§ 548) wear mourning for (*lūgēre aliquem*) [them].

2. Many are wont to set little value (*pendere*) on what is their [own]. No possession, no mass (*vīs*) of gold and silver, is to be valued more highly than virtue. To act with consideration (*cōnsīderātē*) is worth more than to think wisely. No plague (*pestis*) has cost (*stāre*) the human race as much as anger. When (*quum, Ind.*) the weal of the country is at stake (*agī*) we must think less of everything else. Certain (*quīdam*) philosophers have thought nothing of pain and pleasure. I bought this book for a denarius. Chrysogŏnus purchased (*mercārī*) a Corinthian vessel (*vās*) for a high price (*pretium*). The house (*aedēs*) was sold for a round (*grandis*) [sum of] money. Men often subject themselves to the order[s] (*imperium*) of another (*alter*) for hire (*mercēde condūcere*, to hire). Dear did that delay (*cunctātio*) cost him.

LXIV. Interest and Rēfert.

G. 381; A. 50, 4, *d;* A. & S. 219; B. 808; H. 408.

(*On the Sequence of Tenses.*)

G. 510 foll.: A. 58, 10; A. & S. 258; B. 1164; H. 480.

166. 1. It is the interest of all to act right. It was more to the interest of the Athenians to have substantial (*firmus*) roofs on their dwellings (*domicilium*) than the finest ivory statue of Minerva. It is of the greatest importance that I should see personally (*cōram*), how you (*quem ad modum*) accomplish (*subj.*) the matter. Thou wilt perceive how much concerned the State is that all the troops should assemble as soon as possible (*prīmō quōque tempore*). We are both (§ 370, R. 2) interested in being together (*ūnā*). It makes the greatest difference at what time the letter was delivered to you. It makes no difference how many books you have, but how good [they are.] Much will depend on what (*quī*) the temper (*animus*) of the victor, what the issue of things has been. The Spartan state was much interested in the maintenance (*servāre*) of the laws of Lycurgus. I am very much interested in seeing you.

It is a matter of great importance to us for you to be with (*cum*) us. I think that it is not only my interest but yours too that you should come as soon as possible (*quam prīmum*).

2. It makes no difference whether the revolt (*dēfectio*) of the Tarentines took place (*fierī*) this year or the year before (*prior*). What difference will it make a hundred years hence (*ad centum annōs*) whether the games were celebrated (*fierī*) or not? (§ 461). It made a very great difference to the Romans, whether they had Fabius or Otacilius for consul. It makes no difference to me whether you arrive too-late (*sērō*) or not. It is of the utmost importance to you, as a general (§ 381, R. 2), that your soldiers be not (*nē*) killed in [their] beds. It was both to his interest and to yours that the war should be finished before the auxiliaries arrived (§ 579). It was to the interest of Marcellus that Archimedes should not be killed. Gallio said that it was no concern of his that Sosthenes had been beaten (*vāpulāre*) by the rabble. It was greatly to his interest, so-far-as-expense-was-concerned (*ad sūmptūs*), that his aunt should die. It makes no difference to me—as a very (*admodum*) young man—whether I attain (*adipiscī*) the highest honors now or not. What business is it of yours how many slaves he sold?

LXV. Ablative.

G. 384–387; A. 54; A. & S. 254; B. 931; H. 421.

167. 1. Everything there is in this world has been made for the sake of man [*pl.*]. A great quantity (*vīs*) of wood (195, R. 6) was lying on the bank of the river. In [the midst of] the great (*tantus*) [and] general (*omnium*) fear, he alone is not afraid. In [the midst of] his absorbing (*summus*) occupations, he sent (*dare*) me (§ 344, R. 1) for all that a letter. The father lying sick in bed laid (*pōnere*) the letter, which he had received, on the pillow (*pulvīnus*). Our [men] put all [their] hope of deliverance (*salūs*) in their bravery. The Egyptians and the Babylonians bestowed (*pōnere*) all their attention (*cūra*) on astronomy (*cognitio sīderum*). Well painted pictures (*tabula*) should also be put in a good light. The soldier had been put (*collocāre*) on the wall as (*causā*) a guard. Caesar put the army into winter-quarters. [Those] who have been plunged (*dēmergere*) into water cannot breathe (*respīrāre*). Nature has impressed (*imprimere*) on the minds of all the conception (*nōtio, pl.*) of gods. Caesar embarked [= put (*impōnere*) on ships] his legions and [his] cavalry at Brundusium. [The] laws [which] Draco had imposed on the Athenians [were] too (*nimis*) harsh (*dūrus*).

2. The revilers (*vituperātor*) of philosophy are [= have been] sufficiently (*satis*) answered (208) in the book in which philosophy has been defended and extolled (*collaudāre*) by me (*nōs*). The ground[s] of my wish (*voluntās*) I have set forth-fully (*expōnere*) to you in a previous (*superior*) letter. Levies (*dēlectus*) were made (*habēre*) through all Italy. The colonies of the Tyrians were scattered (*diffundere*) over almost all the world (*orbis terrārum*), Carthage in Africa, in Boeotia Thebes (*Thēbae*), [and] (§ 483) Cadiz (*Gādēs*) on (*ad*) the ocean. A raven which happened-to-be (*forte*) flying-by (*praetervolāre, part.*) dropped (*āmittere*) a clod (*glēba*) which he was carrying in [his] claws. I will (*Fut.*) show (*dēmônstrāre*) you his route (*iter*); he set out by the Aurelian road. Caesar hastened (*contendere*) by the nearest land route (*iter terrestre*) to Alexandria (*īa*). Before the rule [of the] Roman[s] the power (*opēs*) of the Etruscans (*Tuscī*) extended (*patēre*) far-and-wide (*lātē*) by sea and by land. The aged (*grandis nātū*) father has been long (221) confined (*tenēre*) to bed. Nobody received the fugitives (*fugiēns*) into the city or (= *ve*, § 497) into [his] house (*tectum*). Ships brought up (*subvehere*) the supplies (*commeātus*) by the Po (*Padus*). Ariovistus in those days kept his infantry (*Adj.*) troops in camp; a [= in a] cavalry (*Adj.*) engagement he fought (*contendere*) every day. In the battle of Cannae (*Cannênsis*) there fell 45,500 infantry [and] 2700 cavalry. The enemy (*plur.*) was utterly-routed (*fundere et fugāre*), and (= *que*, § 478) there were more killed (*interimere*) in this engagement than in all before (*superior*). Aemilius Paulus defeated Perseus the King of Macedon [= of the Mace-

donians] at (= near) Pydna. Marcus Cato, the son of Marcus, having fallen from [his] horse in the battle, rushed at (*invādere*) the enemy (*pl.*) a-foot (§ 401, R.). In the war against (*adversus*) Caesar, Pompey had got together (*comparāre*) a great (*Superl.*) quantity of corn from Thessaly, Asia, Ēpīrus, and (= *que*, § 478) other (*reliquus*) regions. Among (*Dat.*) the Parthians the signal in battle was given not with the trumpet (*tuba*) but with the drum (*tympanum*). My brother will see thee at Dyrrachium, or somewhere (*uspiam*) in those (§ 291) parts. The cavalry (*pl.*) fell upon (*invādere*) the enemy (*pl.*); the rest stood (*manēre*) still [= on the spot, *locus*]. Want (*inopia*) of corn prevents (*prohibēre*) [us] from remaining longer in these parts. The camp was pitched in a most advantageous (*opportūnus*) position. We shall have a chance (= opportunity, *facultās*) for a fight somewhere or other [= in some place or other (§ 301) a chance of fighting will be given]. The Gauls joined (*committere*) battle on unfavorable (*inīquus*) ground. We will speak of this matter in another place. The sun does not always rise or set in the same place [= not (§ 447) in the same place does the sun always rise or set].

G. 388 foll.; A. 54, 1; A. & S. 251, 242; B. 916; H. 425.

168. 1. The soldier who deserts [his] flag (*signum*) or leaves (*dēcedere*) [his] post (*praesidium*) deserves the bastinado (*fustuārium*). A prodigy was announced [namely] that on the Alban Mountains stones had fallen from heaven. Wearied by the long-duration (*diuturnitās*) of the battle, they withdrew (*excēdere*) from the engagement. Scarcely (*vix*) did they keep off (*arcēre*) the onslaught (*impetus*) of the enemy from the gates and (=*que*) walls. The missile (*tēlum*) flew (*fugere*) out of [his] hand. The Pythagoreans abstained from (*abstinēre*) beans (§ 195, R. 8). Relieve (*levāre*) me of this burden. I have rid (*exsolvere*) myself of engagements (*negōtium*). The Suēvī could not (*Perf.*) drive the Ubii out of [their] territory. Storms kept the enemy (*pl.*) from fighting (*Subst.*). Compelled (*cōgere*) by the violence of the storm, he desisted from his undertaking. The enemy desisted from the assault (*oppugnātio*). Volusenus did not venture to go out (*ēgredī*) of the ship. The Gauls were driven from the territory (*agrī*) and the borders of Italy. Clodius tried to drive Quintus Varius from his possessions. The Haedui could not defend themselves and their [property] against [= from] the Helvetii. Dejotărus would not wage war (*bellum īnferre*) on the Roman people, but only protected (*tuērī*) his territory from inroads (*excursio*) and forays (*latrōcinium*).

2. Ye have deprived Sulpicius of [his] life. Prūsias [was] robbed (*spoliāre*) of [his] kingdom and forsaken (*dēserere*) even by his slaves. Lucius Brutus liberated the state (*cīvitās*) from royal despotism (*dominātus*). On either side (*utrimque*) the Punic line (*aciēs*) was (*plupft.*) stripped (*nūdāre*) of cavalry (*eques, sing.*, 195, R. 8). The mother was bereaved (*orbāre*) of her son. After the death of Thēramenes, Greece was filled (*replēre*) with Athenian exiles [= exiles of the Athenians]. [It is] not by strength (*vīrēs*) or quickness of body (*plur.*) [that] great deeds are accomplished (*gerere*), but by wisdom (*cōnsilium*) and influence (*auctōritās*), and-of-these (§ 612) old age is not generally [= is not wont to be] deprived (*orbāre*). The viceroys (*praefectus*) of the King of the Persians used to cheat (*fraudāre*) the soldiers of [their] pay. The tribune wished to cheat the consul of the fruit of the victory. The kingdoms of Asia have always abounded in gold. Germany is bountifully-supplied with brooks and rivers. Sicily was at the height of (*flōrēre*) power (*opēs*) and wealth (*cōpiae*), there were great works of art (*artificium*) on the island, but especially was Syracuse (*Syrācūsae*) rich (*abundāre*) in statues. No part of life can be free from duty. No one lacks a good thing, if he does not need it. The army had an abundant supply of water and fodder (*pābulum*).

I have need of a physician. I have need of travelling-money (*viāticum*). The body needs much food [and] much (286, R. 1) drink (*pōtio*). Books are wanted, not many but good [ones]. In a [well] known matter witnesses are not wanted. I know that you want cash (*nummī*) to get up (*apparātus, Subst.*) the triumph. We want action (*facere*), not deliberation (*cōnsulere*).

G. 392; A. 55, 1; A. & S. 253; B. 949, 950: H. 426.

169. Plato died in [his] eighty-second year [while in the act of] writing. On that day a great (*superl.*) number of the enemy were wounded and killed. The consuls and praetors of Rome [= of the Romans] entered upon office (*inīre magistrātum*) on the Ides of March (*Martius, a, um*). Rome was built in the four hundred and thirty-first year after the destruction (*excīdium*) of Troy, in the third year of the sixth Olympiad (*Olympias, ădis*). In summer the nights are shorter than in winter. I am writing (244) in the third hour of the night. Milo came at midnight (*media nox*) with a great band (*manus*) into the Campus Martius. Flaminius arrived at sunset (*occāsus sōlis*) at Lake Trasimene. Thy two letters I received at once [= at one time]. At the death of Numa there was a return (*rēs redit*) to an interregnum. Forsake (*dēserere*) those by whom you will be forsaken in a short time. Astronomers (*mathēmaticī*) teach [us] that the earth completes (*cōnficere*) her revolution (*cursus*) around the sun in 365 days. Quintus Cicero, the brother of Marcus, had finished (*absolvere*) four tragedies in sixteen days. The cities of Africa, for nearly (*prope*) fifty years after Marcus Atilius Regulus (*ē*) had seen no Roman army. In the docks (*nāvāle*) there were old ships, which they had not used for many years. These they refitted (*reficere*), and so in a few days, contrary to the universal (*omnium*) expectation (*opīnio*), they completed twenty-two quadriremes (*-rēmis*) [and] five quinqueremes. Four and twenty years was there fighting (*certārī*, 199, R. 1) with the Poeni in the first Punic war. In the war with the Latins, the dictator Postumius fought (*dīmicare*) an [= in an] engagement with Octavius Mamilius. The Roman people was overcome in many battles, but (*vērō*, § 489) in war never. Hannibal confessed in the senate (*cūria*) that he was beaten not only in the battle, but [also] in the war. I return to what [= those things which] I said in the beginning. Marcus Crassus laughed

[only] once in [his] life. You have an estate (*praedium, villa*) in Bruttium from which (*unde*) you can hear news scarcely three times a year. I have despatched (*dare*) three letters in an hour. The senate decreed that the ambassadors of Jugurtha, King of Numidia, should withdraw (*dēcēdere*) from Italy within the next ten days. We have understood (*accipere*) that Marcus Cato learned Greek (*Graecae līterae*) in [his] old age. In my chequered (*varius*) fortunes (*tempus*), I have seen and fully (*penitus*) appreciated (*perspicere*) thy feelings-of-solicitude (*sollicitūdo*, 195, R. 5). Often have the Carthaginians, in peace and during (*per*) truce (*indutiae*), perpetrated (*facere*) nefarious deeds (*facinus*). In war luck has most power (*posse*). The old Romans advanced (*cūrāre*) their state by two methods (*ars*): by boldness in war, by justice in peace [= in peace by justice].

G. 395–6; A. 54, 2 10; A. & S. 246, 256, R. 16; B. 918; H. 425.

170. The queens of the Amazons boasted (*praedicāre*) that they were begotten (*gignere*) of Mars. Catiline was born of a noble house (*locus*). Cicero sprang (*orīrī*) from a family of equestrian rank (*locus equester*). Thales, one of (*ē*) the seven wise men, says that everything consists (*constāre*) of water.* In the senate house (*cūria*) at Syracuse [there] was a statue of Marcus Marcellus made of bronze.

The Epicureans measure the highest good by advantages, not by moral-worth (*honestās*). Sins are not to be measured by the result (*ēventus*) of things, but by the faults of men. Not by [their] fortune will I value (*aestimāre*) men, but by [their] character. Everything that is pleasant (*jūcundus*) is judged by the bodily feeling (*sēnsus corporis*). Some are human beings not in reality (*rēs*) but in name. We ought to restore (*reddere*) what we have received according to the same measure, or even in more abundant (*cumulātus*) [measure] if we can (*Fut.*). A man may be an old man in body, a youth in feeling (*animus*) Friends are usually (*solēre*) like [each other] in habits. Ariovistus was by nation a German. Parmenio was next to Alex

* Material is expressed by EX with Abl.; seldom by Ablative alone.

ander in dignity. Caesar, according to custom, posted (*dis-pōnere*) sentinels (*vigiliae*) before (*pro*) the camp. The leaders of the Gauls determined to fortify (*mūnīre*) their camps after the manner of the Romans. In learning and every (*omnis*) kind of intellectual-accomplishment (*līterae*), Greece surpassed the Romans; in the art of war and military discipline the Romans were superior.

G. 398; A. 54, 5; A. & S. 256; B. 395; H. 417.

171. No animal (*bēlua*, *Part. Gen.*) is more sagacious (*prūdēns*) than the elephant. No place ought to be dearer (*dulcis*) to thee than thy country. Nothing dries (*ārescere*) sooner (*cito*) than tear[s]. Nothing was further from (*longius aberat ā*) Caesar than cruelty. Who was more famous in Greece than Themistocles? Nothing is more shameful (*turpis*) for a man than womanish (*muliebris*) weeping (*flētus*). What is more shameful than an effeminate man? Deeds are weightier than words. Fortune has more power (*pollēre*) than human counsels. I have received many letters from you at the same (*ūnus*) time, each more agreeable than the other (*alius-alius*).

Pompey was two years (*biennium*) older (*major nātū*) than Cicero. The sun is many times (*pars*) larger and more capacious than the whole (*ūniversus*) earth. This verse is a syllable too short (§ 312). There are much fewer (*pauciōrēs*) [good] orators than good poets [to be] found (*reperīre*). The city was fortified (*mūnīre*) not only by walls, but much more still (*etiam magis*) by [its] natural position (*nātūra loci*, § 357, R. 2). Thou hast received much more good (*pl.*) than thou hast suffered (*perpetī*) evil (*pl.*). The more (*plūra*) men have, the (*eō*) more (*ampliōra*) they desire. The greater the engagement, the more famous (*clārus*) is also the victory. You will much prefer (*antepōnere*) virtue to all things. One camp was two miles (2000 paces) from (*distāre*) the other [= camp from camp]. I set out with Quintus Fabius from Capua, and five days after we arrived at Tarentum. The very thing (*id ipsum quod*, § 375, R. 1) you remind me of, I had written to you four days (*quadrīduum*) before. Long [= much] before, I foresaw (*prō-*

spicere) the coming (*futūrus*) storm. Numa Pompilius lived (*esse*) many years before Pythagoras. Yesterday, not long [= not much] after you went away (*discēdere*) from me, the letter was handed (*trūdere*) to me. Carthage was founded eighty-two years before Rome. The money was carried off (*auferre*) and not recovered until many years afterward [not until = *dēmum*].

G. 401 foll.; A. 54, 6, 7; A. & S. 247, 249; B. 888; H. 414.

172. He prosecuted (*versārī in*) this study with talent (*ingenium*) and not without industry. Marcus Crassus perished on the other side of the Euphrates in shame and disgrace (*ignōminia et dēdecus*). You have written this with great care and diligence. I have consulted your interests to my cost (*magnum damnum*). The Marseillese (*Massiliēnsēs*) kept [their] treaty with the Romans with the greatest (*summus*) fidelity. Cato spoke against Servius Galba before (*ad*) the people with the greatest (*summus*) energy (*contentio*). The legions set out in high spirits (*alacer animus*). In anger nothing can be done well (*rectē*). The Gauls suffered the army of Hannibal to pass (*trānsmittere*) through their territory in peace-and-quiet (*bona pāx*). The general extended (*longius porrigere*) his line of battle, and in this way advanced (*prōcēdere*) against (*ad*) the camp of the enemy. The tribune of the commons, Gajus Memmius, excited (*accendere*) the feelings (*animus*) of the commons in every (*omnis*) way. The war ought (*Ger.*) to have been carried on in a far different (*alius*) method. Swans (*cygnus*) die amid song and pleasure (*voluptās*). The Greek rhetoricians (*rhētor, ōris*) used-to-sit (*assidēre*) in school amidst a great attendance (*frequentia*) of the public (*hominēs*). He lived to extreme (*summus*) old age in the best health. Hares sleep with [their] eyes open (*patēns*).

Aristotle, a man of great (*summus*) genius and knowledge, combined wisdom (*prūdentia*) with eloquence. Men of the highest (*praestāns*) gifts (*ingenium, pl.*) have devoted themselves to (*sē cōnferre ad*) the study of philosophy. The sun is of such a size that it illuminates (*collūstrāre*) and fills everything (*cūncta*) with its light. The war was great and bloody (*atrōx*) and of varying victory. More (*plūra*) I cannot write, so (*ita*) shocked (*percellere*) and depressed (*abjicere*) are my feelings [= of so shocked and depressed feelings am I]. Ibises (*Gen. is* or *idis*) are tall (*excelsus*) birds with stiff (*rigidus*) legs, with horny (*corneus*) and projecting (*prōcērus*) bills; they kill and devour a great quantity (*vīs*) of snakes (*anguis*). I feel [= am in] extraordinary (*incrēdibilis*) solicitude about thy health. The name of Hannibal was very famous [= of great fame] among (*apud*) all.

G. 403 foll.; A. 54, 6; A. & S. 247, 250; B. 873, 890; H. 414, 429.

173. Bulls protect themselves (*sē tūtārī*) with [their] horns, wild boars with [their] tusks (*dēns*), lions with [their] teeth (*morsus, sing.*), some animals by flight, some by hiding (*occultātio*). Pyrrhus was killed (*interīre*) by a blow with [= struck by] a stone. Darius was bound by his relations (*propinquus*) with golden fetters and chains. The enemy has devastated the whole region with fire and sword (*ferrum ignisque, Abl. in ī*). To win (*colligere*) the good will of [one's fellow-] citizens by flattery is disgraceful. The highest hope of his [fellow-] citizens he has surpassed (*superāre*) by incredible bravery. We will (*fut.*) examine [= explore] this thing by means of active (*impiger*) young men.

Country life (*res rūsticae*) is pleasant (*laetus*), not only on account of the crops and meadows and vineyards (*vīnētum*) and shrubbery (*arbustum, pl.*), but also on account of the gardens and orchards (*pōmārium*), then on account of the pasturage (*pastus*) of cattle (*pecudēs*), the swarms (*exāmen*) of bees [and] the variety of all [manner of] flowers. He fears [his] father on account of his guilty conscience (*dēlictī cōnscientia*). Nero, on account of the remembrance (*recordātio*) of his crimes (*facinus*), was never free from fear. For want of water the enemy begged for a parley (*colloquium*). On account of the great occupations of him, of whom everything is sought (*petere*), access (*aditus, pl.*) to (*ad*) him was more difficult [than usual]. From fear of envy he dares not say what he thinks (*sentīre*).

Thy grandmother died from longing after thee (§ 363). From the brevity of the letter you will [= be able to] see (*scīre*) that he is very much occupied. The want of everything increases in consequence of the long siege. All good men mourn (*maerēre*) over the loss (*interitus*) of their [beloved] ones. The boy exults for joy. From excessive (*nimius*) joy I was almost beside myself (*dēsipere*).

G. 408 foll., comp. 667 foll.; A. 54, 10, *b*; A. & S. 257; B. 965; H. 531.

174. The greatest earthquake (*terrae mōtus*) took place (*exsistere*) under the emperor Tiberius, when many cities of Asia fell-in-ruins (*corruere*) on the same day. Cicero was in the habit of writing [down] his speeches after the cases had been already settled (*trānsigere*). Anxur (*neut.*) in [the land of] the Volscians was recovered (*recipere*) in a short time, because the watches (*custōdiae*) had been neglected on a holiday (*diēs festus*). When appetite (*libīdo*) is mistress (*dominārī*) there is no room (*locus*) for self-control (*temperantia*). When piety toward God is done away with (*tollere*), faithfulness and fellowship (*societās*) of the human race are done away with also. In the heat (*ardēns tempus*) of summer the dog star (*canīculae sīdus*) rises (*exorīrī*) as the sun enters (*ingredī*, with *Acc.*) the first part of Leo. If he himself were present, I would speak more timidly of his virtue. Mucius Scaevola came into the camp of Porsenna and undertook (*cōnārī*) to kill him, although death stared him (*sibi*) in the face (*prōpositum esse*). Although everything (*omnēs rēs*) be lost, nevertheless virtue can maintain itself (*sē sustentāre*). After the expulsion (*exigere*) of the kings, consuls were chosen. After the murder of Darius, Bessus (*ē*) fled (*aufugere*) with a few [attendants]. To-morrow (*crastinus diēs*) at sunrise return to the fight! At the occupation of Jerusalem (*Hierosolyma, ōrum*) the victor Pompey touched nothing in (*ex*) that temple (*fānum*). Xerxes, king of Persia [= the Persians], previously (*anteā*) the terror of the nations (*gēns*), after [his] disastrous campaign (*bellum īnfēlīciter gerere*) in Greece began to be an object of contempt (§ 350) even to his own [followers]. I received the letter which you had written at the beginning (*incipere*) of [your] fever. Of (*dē*) a departure (*profectio*) I am not thinking, except (*nisi*) with your approval (*approbāre*). The Gallic war was carried on under the command (*imperātor*) of Caesar. Augustus was born in the consulship of Cicero and Antonius. This crime (*facinus*) the youth has committed (*facere*) at thy instigation (*auctor*). All this did Quintius at the instigation and advice (*suāsor*) of Naevius. The son died in [his] father's lifetime. The poems of that poet were [held] in such (*tantus*) honor in our boyhood that we learned them by heart (*ēdiscere*). Even in a clear (*serēnus*) sky it thunders sometimes (*aliquando*). The wolf escaped (*ēvādere*) in the midst of a great tumult [on the part] of [his] pursuers (*cōnsectārī*).

The Gauls routed (*fundere*) the army of the Romans on the Allia and approached the walls of the city. Pyrrhus sent ambassadors into the city and exerted himself (*adnītī*) in every way to have a treaty made (*Pass.*) and to be received into the friendship of the Romans. After Caesar had made (*habēre*) this speech and roused (*excitāre*) the courage (*animī*) of all, he gave the centurions the commission (*negōtium*) of (*ut*) suspending (*intermittere*) all other works (*opus*) and throwing [their] energy on (*animum cōnferre ad*) digging (*fodere*) wells (*puteus*). Caesar, after spending (*cōnsūmere*) a few days in Syria, gave Sextus Caesar, his friend and kinsman (*propinquus*), the command of (*praeficere*) the legions and the province. Caesar convoked an assembly (*cōntio*) and bestowed (*tribuere*) on every (*quisque*) brave [man] (§ 305) rewards. The besieged (*oppidānus*) made a sally (*ēruptio*) and killed a great number of the enemy (*pl.*).

THIRD COURSE.

PART II.

LXVI. Predication.

G. 197; A. 46, 2; A. & S. 210; B. 666; H. 362.

175. With the exception of (*praeter*) virtue, everything that is considered (*putāre*) a blessing of body and fortune seems insignificant (*exiguus*) and paltry (*minūtus*). No one has [ever] become immortal by cowardice. In consequence of (*ex*) unbounded (*infīnītus*) license, the minds of the citizens become (*ēvādere*) fanciful (*fastīdiōsus*) and effeminate (*mollis*). Caesar became famous by his clemency. Cicero stood forth (*exsistere*) as the advocate (*patrōnus*) of Sextus Roscius. You proved (*exsistere*) a helper (*adjūtor*) to me in [time of] danger. After the fall (*interitus*) of Sejanus, Tiberius became rampant (*saevissimus*). Every burden is made lighter by patience. Constantine was chosen emperor in Britain (*Britannia*) by the soldiers. Marcus Tullius Cicero and Gajus Antonius were declared consuls. No one is held [to be] a great general without the greatest knowledge of military matters (*sing.*). The race (*gēns*) of the Scythians has always been held [to be] the oldest. Dejotarus was thought (*existimāre*) by the senate worthy of the royal title (*rēgāle nōmen*). Antony was declared (*jūdicāre*) by the senate an enemy of the country. Among the old Romans [he] was called an enemy whom following-generations called a foreigner (*peregrīnus*). Justice toward (*adversus*) the gods is called religion; toward parents filial-duty (*pietās*). Cluilius, the Alban general [= the general of the Albans], surrounded his camp with a ditch; the ditch was called for (*per*) several centuries (*saeculum*), from the name of the leader, the Cluilian. My father was Antimachus; my name is (= I am called, *vocārī*) Lycōnidēs.

G. 334; A. 46, 2; A. & S. 230; B. 715; H. 373

176. Necessity makes even the timid brave. The uncle, being attacked (*afficere*) by a grave malady, made his sister's son [his] heir. The Romans chose Aemilius Paullus [to be their] consul against Hannibal. I have always considered him half crazy (*male sānus*), now I consider him besides that [= also] a scoundrel (*impūrus*) and a villain (*scelerātus*). Socrates regarded (*arbitrārī*) himself [as] an inhabitant and citizen of the whole world. Verres despised the Sicilians (*Siculī*); he did not look upon them as (*dūcere prō*) human beings. The old poets call the fruits-of-the-field (*frūgēs*) Ceres; wine, Liber or (*sīve*) Bacchus. The consul Lucius (*ū*) Furius appointed (*dīcere*) Lucius Papirius Cursor dictator, by whom Quintus Fabius Maximus was appointed Master of Horse (*Magister Equitum*). Our ancestors used to call the supreme council, the senate. Romulus called (*vocāre*) the city after (*ex* or *ā*) his name, Rome. The ancients called Spain after the river Iberus (*ē*), Iberia. Gajus Quinctius is dead; [as his] heir he left by will (*ex testāmentō*) his brother Publius Quinctius. I have left the matter untouched (*integer*). I have you [as] witnesses. To have all citizens [for one's] friends would be (246, R. 1) a nuisance (*operōsus*, *Adj.*); it is enough not to have them [for] enemies. We consider (*habēre prō*) certain what is perceived by the senses. Verres had made (*reddere*) the well-furnished (*exornātus*) and [well-] arranged (*īnstructus*) house of Sthenius almost entirely-empty (*nūdus et inānis*). I show (*praestāre*) myself grateful to [those who have] deserved well (*bene meritus*) of (*dē*) me. Show yourself [to be] the (*tālis*) man that we have always known you to be thus far (*hūcusque*). Nerva showed himself [to be] a just (*Superl.*) and mild prince. Gnaeus Pompey showed himself (*sē exhibēre*) the author of my salvation

Predicative Attribution and Apposition.

G. 324; A. 46, 47, 6; A. & S. 204, 205, R. 15; B. 622; H. 363.

177. Socrates drank (*haurīre*) the poison joyous[ly]. The army was brought (*dēdūcere*) into winter-quarters victorious (*victor*) and laden (*onustus*) with spoils. The soldiers did not keep (*servāre*) their ranks [but] fought singly (*rārus*) and scattered (*dispergere*). Men of business (*negōtiātor*) go unwillingly and rarely (*rārō*, *Adv.*) from the provinces to Rome. Marius, for the seventh time (*septimum*) consul, died in his house at an advanced age (*senex*). We will be present at the right time to save you [= as saviours, *vindex*]. The augur Attus Navius [when] a boy, on account of (*propter*) poverty was a keeper of (*pascere*) swine. The temple of Welfare (*Salūs*), which Gajus Junius (*ū*) had vowed as consul [and] let the contract of (*locāre*) as censor, he dedicated as dictator. The whole summer the Nile keeps (*tenēre*) Egypt (*Aegyptus*) entirely overflowed (*obrutus et opplētus*). Very fortunate was Quintus Metellus, who saw three sons consuls, one [of them] also a censor and triumphing [general], and left them in good health (*salvus*), and three daughters married. We must follow nature as [our] guide. Hector, [when] dying, told of (*dēnūntiāre*) the death of Achilles as near at hand (*propinquus*). When (*quum*, with *Indic.*) a good man has to give (*dicere*, *Gerundive*) [his] opinion under oath (*jūrātus*), he will remember (*meminisse*) that he brings in (*adhibēre*) God as [his] witness. Crassus had in (*ūtī*) Asclepiades a friend and physician. In this matter I shall have the assistance of your brother and yourself [= I shall use you and your brother as helpers].

No one ever heard me complain of my lot (*sors*) or say that I never saw any one undergo (*subīre*) such toils. He found the state in a far different condition (*longē aliter sē habēre*) than (§ 646) he had expected. The great (*summus*) poet makes (*facere*) the old king curse (*exsecrārī*) his daughters. The seer (*augur*) Tīrĕsias, whom the poets represent (*fingere*) as a wise man, they never bring in (*indūcere*) deploring his blindness (*caecitās*).

178. Pompey alone has more power (*plūs posse*) than all the rest. Bad citizens would rather (*potius*) perish with all than alone. It is the wise man alone who has the good fortune (*contingit*) to (*ut*) do nothing against his will (*invītus*), nothing under compulsion [= forced]. It is a common (*ūsitātus*) consolation: you are not the only one to whom this has happened. Quintus is entirely changed (*commūtāre*). Spain was the last (*postrēmus*) of the provinces that was completely-subjugated (*perdomāre*). Sicily was the first of all to be made a province Marius wounded-the-pride-of (*laedere*) the nobles, now (*modo*) singly, now in a body (*ūniversī*). Zeno (*ē*) thought that a happy life depended (*positum esse*) on virtue alone. Tullia was the first to salute her consort as king. Lead was first brought (*apportāre*, *Active construction*) by Midacritus from a Cassiteridan island (*Cassiteris, idis*). The nation of the Phrygians (*Phryges*) first yoked (*jungere*) a two-horse chariot (*bīgae*). A trial for life (*jūdicium capitis*) was first held on the Areopagus. In the senate Pompey was generally (*plērumque*) asked his opinion first. Racilius first asked me [my] opinion. Racilius asked me first [my] opinion. Of the two sisters the younger died first. The senate was at once convoked, and met, with a full attendance (*frequēns*). The knights were standing in great numbers (*Superl.*) on the steps of [the temple of] Concord. At first I loved him, afterwards I despised him. We first endure (*tolerāre*) [and] then embrace (*complector*).

LXVII. Infinitive.

G. 527 foll.; A. 70, 2; A. & S. 272; B. 1152; H. 551.

179. We know that the alternation (*vicissitūdo*) of day and night is caused by the revolution (*mōtus*) of the earth around its axis. Who believes that there [ever] was a Centaur or a Chimaera? Reflect (*cōgitāre*) that an enemy [= from an enemy] may become a friend. We have understood that Pythagoras

Democritus, [and] Plato travelled over (*per agrāre*) the most distant (*ultimus*) lands. The physician assures (*cōnfirmāre*) [us] that you will be well (*valēns*) shortly (*propediem*). Dēmarātus informed (*certiōrem facere*) the Lacedaemonians by letter that Xerxes was getting ready for war (*bellum parāre*). The story (*fāma*) went (*ferre, Impf.*) that the temple of Diana of Ephesus (*Ephesius*) was built (*facere*) in common (*commūniter*) by the states (*cīvitās*) of Asia. I grant (*fateor, cōnfiteor*) that I have but now (*nunc dēmum*) learned (*cognōscere*) this thing. The ancients were of opinion (*cēnsēre*) that the future [= future things] could be known (*intelligere*) and foretold by soothsayers (*vātēs*). The news was brought (*afferre*) that the enemy had entered the country (*fīnēs ingredī*). I find (*reperio*) that Plato came to Tarentum in the consulship of Lucius Camillus [and] Appius Claudius.

I admit having done you wrong. He denied having spoken with you. The youth hopes to live a long time [yet]. I hope to be at Athens in the month [of] September. There is no hope of his returning soon. I hope to finish this work. Cleon promised to finish (§ 424, R. 3) the war in twenty days. I promise to undertake this service (*officium*).

G. 528; A. 70, 2; A. & S. 272; B. 1152; H. 551, I.

180. They say (*dīcunt, ferunt*) that tortoises (*testūdo*) and crocodiles bury (*obruere*) their eggs in the sand. They say that Plato came to Italy to make-the-acquaintance-of (*cognōscere*) Archȳtās (*Gen., ae*). The story goes (*trādunt*) that Romulus (*ō*), the founder of Rome, was reared (*nūtrīre*) by a she-wolf; Cyrus, the king of Persia [= of the Persians], by a bitch.

The woman seemed (*Perf.*) to be filled (*afficī*) with great joy. It seemed to me that your brother was greatly rejoiced [= filled with great joy] by my arrival. It is thought (*existimāre*) that you have equipped (*parāre*) an army. It is believed that intellectual-pursuits (*doctrīna, līterae*) were invented in Greece. It is said that Cyrené, a virgin of extraordinary beauty, was carried off by Apollo. It is said (*trādere*) that, at the advice (*auctor*) of the magi, Xerxes set the temples of Greece on fire (*īnflammāre*). There is a tradition (*trāditum est*) that Aristīdes was the most just of men (*ūnus omnium*, § 317). It was believed (*crēditum est*) that the mice ate the cheese (*cāseus*).

The Phoenicians, it is said, were experienced (*Superl.*) sailors. Romulus, they believed, had gone (*trānsīre*) to the gods. Ulysses and Nestor, we have learned, were the wisest of men. Many fables which, they say, were written by Esop (*Aesōpus*), have been made by moderns (*recentiōrēs*). The general hurried (*occurrere*) with the cavalry to the aid of his [men], who, he had learned (*accipere*), had been already beaten (*pellere*). They brought to Caesar those, by whom they thought (*exīstimāre*) the common people (*plēbs*) had been stirred up (*concitāre*).

It seems as if my brother can do nothing without your advice. It seems as if Sicily once stuck on to (*adhaerēre*, with *Dat.*) Italy. It seems as if I shall never return to [my] country. It seemed as if the whole army was about to perish.

G. 532; A. 57, 8, *d*; A. & S. 272; B. 1153; H. 551, II.

181. The Pythian (*ȳ*) Apollo bids us know (*nōscere*) ourselves (*nōsmet*). The teacher bids the scholar come at nine o'clock (*nōna hōra*). The father forbids his son to come into his sight (*cōnspectus*). The consul ordered the men to be thrown (*conjicere*) into prison (*carcer*). Cyrus ordered Croesus to be burned [the burning [of] Croesus] alive. The general ordered the distribution of (*Inf.*) the troops through (*per*) the province. A storm rising, the admiral (*praefectus clāssis*) ordered the sails to be reefed (*contrahere*) and the yards (*antennae*) lowered (*dēmittere*). The praetor had [= ordered] the man arrested and hanged on (*in*) a (*quīdam*) wild-olive (*oleaster*, *Masc.*), a tree which (§ 618) stood [= was] on the market-place of the city.

G. 535; A. 57, 8, *b*; A. & S. 272; B. 1150; H. 549.

182. It was the custom that when (*Abl. Abs.*) the sacrifice for purification (*lustrātiōnis sacrum*) was finished (*peragere*), the army should pass-by-in-review (*dēcurrere*). It is [high] time that we should now (*jam*) think of (*dē*) the eternal (*perpetuus*) [life] to come (292), [and] not of this present (§ 290) brief (*exiguus*) life. It is not right that the greater should obey the less. It is credible that the world was made for man (*pl.*). It is meet (*pār*) that I know [= should know] your plans. It is certain that children are loved by [their] parents. That a great multitude of Germans should have come to Gaul, was dangerous to the Roman people. It is clear that we are born for action (*agere*). It was known that Caesar would make war upon (*bellum īnferre*) the Venetians. It is known that you were absent on that day. An orator must have a good memory (§ 349, R. 4). If there is much dust on his shoes (*calceus*), he must come from (*ex*) a journey. You must be stout-hearted (*animus*). It has delighted (*juvāre*) me that your studies (*līterae*) have been of advantage (*prōdesse*) to you. It is not necessary that I write to (*ad*) you what [= that which] is known to you.

LXVIII. Gerund and Gerundive.

G. 426 foll.; A. 72. 5, 73; A. & S 274 foll.; B. 1304 foll.; H. 559–566.

183. The Lacedaemonians were fired (*īnflammātus*) by the desire of conquering. The carefulness of your writing [= your carefulness of writing] has pleased me very much. I will undertake (*aggredī*) the matter, not so much (*tam*) with the hope of accomplishing [it] as with the wish to try [it]. The alternation (*vicissitūdo*) of day and night preserves living-beings (*animāns*) [by] assigning (*tribuere*) [them] one (*alius*) time for action, one for rest. We came into the garden for the sake of taking a walk. I have written much to you by way of [= for the sake of] admonition. God has made the animals for the sake of man, as-for-instance (*ut*) the horse for (*causā*) riding (*vehī*), the ox for ploughing [= for ploughing the ox]. Man is naturally eager to learn. The soldiers were eager to fight. Wrapping-paper (*charta emporētica*) is worthless (*inūtilis*) for writing. We see that some (*aliī*) by [their] swiftness (*vēlōcitās*) are good (*valēre*) at running, others by [their] strength (*vīrēs*)

[good] at wrestling (*luctārī*). We are not only (*sōlum*) inclined (*prōpēnsus*) to learn but also to teach. To think aright (*bene sentīre*) and to act aright (*rectē*) is enough for living well and happily. The character (*mōrēs*) of boys reveals (*dētegere*) itself in [their] games (*inter, lūdere*). The best orator is [he] who by speaking instructs (*docēre*) the minds (*animus*) of [his] hearers (*audiēns*) as well as (*et-et*) delights and excites (*permovēre*) them. There is often more misfortune in the fear [= fearing] than in the misfortune itself. He has no time free (*vacāre*) [= no time is free to him] from writing or from thinking. My feelings (*animus, sing.*) are averse to (*abhorrēre ā*) writing.

184. Catiline and his associates (*Passive construction*) had made (*inīre*) plans to destroy the city, to massacre (*occīdere*) the citizens, to annihilate (*exstinguere*) the Roman name. All [my] hope of alleviating this annoyance is fixed on (*positum esse in*) your kindness. The Gauls maintained for a long time the (*ille*) monstrous (*immānis*) custom (*cōnsuētūdo*) of sacrificing human beings. Caesar gave up (*omittere*) for the moment (*in praesentiā*) the plan (*ratio*) of following Pompey. To avoid the heat (*calor*) we rested (*acquiescere*) three hours under a shady tree. I rejoice that (*Acc.* with *Inf.*) you are eager to restore (*conciliāre*) peace among the citizens. The soldiers of Marcellus were highly-skilled (*perītus*) in besieging (*oppugnāre*) towns. Everything that (*quidquid*) was calculated (*idōneus*) to feed (*alere*) the fire, was heaped (*ingerere*) upon the works (*opus*). The physician was busily (*sēdulō*) preparing whatever was necessary for treating (*cūrāre*) the wound. A supplication was made for the expiation of the [evil] omens. There are some games (*lūsus*) [that are] right useful (*nōn inūtilis*, 448, R. 2) for sharpening the wits (*ingenium*) of boys. By nature we are inclined (*prōnus*) to love (*dīligere*) men. Stormy weather (*tempestātēs*) is not suitable (*idōneus*) for catching fish (*pl*). Iron is necessary for the cultivation of land (*agrī*). The eyelids (*palpebrae*) are admirably-adapted (*aptissimē factus*) for covering [= shutting] and uncovering [= opening] the pupils (*pūpula*). Nature has

given us eyes as [it has given] the horse and the lion, mane (*sētae*), tail, [and] ears, in order to show (*dēclārāre*) the emotions (*mōtus animōrum*). You will be of the greatest service (*usuī*, § 350) to me in [= for] regaining (*conciliāre*) the good-will (*voluntās*) of my opponents (*adversārius*). The hand is calculated (*aptus*) for painting, for moulding (*fingere*), for chiselling (*sculpere*), for drawing out (*ēlicere*) the tones (*sonus*) of stringed-instruments (*nervus*) and of flutes (*tībia*). By doing away with (*tollere*) superstition, religion is not done away with. By giving and receiving benefits, friendships are made (*parāre*). He had written to (*ad*) me about the purchase (*emere*) of a garden. Virtue shows itself (*cernitur*) especially (*maximē*) in the contemptuous-rejection (*spernere et repudiāre*) of sensuous-enjoyment (*voluptās*); bravery in undertaking (*subīre*) exertions and dangers. Old age draws [us] off from active life (*rēs gerendae*). Collatinus, in the expulsion of the royal family (*rēgēs*), was privy (*socius*) to the plans of Brutus. Cicero begged Luccejus to undertake (*suscipere*) the writing of the history of his consulship. Quintus Catulus let (*locāre*) the repairing (*reficere*) of the temple. Six boys were sent to Germany for their education (*ērudīre*). He contracted for (*condūcere*) the assassination (*necāre*) of the mayor (*praetor*) of the city. The Egyptians give [their] dead to the priests to embalm (*condīre*). Diomedon undertook to bribe (*pecūniā corrumpere*) Epaminondas. Tarquin gave the Sibylline books to two keepers to preserve in the shrine (*cella*) of Jupiter. When Catiline was planning (*mōlīrī*) a revolution, two knights undertook to kill Cicero in his house and to bribe his slaves. I have given him my only son to bring up.

G. 243; A. 73; A. & S. 274, R. 11; B. 1308 foll.; H. 559.

185. When the victory is won (*parere*, *Abl. Abs.*), the conquered must be preserved. God is to be honored (*colere*) not with sacrifices (*immolātio*), but with a pure heart (*mēns*). The honorable (*honesta*) as such (*per sē*) is to be sought after (*expetere*). Riches are to be lightly esteemed. [We] must show the stranger the way, that he may not fall (*incidere*) into dangers. I must bear these annoyances (*molestia*). You must not neglect these directions (*praeceptum*). I must sleep. You must take a walk. You (*pl.*) must read this book often. One must adapt himself (*servīre*) to the crisis (*tempus*). Eloquence must be studied (*studēre*), although some (*quīdam*) abuse it. You must avail yourselves (*ūtī*) of the [favorable] opportunity which offers itself (*darī*, 209). The conquered must be spared (*parcere*).

Too little (*parum*) life is left me to enjoy my riches. My father went to Bajae for the sake of curing (*medeor*) [his] gout (*podagrā*). We are all inclined (*prōnus*) to make use of the assistance (*opera*) of others.

LXIX. Supine.

G. 435 foll.; A. 74; A. & S. 276 foll.; B. 1360 foll.; H. 569.

186. The people of Veji, quelled (*subigere*) by [their] defeat (*adversa pugna*), sent envoys (*ōrātor*) to Rome to sue for peace. When the war with the Helvetii was finished, ambassadors from (*Gen.*) almost the whole of Gaul came to Caesar to congratulate (*grātulārī*) [him]. The viceroys (*praefectī*) of the king of Persia sent ambassadors to Athens to complain that (*quod*, § 539) Chabrias was waging war against the king in conjunction with (*cum*) the Egyptians. He sent his son to the oracle to inquire (*scīscitārī*) what would be the result (*ēventus*) of the war. I hired (*condūcere*) ten men to whitewash (*dealbāre*) the palace. William (*Guilelmus*) had gone to the shore to catch mullets (*mullus*). Hannibal, incredible to relate, in two days (*bīduum*) and two nights reached (*pervenīre*) Adrumetum, which is (*distāre*) about (*circiter*) three hundred miles from Zama. It is impious (*nefās*) to say that no old age can be happy. Many things happen [that are] hard to bear (*tolerāre*). A horrible sight! the old man had his eyes gouged out (*effodere*). You must do (243) what seems [= shall seem] best to do.

LXX. Imperfect.

G. 222; A. 58, 3; A. & S. 145, II.; B. 1087 foll; H. 468.

187. Quintus Fabius Maximus remembered (*memoriā tenēre*) all the wars, not only the domestic but also the foreign (*externus*) [wars]. The Lacedaemonians had two kings. Verres used to live in the winter (*hībernus*) months at Syracuse. In the spring he gave himself up (*sē dare*) to work and travelling (*itinera*); he was carried in a litter (*lectīca*), in which there was a pillow (*pulvīnus*) stuffed (*farcīre*) with roses (*rosa, sing.*, § 195, R. 8). he himself, moreover (*autem*, § 486), had one (*ūnus*) wreath on [his] head, another about (*in*) [his] neck, and applied (*admovēre*) to [his] nose (*nārēs*) a net-bag (*rēticulum*) of the finest (*tenuis*) linen (*linum*) full of roses. After [his] journey was finished (*Abl. Abs.*), he had himself carried (*dēferre*, § 210) in the same litter to [his] very (*usque*) room (*cubiculum*). The long, covered ships were invented by [*active*] the Thasians; before (*anteā*), the fighting was done (*pugnārī*, § 199, R. 1) only from (*ex*) the prow and the stern. From (*ex*) the tongue of Nestor (*Gen. ŏris*), as Homer says (*ait*, § 651, R. 1), speech flowed more sweet than honey.

King Artaxerxes gave Conon, who was living-in-exile (*exsulāre*) at the-court-of (*apud*) Evagoras (*Euagorās*) the command of (*praeficere*) the fleet. Regulus returned to Carthage; he knew full well (*nōn ignōrāre*, § 448, R. 2) that he was setting out to [meet] a cruel (*Superl.*) enemy and exquisite tortures (*supplicium*), but he thought that an oath had to be kept (*servāre*).

LXXI. Future and Future Perfect.

G. 234–7; A. 58, 4, 7; A. & S. 149, III., VI.; B. 1090–98; H. 470–73.

188. Let the man who desires to gain (*adipiscī*) the true glory, discharge the duties of justice. Let any one get angry who will. Nothing holds the commonwealth together (*continēre*) more powerfully (*vehementer*) than credit, and that (§ 612) cannot (§ 304, R. 2) exist unless payment (*solūtio*) for articles-purchased-on-credit (*rēs crēditae*) is necessary. When we meet (*congredior*), then will we confer (*cōnferre*) together (§ 212) personally (*cōram*). Before I settle (*cōnsīdere*) in some place or other, you are not to expect long letters from me. Since (*quoniam*) you are a scholar (*grammaticus*), I will ask you this question (§ 331, R. 2); and if you will solve it (§ 612) for me, you will relieve (*līberāre*) me of great annoyance. If he is made consul, he will conquer with less crime than he began with [= than [that] with (*Abl.*) which he began (*ingredior*)]. If you will convey (*dēportāre*) the arms that remain over (*superāre*) to Brundusium, you will do a vast service (*vehementer prōdesse*) to the commonwealth. Nowhere shall I more easily bear-the-burden-of (*sustentāre*) this wretched life, or (*vel—vel*, § 496)—which is far better—throw it off [for good]. When you return from Ēpīrus, I want you to write to me about the state-of-public-affairs, if there is anything that (§ 634) you nose-out (*odōrārī*). If I have a talk (*colloquī*) with Antony, I will write to you what has been done. They are (*sē habēre*) so far (*hōc*) better off than we, in that (*quod*) when they come to Italy, they come home. Unless my exercise (*scrīptum*) is finished (*absolvere*) to-day, I shall not consider myself acquitted (*līberāre*) of laziness. It will do no harm for you to have [= if you have] a short talk (*aliquid loquī*) with Balbus. If you examine (*īnspicere*) the gardens, you will give me something to (§ 634) write to you.

LXXII. Indirect Question.

G. 469; A. 67, 2; A. & S. 265; B. 1182; H. 524. (*On the Sequence of Tenses, see* G. 510 foll.; A. 58, 10; A. & S. 258; B. 1164; H. 480.)

189. That the sun is great, the philosopher will prove (*probāre*); how great it is, the mathematician (*mathēmaticus*) will prove. You will see yourself what is worthy of a brave and wise man. We must decide (*jūdicāre*) [for] ourselves what the case (*causa*) requires. I wish to know what you have done. The magnet (*magnēs*) is a stone which lures (*allicere*) and attracts (*ad sē attrahere*) iron; the reason (*ratio*) why it happens, I cannot (*nequeo*) tell (*afferre*); that it actually (*omnīnō*) happens you will not deny. You see clearly [= it does not escape (*fugere*) you] how difficult this thing is. What the nature of the mind is, the mind itself does not know. Many tribes (*gēns*) do not know why the moon is eclipsed [= fails, *dēficere*]. Alexander['s] friends asked [him] whom he made heir of the throne (*regnum*). The physician asked the sick man how (*quemadmodum*) he was (*sē habēre*). Sicily was the first to teach the Romans how splendid (*praeclārum*) it is to lord it over (*imperitāre*, with *Dat.*) foreign nations. What the character (*quālis*) of Pompey's first speech-to-the-people (*cōntio*) was, I have [already] written to you. I do not know what he will do. I do not know what I am to do (§ 467). We do not know when the holidays (*fēriae*) will come (*esse*). A maritime enemy scuds in (*advolāre*) suddenly, and does not let it be known (*prae sē ferre*) who he is or whence he comes, or even what he wants (*velle*). Eumaeus asked Ulysses who he was and whence he came. Evander asked Hercules what sort of man he was. I will inform you in what parts (*locus*) I am. I remember what piece of advice you gave me (*aliquid suādēre*, to give a piece of advice). I do not know what [sort] of a plan (§ 371) our friend has adopted (*capere*). I do not know (*ignōro*) what we have to do (§ 353).

LXXIII. Reflexive Pronoun.

G. 295, 521 foll.; A. 19, 3; A. & S. 208; B. 1018; H. 448.

190. I expect the father and his sons. The father and his sons are arrived. The father has brought (*addūcere*) his sons. The father is arrived with his sons. When the father returned home, his sons were away (*abesse*) from home. I like (*dīligere*) Fabius on account of (*propter*) his great (*summus*) kindliness (*hūmānitās*). Fabius is loved by me on account of his great kindliness. King Cyrus put Soëbares in command of (*praepōnere aliquem alicuī*) the Persians and gave him his sister in (*in w. acc.*) marriage. Soëbares, put by Cyrus in command of the Persians, married his sister. Men can use animals (*bestia*) for (*ad*) their service (*ūsus*) without [doing] wrong. When Alcibiades had been cast out (*prōjicere*) unburied and lay [there] forsaken (*dēserere*) [a woman who was] a friend [to him] covered his body with her cloak (*pallium*). The Romans conquered the Corinthians and carried off (*trānsportāre*) their works of art (*ornāmenta*) to their city. Cleopatra applied (*admovēre*) an asp (*aspis, idis*) to (*ad*) her breast and was killed (*exstinguere*) by its venom.

Word was brought (*nūntiāre*) to Cincinnatus [while] ploughing, that he had been made dictator. Cincinnatus [while] ploughing received the news (*nūntius*) that he had been made dictator. Caesar declared (*cōnfirmāre*) that he had conquered not for himself but for [his] country. Caesar's friends declared that he had conquered not for himself but for [his] country. Numa pretended (*simulāre*) that he had (*esse*) conferences by night (*congressus nocturnus*) with the goddess Egeria. Caesar went on board (*cōnscendere*) a ship and bade the whole fleet follow him. Brutus begs you to receive him into your friendship. Eurystheus ordered (*imperāre*) Hercules to bring (*afferre*) him the arms of the queen of the Amazons. I have been informed by a letter from Atticus of your great (*summus*) generosity (*līberālitās*) towards him.

LXXIV. Miscellaneous Exercises. (On the Cases.)

191. 1. Of all the nobles Gajus Sulpicius Galba studied (*Perf.*) Greek literature most (*maximē*). Few [= among] orators have equalled the reputation of Demosthenes. I have been associating (*ūtī* § 221) with Trēbonius on the most friendly terms for many years. From fear of death many have endured (*perferre*) the violence (*vīs*) of the rack (*tormenta, ōrum*). The position (*dignitās*) of the man (*homo*) gave his speech some (*aliquantum*) weight (*pondus*). Who of the Carthaginians was (*Pf.*) worth more than Hannibal? The soul during (*per*) sleep is free from sensations and cares. Atticus abstained from food two days (*bīduum*). The cavalry, which the Haedui had sent to Caesar's help (§ 350) was commanded (*active construction, praeesse*) by Dumnorix. Distress (*aegritūdo*) has deprived me of sleep.

In military matters (*sing.*) the Romans were (*Perf.*) very powerful (*multum valēre*), not only (*quum* § 589) on account of [their] bravery, but also and more especially (*tum plūs etiam*) in consequence of [their strict] discipline. The Tyrians made Alexander a present of a crown of gold of great weight. Atticus had the advantage of (*ūtī*) a very careful (*dīligēns*) father. You ought not (*dēbēre*) to abuse (*male dīcere*) the excellent man. You are not unacquainted with (*nōn fugere aliquem*) the examples of the famous (*superl.*) men, whom we ought to resemble (*similem esse*). Oh! the fallacious hope of men and fickle (*fragilis*) fortune and our idle (*inānis*) exertions (*contentio*)! The besieged (*oppidānī*) had laid (*collocāre*) on the wall stones (*saxum*) of great weight, and beams pointed at-the-end (*praeacūtus*). In an engagement [it is] always those who are most afraid (*maximē timēre*), who are most in danger (*est alicuī perīculum*).

2. Philopoemen equalled any (*quīvīs*) of the renowned generals in bravery. Put on (*impōnere*) me any burden you choose (*quidvīs* § 371); I will bear [it]. Men decide (*jūdicāre*) far more (*plūra*) by hate or love or hope or fear or any mental excitement (*permōtio mentis*), than by the truth. Socrates, according to the testimony of all cultivated men (*ērudītus*) and according to the judgment of all Greece, was, both (*quum*) in wisdom (*prūdentia*) and eloquence, the prince of all philosophers. I perish by my [own] ill desert (*vitium*); chance has done (*afferre*) me no (*nihil*) harm [= evil]. It has been all brought upon [me] (*contrahere*) by my own fault. How much money (*argentum*) do you want (§ 390)? [There is] nothing [that is] either (§ 444) more profitable (*ūber*) in the matter of utility (*ūsus*) or handsomer (*ornātus*) in the matter of appearance (*speciēs*) than a well tilled (*colere*) field. In consequence of your arrival, I have much more courage (*animus*). With the multitude of trees, there could be no lack of (*dēficere*) timber (*māteria*). I am accused by you without ground of sending (*missio*) the letter. According to the civil law (*jūs*) [he] is free, who is [born] of a free mother. A great man (*Gen.* § 365)

holds firmly to (*retinēre*) [what is] right and honorable in every situation (*fortūna*). When Caesar had crossed the Rubicon, everything was full of fear and confusion (*error*). The virtue of distinguished (*excellēns*) citizens deserves (*dignum esse*) imitation, not envy. We finished the march (*iter*) by a hot (*aestuōsus*) and dusty (*pulverulentus*) road. In that engagement [there] fell some Roman knights. The land (*ager*) is now worth more than formerly [= than it had been heretofore, *antehāc*]. The greatest evil is avarice; for many have been greatly injured by it [= for many has avarice affected with great disadvantage, *incommodum*]. In this solitude [of mine] I forego (*carēre*) all conversation [= the conversation, *colloquium*, of all].

3. After the capture (*capere*) of Syracuse, Marcellus brought to Rome the works of art (*ornāmenta*) of the city, statues and paintings, in which Syracuse abounded. Your early (*mātūrus*) arrival was necessary to us. After murdering Darius, Bessus fled with a few [attendants]. The Albans with an enormous (*ingēns*) army made an attack (*impetus*) on the Roman territory (*ager*). The Arabians (*Arabs*) because (*quod*) they occupy themselves (*ūtī*) especially (*maximē*) with the grazing (*pastus, ūs*) of cattle (*pecus pecudis, Pl.*) wander over (*peragrāre*) plains (*campī*) and mountains, summer and winter. In the Peloponnesian (*Peloponnēsiacus*) war the Athenians upon the advice and under the influence (*auctōritās*) of Alcibiades declared war against (*bellum indīcere*) the Syracusans. Alexander made himself master (*potīrī*) of all Asia in a few years. In civil strife (*dissēnsio*) we ought to take (*sequī*) the better (*honestus*) side (*pars*). Nothing is more praiseworthy (*laudābilis*), nothing more worthy of a great and renowned (*praeclārus*) man, than a forgiving and merciful disposition (*plācābilitās, clēmentia*). In Africa there is a race of people of sound (*salūber*) body and capable of bearing fatigue (*labōrēs*). Without accomplishing their purpose (*rē īnfectā*), the ambassadors returned home. I will go into the country and remain there. Pericles ruled (*praeesse*) the state (*cīvitās*) by his great (*superl.*)

influence many (*plūrimī*) years in peace and in war. You act (*facere*) as (*ut*) is becoming to you. The noble (*honestus*) man is ashamed to play the slave (*servīre*). I repent of my laziness. That my friends should know this is a matter of importance to me and to them (*ipsī*). Thy presence at Rome is a matter of great importance to us.

192. 1. At the outset (*principium*) of [his] speech (*dīcere*) the orator turned pale (*exalbescere*) and trembled in every (*omnis, pl.*) limb (*artus, ūs*). Although Themistocles, as general in the Persian war, had liberated Greece from slavery, when driven into exile on account of envy [= when Themistocles had liberated and (*-que*) had been driven], he did not bear (*ferre*) the injustice of [his] ungrateful country; he did the same that Coriolanus had done twenty years before; he joined (*sē jungere*) the enemy. The spendthrift (*prōdigus*) sold for a small amount all that he had received from his ancestors (*majōrēs*). It is the duty of him who stands at the head of (*praeesse*, with *Dat.*, *Subjunct.*, § 631) the citizens to labor for (*servīre*) their interests (*commodum*) and welfare. Alexander died at Babylon of disease, aged thirty-three years and one month. I have got (*pōnere*) you into favor with (*apud*) him. Epicurus preferred (*mâlle*) calling (*dīcere*) the gods like men to [calling] men like the gods. We have received the stranger into our house (*tectum*). Caesar set out from Egypt by land for Syria. I want very little (*perexiguum*) time. That ship best completes [its] course that has (*ūtī*) the most expert (*sciēns*) pilot (*gubernātor*). He had sent me (*ad mē*) a letter full of all [manner of] insults (*probrum*) to (*in*) me. It is a saying (*dictum*) of Chīlo of Lacedaemon, one-of (*ex*) the seven sages (*sapiēns*), [that] it is becoming to forget a benefit conferred (*dare*), to remember [a benefit] received. Nothing can be more pleasant to me than this book. The little Ciceros (*Cicerōnēs puerī*) are learning and practising (*sē exercēre*); but the one, as Isocrates said in the case of (*in*) Ephorus and Theopompus, needs the rein (*frēna*), the other the spur (*plur.*). The Parthians had crossed the Euphrates under the leadership of

Pacŏrus, with almost all their forces. Cluentius had not seen any (*nihil*) misfortune in [his] life.

2. When (*quum*, with *Ind.*) we are relieved (*prīvāre*) of pain, we rejoice at the mere (*ipse*) release (*līberātio*) and freedom (*vacuitās*) from (*Gen.*) all annoyance (*molestia*). Jugurtha was vigorous (*validus*) of intellect (*ingenium*), ready in action (*manū prómptus*) [and] eager (*appetēns*) for military glory. Foolish people do not remember past blessings, do not enjoy the present, only (*modo*) look forward to (*exspectāre*) the future. **I [am old enough to] remember* Cinna, I have seen Sulla.** In **the battle of (*apud*) Zama, the Roman was superior in number[s]** and in courage. Grateful people imitate fruitful fields, which yield (*efferre*) much more than they receive (§ 625). After reading the letter, Sextius hurried (*advolāre*) with incredible speed to (*ad*) the city. If wild beasts love (*dīligere*) their young (*pullus*) how indulgent [= of what indulgence] should (*dēbēre*) we be toward our children. The soldier showed the sword besmeared (*oblinere*) with blood, which he had made bloody (*cruentāre*) in the battle by slaying (*Abl. Abs.*) many of the enemy [= many enemies]. The welfare of men depends (*nītī*) not only on virtue but also on reputation (*fāma*). You are abusing my patience. Man alone of (*ex*) so many kinds of living-beings (*animāns*) has [= partakes of] reason. A strong and elevated (*excelsus*) mind is free from care and distress (*angor*). After the death of Thēramenes, Greece was filled (*replēre*) with exiles. Magistrates are necessary, for without their [= without whose, § 627] foresight and carefulness a state cannot exist (*esse*). The consul went (*proficiscī*) to Africa with a hundred ships. Jugurtha surrounded (*circumvenīre*) unexpectedly (*dē imprōvīsō*) the camp of Aulus Postumius with a multitude of Numidians (*Numidae*).

3. The Romans made use of auspices (*auspicia*) not only in time of peace but also in time of war. As [it was] now the tenth day [that] I had been suffering (*Impf.*) in my bowels (*ex intestīnīs labōrāre*), I ran into the country. There is noth

* In this sense, meminī takes accusative.

ing more useful for the body (*plur.*) than salt and sun. The more violence (*vīrēs*) storms (*procellae*) have, the less [their] duration (*tempus*). The soldiers occupied (*capere*) a somewhat higher (*ēditus*) point [= place]. Lūcius Sextius was the first of (*dē*) the commonalty (*plēbs*) to be made consul 388 years after the building of the city, 366 before the birth of Christ. The old man had [= was of] a very large body and terrible countenance (*faciēs*) [terrible] because (*quod*) he was black and had long hair (*capillus*) and a flowing (*prōmissus*) beard. The highest hope of his [fellow] citizens he surpassed by incredible bravery. The Numidians live chiefly (*plērumque*) on milk and game (*caro ferīna*). The boy for the last (*hic*) six months has not deserved (*dignum esse*) even (*nē—quidem*) the slightest blame (*reprehēnsio*). We need the eyes for seeing (*cernere*). For the common welfare of the citizens good laws are necessary. Crassus returned home with a fever. I am pained (*dolēre*) at his undeserved (*injustus, superl.*) misfortune (*calamitās*). Neither [= not] in courage nor [= not] in arms, not in military art nor strength (*pl.*) of body was the Tarentine a match (*pār*) for the Roman. The father was fifty years older than the sons. Aulis is separated (*distāre*) from Chalcis (*Gen. idis*) by a space of 3,000 paces (*passus*). One consul fought on (*ad*) the river Ticīnus, both together (*ambo*) somewhat later on the Trebia.

4. He went from the town of Fregellae to the city of Rome. Expelled from the obscure (*ignōbilis*) island of Mycŏnos, he took refuge (*confugere*) in the celebrated city of Corinth. Crispus halted (*consistere*) at Praeneste, a charming (*amoenus*) town. How far is (*distāre*) Rome from Bajae? The general led his troops in three days (*trīduum*) from Naples to Rome. The thief took away a golden image from the temple of Diana at Ephesus. I sent the message to my uncle at Rome. She lived twelve years at Paris (*Lutētia*) in a refined (*pūrus et castus*) household.

FOURTH COURSE.

SYNTAX OF THE VERB.

COMPOUND SENTENCE.

LXXV. Interrogative Sentences.

G. 451 foll.; **A.** 71; **A. & S.** 198, 11, 265; **B.** 1040, 1182, 1101 **H.** 346, 486, 525 foll.

193. Have you seen the sunset at Naples (*Neāpolis*)? Have you ever been at Athens? Do not men often despise the better? Did Hannibal carry on war against Rome from hate? Was his hatred unjust? Is the science of war nothing because a great (*summus*) general sometimes runs (*fugere*)? All wicked (*improbus*) men are slaves. Or is he free who is a slave to [his] lust? You remember those magnificent temples which you saw in Italy. Or perhaps you are too young to remember them. Are you still (*etiam nunc*) hesitating? Or do you not know the law of Solon, who laid the death penalty on any one who (*capite sancīre sī quis*) in time of (§ 393) civil-faction (*sēditio*) did not belong to (*Plpf. Subj.*, § 365, R. 1) one party or the other (*alteruter*)?

194. Have your forces been diminished (*imminuere*), or theirs increased? Is the world governed by the providence of God or by chance? Is the cup gold or silver? Does wisdom alone make (*efficere*) us happy or not?

195. He asked the boy whether he wanted to go back to his father. I want (*velim*, § 250) you to write me under what consuls Clodius was tribune of the Commons. When I get to Rome and find out (*intelligo*) what the business is, I will write to you at what time I shall return. I should like you to be with me when Lewis (*Ludovīcus*) comes (*Fut.*). It is of great importance to me that we should be together then. You will know when it will be [= when that day will be], if you will (§ 236) instruct (*negōtium dare ut*) your servant to inquire. You will perceive (*intellego*) whether they [really] think so (*id sentīre*), or [only] make believe (*simulāre*).

LXXVI. Interrogative Sentences.

196. What difference does it make whether I come now or ten years hence (*ad decem annōs*)? Let me know whether you will be long at your country-seat (*vīlla*) or not. If anybody asks why I am not at home, answer: "It is none of your business." I ask, whether it was none of my business how my friend was [*quid agis?* = how are you?]. Write me whether Clodia was alive or not when her son died.

197. Urged (*adductī*) by famine and want, the soldiers went secretly out of camp to try if they could find anything to eat (§ 634) in the fields. The general began to reconnoitre (*circumspectāre*) in case he could attack (*adorīrī*) the enemy in the rear. An effort was made (*rēs temptāta est*) in the hope that the brother of the accused (*reus*) might be permitted (*licēre*) to console him, [as he was] dying. I opened (*solvere*) the package (*fasciculus*) to see if there was a letter to me in [it].

198. I am half-inclined to think it is better to travel abroad (*peregrīnārī*) than to sit [still] at home. I have sent you a copy (*exemplum*) of my letter to Gajus, because I am half-inclined to think that it would have been better not to have written it. I doubt but he will turn [his] wife out of doors (*forās ējicere*). I do not doubt that he will turn [his] wife out of doors. He will not hesitate to turn his wife out of doors (§ 551, R. 3). I am disposed to think he will not turn his wife out of doors. I am inclined to think that Hannibal was more wonderful (*mīrābilis*) in adversity than in prosperity (*adversae, secundae rēs*). It may be (*forsitan*) that I did not (*parum*) understand you.

LXXVII. Interrogative Sentences.

199. What was I to answer? Was I to kill the impudent varlet (*homo*)? Whither am I to betake myself (*sē cōnferre*)? They did not know what to seek or what to avoid. They took counsel (*cōnsultāre*) in what way the enemy was to be met (*obviam īre*, 208).

200. Somehow or other the remedy (*medicīna*) is worse (*gravis*) than the disease. Archimedes was killed by some soldier or other, who-did-not-know (*ignārus*) who he was. It is extraordinary what an amount of labor men spend on (*pōnere in*) trifles (*rēs levissimae*).

201. You know what a troublesome (*molestus*) creature Peter (*Petrus*) is. What madness has seized him that he [= by what madness seized, *captus*] comes to my house daily? Whither was he going that you asked him so angrily whether his mother knew that he was out (*forās exīsse*)? With what genius are you endowed that you hope to obtain the highest honors in the state? Do not keep back (*silēre*) what you have come to ask [= asking]. I am going to bed. To do what (*quid ut*)? I crossed the ocean. To see what? He came early in the morning (*māne*). What was to be done?

LXXVIII. Non dubito quin.

G. 551; A. 65, 1, *b*; A. & S. 262, R. 7; B. 1232; H. 498.

(*Sequence of Tenses:* G. 510 foll.; A. 58, 10; A. & S. 258; B. 1164; H. 480.)

202. I do not doubt that a ruinous (*exitiōsus*) war is impending. I do not doubt that Caesar has arrived at Brundusium. I do not doubt that if anything of the sort (*ējusmodī*) happens, you will hurry (*advolāre*) to me. I do not doubt that if the king had found out the approach of the enemy, he would have crossed the river.

I did not doubt that we could not accomplish the journey. We did not doubt that the house had been adjudged (*adjūdicāre*) to us. It was not doubtful that if he walked briskly (*rectē*) he would arrive before day (*lūx*). There was no doubt that if he had written the letter, I should have been relieved of very great annoyance (*molestia*).

There is no doubt that the conservatives (*bonī*) would have conquered, if Caesar had been their leader. There is no doubt that they will make (*efficere*) him dictator.

I did not doubt that my brother and myself ought to make our way (*sē cōnferre*) to Brundusium.*

I did not doubt that he would have come to his senses (*resipiscere*)† if he had followed (*ūtī*) your advice.

LXXIX. Verbs of Emotion.

G. 533; A. 70, 5, *b*; A. & S. 273, 5 (3); B. 1154; H. 552, III.

203. I am glad that you have got well (*convalēsco*). I thank you (*grātiās ago*) for having come to my assistance. Are you sorry or glad that your mother-in-law (*socrus*) has hanged herself (*suspendiō vītam fīnīre*)? I am astonished at your not having been beaten (*vāpulāre*) by your own servants. He was indignant (*indignē ferre*) at being envied by his own brothers.

G. 542; A. 70, 5, *b*; A. & S. 273, 5; B. 1258; H. 520.

204. We regret that we do not know when we shall see you. Aristides is praised for his justice and integrity; Alcibiades is blamed for having from lust (*cupiditās*) of vengeance (*ulcīscī*) betrayed his country to the Lacedaemonians. Valerius used to praise the [good] fortune of Brutus in having found his death (*mortem occumbere*) [while] fighting for his country. The legions thanked the general for having given so good (*superl.*) an opinion (*jūdicium facere*) of them. The generals of the king of Persia sent ambassadors to Athens to complain (*querī*) that Chabrias was waging war on the king of Persia in conjunction with the Egyptians. Are you sorry that I have

* The subjunctive after QUIN may be an original subjunctive. Nōn dubito quīn statim veniam, CIC., *I do not doubt that I ought to come at once.* Mihi vidēbāre nōn dubitāre quīn cēderem, CIC., *It seemed to me that you did not doubt that I ought to withdraw.*

† In the absence of periphrastic tenses use the forms of POSSE.

brought the army across (*trādūco*) safe? (*Negative idea. What mood?* comp. 540, R. 1). Xerxes thanked Dēmarātus for having been the only one to tell him the truth.

G. 534, 560; A. 57, 8, *g*; 70, 4, *c*; A. & S. 270, R. 2; B. 1159; H. 553, III.

205. I whom some consider the father of my country, [I] bring hordes of outlandish-foreigners (*barbarī*) to devastate Italy! [To think] that he should have entertained (*cōgitāre*) such cruel [projects]! The idea of your having done anything that would benefit (*prōdesse*) the human race! That he, who [though] victorious at (*ad*) Cannae had not dared (*Subj.*) to go toward Rome, should, after being repulsed from Capua, have conceived the hope of possessing himself of the city!

LXXX. Sentences of Design.

G. 543 foll.; A. 64; A. & S. 262; B. 1025; H. 497.

206. Before old age, let us see to it (*cūrāre*) that we live well, in old age that we die well. I have toiled (*labōrāre*) to get the prisoners spared [= that the prisoners might be spared, § 208]. The father begged (*rogāre*) each individual (*ūnusquisque*) senator (*Gen. pl.*) with tears (*part.*) to spare his son; afterwards he begged and besought the opposite party (*adversāriī*) not to attack (*oppugnāre*) his son. Beware (*cavēre*) of considering (*habēre*) the unknown as (*prō*) well known. There are letters extant (*exstāre*) from Philip to (*ad*) Alexander, in which he advises (*praecipere*) that he win (*allicere*) the hearts (*animus*) of the masses to love him (*ad benevolentiam*) by kind (*benignus*) language (*ōrātio*). Alexander made an edict (*ēdīcere*) that no one should paint him except (*praeter*) Apelles. Metellus persuaded the ambassadors of Jugurtha to deliver (*trādere*) to him the king alive or (*aut—aut*) dead (*necātus*). The general ordered his men to march as much as possible to the left that they might not be seen from any quarter (*nēcunde*). Lucullus says with regard to his history (*plur.*), which he had written in Greek, that in order to prove more readily that it (*ille*) was the work of a Roman (§ 365, R. 1) he had inserted (*īnserere*) certain solecisms (*soloecismus*).

I readily convinced (§ 546, R. 2) him that I was not free to do what he asked (*Subj.*). I am convinced that this thing will be rather (*potius*) to your credit (*laus*) than to your discredit (*vituperātio*). Pompey reminded me that I had promised him not to go into the senate until I had (*Plpf. Subj.*) finished the business.

LXXXI. Sentences of Design.

Sentences of Design take as a rule only the Present and Imperfect Subjunctive.

207. Birds of prey (*rapāx*) are endowed (*praeditus*) with a very keen (*ācer*) vision (*vīsus*) in order that they may be able to see [their] prey from a great distance (*ē longinquō*). The men of Clusium (*Clūsīnī*) sent ambassadors to Rome to beg the senate for help. The thirty tyrants sent people (§ 623) to kill Alcibiades. Isocrates used to write speeches for others to use in court (*in jūdiciō*). Caesar had given orders before the engagement for the horses to be removed in order that the hope of flight might be taken away (*tollo*) thereby. Tarquinius Superbus chose (*legere*) no one senator [= into the senate], that the estate (*ordo*) might be the more despised (*contemptus*) by reason of [its] meagre-numbers (*paucitās*).

No sensible man (*nēmo prūdēns*) punishes because a sin has been committed (*peccātur*, 199, R. 1), but to prevent its commission. The proconsul Metellus avoided [= fled] the sight (*cōnspectus*) of Marius, who was his successor (*in locum alicūjus succēdere*) in order not to see a low-born fellow (*homo ignōbilis*) with the [consular] power and the fasces.

I omit to name many [who are] worthy of praise, in order that no one may complain (*querī*) that he is passed by (*praetermitto*). The conspirators bound themselves by a solemn oath (*inter sē sancīre*) that no one should divulge (*nūntiāre*) the thing. We demand (*flāgitāre*) that you determine (*statuere*) nothing about the accused (*reus*) in his absence without investigation of the case (*causā incognitā*). A law was passed (*ferre*) that no one should be accused of past offences (*ante actae rēs*) nor fined [therefor].

The army begged Alexander with tears (§ 546, R. 3) to put an end to the war. Herod (*Hērōdēs*) gives orders (*imperāre*) for the children (*parvulī*) to be slain. Let me perish rather than be a burden to you.

LXXXII. Verbs of Hindering.

G. 547; A. 50, 3, *e*; A. & S. 262, R. 9; B. 1231; H. 498.

208. I will not hinder that being done. I do not deter you from changing your opinion (*sententia*). The humble origin (*ignōbilitās*) of Marius and Cicero did not stand in the way of their working up (*ēnītī*) to the consulship (*pl.*). Much may stand in the way of the accomplishment (*verb*) of your endeavors (*cōnātum.*) It was the fault of the general (*per aliquem stāre quōminus*) that the blow (*clādēs*) received at Cannae was not repaid (*reddo*) to the enemy.

LXXXIII. Verbs of Fearing.

G. 552; A. 70, 3; A. & S. 262, R. 7; B. 1215; H. 492, 4.

209. I fear (*vereor*) that I am troublesome (*molestus*) to you I fear that I have preached my sermons (*praecepta canere*) to deaf ears. I was worried (*ango, Impf.*) [for fear] that I had let something disgraceful (*dēdecus*) come-to-my-charge (*admittere, Pass. constr.*). I fear he has not received the letter. I do not fear that the enemy will not be conquered.* I fear that, if I give this letter to him, he will open it (*solvere.*)

LXXXIV. Sentences of Tendency and Result.

G. 553 foll.; A. 65; A. & S. 262; R. 3; B. 1218, H. 494.

Sequence of Tenses, G. 510 foll.; A. 58, 10; A. & S. 258; B. 1164; H. 480.

210. The severity (*gravitās*) of the sickness makes us need (*egēre*) medicine. [It is] by obedience (*obsequium*) [that] you have brought it about (*efficere*) that no one is dearer to the prince than you.

* NE—NŌN, more frequently after negatives.

It often happens that the most perspicacious man fails to notice (*fallit mē* = it escapes my notice) what lies (*positum est*) before [his] eyes. The proconsul took many cities and plundered the temples of the gods; and hence it came about that he had a [super]abundance of gold and silver. It happened accidentally (*forte*) that we met (*obviam esse*) the line of march (*agmen*). He ought to be a greater friend to me than to those men, who have always been bitter enemies to us [and § 639], by whose artifices it has been brought about that the state is (§ 512, R. 2) in its present (*hīc*) condition. If this statement (*ēnūntiātio*) is not true, it follows that it is false. It is owing to (*fierī* with *Abl.*) your dilatoriness (*cunctātio*) that Hannibal has had (§ 221) Italy as a province for more than nine years (*jam decimum ānnum*) [and] has lived here longer than in Carthage.

Some animals as-for-instance (*ut*) the tiger (*tigris*) and the hyena (*hyaena*) are so savage (*ferōx*) that they cannot be tamed in any way. The enemy rushed up (*advolāre*) so quickly that the people in the fields were surprised (*opprimere*). The ways of living [= institutions of life] are so (*sīc*) different (*distāre*) that the Cretans (*Crētēnsis*) deem it honorable to commit highway-robbery (*latrōcinārī*). So much [and only so much] meat (*cibus*) and drink (*pōtio*) is to be taken (*adhibēre*) as to restore (*Pass.*) the strength (*vīrēs*), not overpower (*opprimere*) [it]. There arose (*exorīrī*) a violent storm (*turbida tempestās*) [so] that we could not leave (*proficīscī*) the harbor.

LXXXV. Sentences of Tendency and Result.

211. It is rare for a man to respect (*verērī*) his own judgment sufficiently. It is true that Scipio (ī) surpassed all-other (*cēterī*) generals in good luck, it is not to be denied (*īnfitiārī*) that Hannibal excelled (*praestāre*) Scipio in skill (*prūdentia*). It is not right that envy should be an attendant (*comes*) of worth.

Tantum abest ut.

212. So far from his changing my plan, I think that he himself ought to be sorry for having given up (*dēcēdere dē*) his own

So far from grieving that his mother-in-law (*socrus*) was dead, he got up (*īnstruere*) a party (*convīvium*) three days (*trīduum*) after she was buried (*efferre*, § 566). So far were the ancient Romans from luxury that they used to swear at the Megalensian games not to take (*ūti*) any wine except (*nisi*) native (*patriae*).

Exceptional Sequence of Tenses in Sentences of Result.

G. 513 A. 58, 10, *c*; A & S. 258; R. 3 (*c*); B. 1168; H. 488, 2.

213. The desire of driving the Romans from Sicily went so far (*adeō prōcēdere*) that even the besieged (§ 566) at Syracuse plucked up courage (*animōs tollere*). All the roads were blocked (*praeclūdere*) by cavalry so that of that great (*tantus*) multitude scarcely a thousand got off (*ēvādo*). The army was so (*eō usque*) cut to pieces (*caedere*) that of (*ex*) eighteen thousand men not more [than § 311, R. 4] two thousand escaped. Twenty-five jurymen (*jūdex*) were so brave as to have preferred to perish themselves rather than ruin the State. It happened (*ēvenīre*) that both consuls came to Praeneste on the same day. So many ships were collected that you would have thought (§ 252) that all the forests of Italy had not been sufficient for building so great a fleet. Such a mixed-multitude (*turba*) of people had filled all the roads that you would have said that Africa was suddenly forsaken (*relinquī*).

LXXXVI. Temporal Sentences.

Antecedent Action.

G. 563; A. 62, 2, *a*; A. & S. 259; R. 1 (*d*); B. 1237; H. 474.

214. After the war was finished (*cōnficere*) the consul returned to Rome and triumphed. After the soldiers had gained the victory, they left the vanquished nothing (*nihil reliquī facere*). When (*quum*) Scipio said this, he suddenly caught sight of (*cōnspicere*) Lūcius Fūrius coming, and as-soon-as (*ut*) he [had] saluted him, laid hold of him (*apprehendere*) in the most cordial [= friendly] manner, and seated him (*pōnere*) on his sofa (*lectus*). As soon as (*quum prīmum*) I got to Rome, I thought there was nothing I had to do (§ 353) sooner than (*quam ut*) congratulate you (*alicuī grātulārī*). Three days after the king came, he put his forces in line (*in aciem ēdūxere*), but after the battle (*pugnārī*) began [his] line gave way (*inclīnārī*). After [he saw that] the men were unwilling to renew (*redintegrāre*) the fight, he withdrew into winter-quarters. After I tell you what I think, you ought to believe me. After I have thought out (*excōgitāre*) a plan, you ought to try (*ūti*) [it].

Postquam.

G. 564–5; A. 64, 2, *a*, R. 1; A. & S. 259; R. 1, *d*; B. 1249.

215. The besieged (*oppidānī*) surrendered (*i. e.* themselves) forty-seven days after we began to besiege them. Fifty years after Themistocles left Athens because (*Rel.*) he could not defend it, Pericles refused to do the same thing, although he held nothing but (*praeter*) the walls. Cimon was recalled to his country five years after he was banished. Gnaeus Scipio was killed eight years after he came to Spain [and] twenty-nine days after the death of his brother.

Iterative Action.

G. 568-9; A. 62, 1; A. & S. 259, R. 4 (3); H. 475, 3, 486, 5.

216. Physicians employ-remedies-for (*medērī*) even the smallest part of the body, if it suffers (*condolēre*). Fortune, for the most part (*plērumque*), makes those blind whom she embraces. As often as (*ut*) a man (*quisque*) killed an enemy, he wasted (*terere*) time by cutting off (*abscīdere*) [his] head. Women in India, when the husband of any one (*quis*, § 302) dies, enter into a contest (*certāmen*) which one he loved (*dīligere*) most. The general did not leave (*ēgredī*) the standing camp (*statīva*) except (*nisi*) when want of forage (*pābulum*) forced him to change [his] position. The whole theatre (*pl.*) cries out (*exclāmāre*) if a verse is one syllable (§ 400) too short (§ 312) or (*aut—aut*) too long. As often as each cohort charged (*prō* *currere*), a great number of the enemy fell. When we see swallows, we think (*arbitrārī*) that summer is beginning. The further they advanced (*prōferre*) [their] camp, the further they were from water. Whenever the enemy made an attack (*impetum facere*) on any part [= on whatever (*quīcumque*) part], they forced our men to give ground (*locō cēdere*). Young ducks (*pullī anătum*) leave the hens, by which they have been hatched (*exclūdere*), as soon as they see the water. Whenever (*sī quando*) you come to my house, you will find a bed ready.

LXXXVII. Temporal Sentences.

G. 570 foll.; A. 58, 2, *e*; A. 263, 4; B. 1239; H. 521 foll.

(1.) *Contemporaneous Action.*

217. While my wife is getting ready (*sē comparāre*), a whole hour passes (*abīre*). While the Romans were making-preparations and consultations (*cōnsultāre*), Saguntum was attacked (*Impf.*) with might and main (*summa vīs*). The consul kept the enemy busy (*tenēre*) as long as there was any (*quidquam*, § 371) [day]light. Cato, as long (*quoad*) as he lived, increased in reputation for virtue (*virtūtum laus*). We favored you so long as (*dum*) we saw that you were a friend of virtue and an enemy of vice. Hannibal went with his army from Spain (*Hispānia*) to Italy, and defeated the Romans with small forces, until at length he was compelled to leave Italy with great loss (*dētrīmentum*). Metellus found in Rhodes an honorable retreat (*perfugium*), and gave himself up to literature and philosophy until he was recalled to [his] country by the authority of the senate and the order of the people. I shall not be able to rest until I ascertain (*rescīsco*) how you are (*quid agis?*). The Thracians did not move a jot (*nihil*) until the Romans passed by. They will not make an end of following until they drive the enemy headlong. Caesar determined to tarry (*morārī*) in Gaul until he knew that the legions were posted (*collocāre*) and the winter-quarters fortified. Let [my] friends perish, so long as [my] enemies go down (*intercidere*) too (*ūnā*). We are ready to bear toils and burdens if we only gain (*adipiscī*) the victory. It is never base to be overcome provided that you do not throw away (*prōjicere*) your arms.

They rested the following day to let the prefect meanwhile [= while the prefect should] inspect the youth of the city. I told him that you had waited for his arrival as long as (*quoad*) you could. I should have preferred to have stayed (*residēre*) in some town or other until I was sent for (*arcesso*).

Exspecto.

218. He waited to get the news from (*certiōrem fierī dē*) the army. If he is waiting until I bring him the newspaper (*acta diurna*), let him begone. He thought that I would wait for the moon to wane (*senescere*). Each (*uterque*) general was waiting [to see, § 462, 2] whether the forces of the enemy would try (§ 515, R. 2) to cross the river. What are you waiting for? [= for what to take place (*quid ut*) are you waiting?].

(2.) *Subsequent Action.*

Ante (Prius) quam.

G. 576 foll.; A. 62, 2, *c;* A. & S. 263, 3; B. 1237, 1241; H. 528.

219. Before I speak of the misfortunes of Sicily, it seems to me (§ 528) that I ought to say a few [words] about the dignity, the antiquity (*vetustās*) [and] the value (*ūtilitās*) of the province. The feelings (*animus*) are often engrossed (*occupāre*) by angry passion (*īrācundia*) before reason can (§ 559) provide against their being engrossed (§ 548; § 512, R. 2). All the enemy turned [their] backs, and did not cease (*dēsistere*) to run until [= before] they arrived (*pervenīre*) at the river Rhine. Although (*etsī*) I understand (*teneo*) what he is ready to say, yet I will make no counter remark (*nihil contrā disputāre*) before he has said [it]. A careful physician, before attempting (*cōnārī*) to apply a remedy (*medicīnam adhibēre*) to a sick man, ought to make himself acquainted with (*cognōscere*) his disease. The Romans wished to protect the Saguntines, but Hannibal took their town before the Romans came to their help. It is better to give before you are asked. You will be conquered long (*multō*) before you perceive that you are conquered. Why should you despair before you try (*temptāre*)? The Achaeans did not dare to begin the war before the ambassadors had returned from Rome. Brutus requested me to correct his speech before publication (*ēdere*).

LXXXVIII. Temporal Sentences.

Quum.

G. 580 foll.; A. 62; A. & S. 263, 5; B. 1237, 1244, 1247, 1250, 1282; H. 515, 517, 518, 3.

220. He who does not ward off (*dēfendere*) an injury nor repel [it] (*prōpulsāre*) when he can, acts (*facit*) unjustly. When a wise man is (§ 234) derided by the foolish rabble, he will not be indignant. Conon was general at the end of (*extrēmus*) the Peloponnesian (*Peloponnēsiacus*) war, when the forces of the Athenians were vanquished (*dēvincere*) by Lysander at Aegos potamoi (*Aegos flūmen*). Tarquin was making-preparations to surround the city with a wall (§ 348), when the Sabine war interrupted (*intervenīre* with *Dat.*) the undertaking. There was a time when (§ 634) I too thought that we should recover (*recuperāre*) our liberty. The time will come when you will feel the-loss-of (*desīderāre*) such brave allies (*fortitūdinem sociōrum*). I have often heard my father say that he had never been able to find a scholar that (*quī quidem*) equalled you in diligence [= your diligence]. It is ten years that I have been living (§ 221) in the country. It is six months since any one [= that (*quum*) no one has] set foot (*pedem inferre*) in this house (*aedēs*).* You have granted me enough in granting that disgrace seems to you a greater evil than pain.

221. A boy finding an oar [as he was] walking on the shore, became eager (*concupīscere*) to build a ship. As Pyrrhus was besieging Argos, he perished (*interīre*) by a blow with a stone [= struck (*īcere*) by a stone]. When Perseus succeeded his

* Lapses of time are treated as designations of time in Acc. or Abl. Multī annī sunt quum (= multōs annōs) in aere meō est—(*It is*) *many years* (*that*) *he has been in my debt*; quum in aere meō nōn fuit = multīs annīs nōn fuit.

father on the throne (*patris imperiō succēdere*), he stirred up (*incitāre*) all the tribes (*gēns*) of the Gauls against the Romans.

Hoping that my friend would return, I remained in the city, but receiving the intelligence (*nūntius*) that he was detained (*retinēre*) at Brundusium by sickness, I departed. Zōpyrus, as no one doubted (*dē*) his fidelity, was received into the city and unanimously (*omnium suffrāgiīs*) appointed leader. The states (*cīvitās*) of Greece (*adj.*) all lost the command (*imperium*) because each one (*singulae*) wanted to command. Man does not need the strength (*vīrēs*) of the elephant, as he is endowed with reason.

I do not consider Marcus Regulus unfortunate; for although his body was captured and tortured (*cruciāre*) by the Punics, his soul (*animus*) could not be captured. It seems to *me* that men, although they are in many things inferior (*humilis*) and weaker, excel (*praestāre*) beasts in this (*hāc rē*) especially (*maximē*) that (*quod*) they have the power of (*posse*) speech (*Inf.*). He did not seek (*petere*) honours, although they were open (*patēre*) to him on account of (*propter*) his position (*dignitās*).

LXXXIX. Conditional Sentences.

G. 590 foll.; A. 59; A. & S. 259, R. 2, 260, II.; B. 1259 foll.; H. 503 foll.

222. If virtues are equal (*pār*) to one another (§ 212), it follows that vices are also equal. If I have said anything by way of jest (*per jocum*), do not turn it into a serious [matter]. If what (*illud quod*) we wish happens (§ 234, R. 1) we shall rejoice, if not (§ 593) we shall bear [the result] with equanimity. If we do not (236, R. 2) lop off (*resecāre*) the passions, in vain shall we endeavor to live happily. Limbs are amputated (*amputāre*), if they begin (§ 569) to be without blood.

223. If you were to know me [well] enough, you would not think that I could betray [my] country. What good man would hesitate to meet death for [his] country, if he should expect (§ 129) to do her good? See in what year Piso was quaestor or tribune; should neither hit (*quadrāre*), see whether he lived at all (*omninō*) at the time of that war. Would a physician (*medicus*), when a patient (*aegrōtus*) had been turned over* (*trādere*) to another physician, be angry with the physician who had succeeded him,* if he were to change some things that he had prescribed (*cōnstituere*) in his treatment (*in cūrandō*)?

224. Most persons cannot do a thing because they will not; they could, if they would. Antigonus would have saved (*servāre*) Eumenes [when he was] captured, if his men had allowed him to do so (*per aliquem licet*), but those who were about (*circā*) [him] did not suffer it, because they saw that they would all be of little value by-the-side-of (*prae*) Eumenes. If I had conquered you, Scipio, quoth Hannibal, I should put myself before all other generals. Quintus would have stayed (*esse*) longer with me, if I had been desirous of it (§ 599, R. 1).

225. If we had been energetic (*impiger*) in bringing help [= if we had brought help energetically] to the Saguntines, we might have averted the whole war. The Gauls had nearly taken the capitol, had not the geese by their noise (*clangor*) waked the soldiers out of sleep. If you had not hastened, we should all have had to die. The commonwealth might be perpetual, if we lived (*vīvitur*) according to (*Abl.*) the constitution (*patria īnstitūta*). If Publius Sextius, who was left for dead [= killed], had been [really] killed, would you have (239) taken up arms (*ad arma īre*)?

226. It is not doubtful that if Caesar had not perished (*exstinguī*) by an untimely (*immātūrus*) death, the condition of Rome under the Empire would have been far different (*alius*). No one doubted [= it was doubtful to nò one] that if the general had come immediately, he might easily have crushed the conspiracy of the soldiers. No one doubts that if the city had been taken, the enemy would have been conquered. He gave so tardily that he would have done a greater favor (*plūs*

* Perf. subjunctive.

father on the throne (*p*[…]
(*incitāre*) all the tribes ([…]

Hoping that my friend […]
but receiving the intelli[…]
(*retinēre*) at Brundusium […]
no one doubted (*dē*) his […]
unanimously (*omnium s*[…]
(*cīvitās*) of Greece (*a*[…]
because each one (*sing*[…]
not need the strength (*v*[…]
with reason.

I do not consider Mar[…]
his body was captured […]
his soul (*animus*) could […]
men, although they are […]
weaker, excel (*praestā*[…]
(*maximē*) that (*quod*) […]
(*Inf.*). He did not seek […]
[…] to him […]
G. 604; […]

[…] quickly. I do not doubt […] my advice, you would not be in such […]

[…] from coming to me […] I beg you to write us soon […] had consented (*velle*) […] of Hannibal, he would have […] nearer to the Tiber than […] *ratio*) of benefits is sim-[…] something comes back, it […] back, it is not a loss. If our […] directions of the physician, […] Sulla was lucky, if there can […] a crime. Solon gave the Atheni-[…] useful laws, that if they had been […] always, they would have had an […] empire.

III. Conditional Sentences.

[…] G. […] 1; A. & S. 261, 2; B. 1277; H. 506.

227. [Those things] which […] are very (*per*) difficult are often to be regarded just as (*perin*[…]) if they could not be done. Those who injure some (*aliī*) […] in order to be liberal toward others, are guilty-of [= in the] same injustice as if they appropriated other people's property (*alie*[…] *in suam rem convertere*). He loves you as if (*tam—quam*) he […] had lived with you. He loved you as if he had lived with you. […] Soldiers enjoy present abundance as if they knew for certain (*exp*[…] *irritum habēre*) that they would never be plagued (*urgēre*, § 240, […]) by want again. Xerxes sent 4,000 armed men to Delphi to p[…] the temple of Apollo, as if he were carrying on war not only with the Greeks but with the immortal gods. I consider (*e*[…]*ssimo*) him to be the best who forgives others (*cēterī*) as if he […] himself sinned daily, but who (§ 630) refrains from sin as if he wo[…] forgive none. My brother treats (*tractāre*) me as if I were a king.

G. 592, R. 2-4 ; A. 61, 4; A. & S. 261, R. 6, 277, R. 16; H. 506.

228. History (***historia***) at that time was nothing except the putting together (***cōnfectio***) of annals. No rule (***imperium***) can be safe except [when it is] fortified by good-will. Of Homer, the prince of poets, almost nothing is known except what nobody would be likely to believe [namely] that he was born blind; unless perhaps we believe that a blind man could have described (***expōnere***) so many and so various things so truly and so clearly. I have received a silly (***īnsulsē scrīptum***) note (***līterulae***) from Peter (***Petrus***), unless perhaps everything that you do not like (*Subj.*) seems silly. What does it concern me what you think of a book, which will not (§ 515) be published (***forās prōdīre***, § 633), unless liberty is recovered (***recuperāre***)?

G. 597, R. 4; A. 61, 4; A. & S. 259, R. 4 (3).

229. Whether you follow the Peripatetics or the Stoics, you must confess that there is in virtue guarantee (***praesidium***) enough for a happy life. "We have to do (***rēs est***)," said he, "with an (***is***) enemy that cannot bear either good or bad fortune. Whether he vanquishes or is vanquished (§ 569), he shows (***prae sē ferre***) the same savage-temper (***ferōcitās***)!" Whether you linger (***cunctārī***) or hasten, you will not find him at home.

XCI. Concessive Sentences.

G. 605; A. 61, 2; A. & S. 271, R. 2; B. 1284; H. 514.

230. Even if there is nothing in glory that it should be sought after [= has nothing in itself for which, ***cūr***, § 634], nevertheless it follows virtue like (***tamquam***) [its] shadow. Although (***etsī***) the ground (***locus***) was unfavorable (***inīquus***), nevertheless Caesar determined to attack the enemy. Even if you had taken away from Sulla nothing but (***nisi***) [his] consulship, you ought (§ 246, R. 1) to be content with that. Who will not be shocked (***offendere***) by such baseness, even if it does not [= should not be likely to, § 239] injure him? No one, no matter how wealthy (***locuplēs***) he may be, can dispense with the aid of others (*aliēnus*). Although (*licet*) I have asked you to come to me, nevertheless I know that you cannot help me. No matter how much pleasure you may have in (*dēlectārī*) the flattery (*adūlātio*) of courtiers (*aulicus*), they will, notwithstanding, lay-plots (*insidiārī*) against you. Granted that Rome was founded before the time (*pl.*) of Romulus, nevertheless the Roman historians (*scrīptor rērum*) begin with (*ā*) him. Granted that our soldiers' courage do not fail (§ 345, R. 1) them [= courage do not fail our soldiers], nevertheless they will not be able to resist the great multitude of the enemy. The wicked do not escape [the charge of] impiety, although (*quamvīs*) they may have watered (= *cruentāre*) altars with much blood. [But] few are so grateful that they think of (*cōgitāre*) what they have received, even if they do not see [it]. They said that they knew that, although (*etsī*) they had deserved ill of the Roman people, they would be in a better condition (*status*) under the Romans, [though] angry, than they had been under the Carthaginians [as] friends.

XCII. Relative Sentences.

G. 612 foll.; A. 48; A. & S. 206; B. 683, 1192; H. 445.

231. The deeds of Hannibal, who is known to have defeated (*vincere*) the Romans so often (*quotiēs*), are admired by all of us (§ 368, R. 2). The boy, while he is [yet] tender, must be steeped (*īnficere*) in (§ 387) those arts from the absorption (*combibere*) of which [= which when he shall have absorbed] he will come better prepared for greater [things]. Great is the admiration felt for (*Gen.*) a man, who speaks eloquently and wisely, for those who hear him think that he is wiser than everybody else. Philosophy contains the doctrine (*disciplīna*) not only (*et*) of duty (*officium*), but also (*et*) that (§ 293, R. 3) of living well, so that he who teaches it (*prōfitērī*) seems to undertake a very important part (*partēs*). The ancient Greeks called fate a blind ruler of gods and men, and thought that even Jupiter, the father of gods and men, was subject to its sway. Defeated, the Carthaginians begged the Romans for peace; and as Regulus would not grant it, except under the harshest conditions, they begged the Lacedaemonians for help.

Let the punishment stop (*cōnsistere*) at those with whom the fault originated (*orīrī*). I did not suppose that there were any (*nullus*) human-beings in whose eyes (*ubi*) my life was hateful (*invīsus*). He betook himself to the Volscians, with whom he had taken refuge (*cōnfugere*) before.

Tell me what you think about public affairs (*rēs pūblica*). To tell you what I [really] think, the state is in the hands of (*penes*) abandoned men. The soldier slipped out (*ēlābī*) through the pickets (*per intervalla statiōnum*) and told the commander of the enemy the facts of the case [= what had been done]. They recounted (*memorāre*) what dangers [= the dangers that] threatened (*portendī*) their respective (*suum quisque*) cities by land and sea, and begged the king for reinforcements (*auxilia*).

G. 616 foll.; A. 48; A. & S. 206; B. 688 foll.; H. 445 foll.

232. A benefit that is bestowed on anybody (*quīlibet*) is a favor (*grātus*) to nobody. Everything (*quīcunque*) we say (*loquī*) cannot be reduced (*revocāre*) to regular laws (*ars et praecepta*). Are you the man that has lost everything? We are the men that have often loaded (*cumulāre*) you with kindnesses (*beneficium*). The Lacedaemonians slew King Agis (*Acc. Āgin*), a thing that had never happened among them before. Aratus of Sicyon (*Adj.*) thought—and this (*Rel.*) showed (§ 365, R. 2) a wise man—that he ought to consult the interest of all his [fellow] citizens. Dionysius was brave and skilled in war, and—which is not easily found in a tyrant—neither a debauchee (*luxuriōsus*) nor avaricious. I have taken refuge with you (*confugere ad*), to whom I am compelled—the most wretched thing in my eyes (*Dat.*)—to be a burden rather than a blessing. The city of Cadiz (*Gādēs*) was founded by a Tyrian fleet, which founded Utica also. All (*ūniversus*) Italy took up (*capere*) arms against the Romans, and while (*ut, ita*, § 484) their (*Rel.*) fortune was horrible (*atrōx*) their cause was just. Of the number of those (*is numerus*) who were (*Perf.*) consuls during those years many are dead. The poet Virgil (*Vergilius*) wrote an epic poem (*carmen epicum*), which is called the Aeneid (*Aenēis*). The Gauls once plundered Delphi, the famous (*superl.*) oracle of Apollo, which was called by the ancients the centre (*umbilīcus*) of the world (*orbis terrārum*). The Arabians have fleet (*vēlōx*) horses and swift camels, which [latter] they call the ships of the desert (*dēserta, ōrum*). This great war that had lasted so long (*diuturnus*), by which [*i. e.* war] all nations were oppressed (*premere*), Pompey brought to an end (*cōnficere*) in one year.

G. 618 foll.; A. 48; A. & S. 206; B. 683 foll.; H. 445 foll.

233. Animals (*bestia*) do not move (*sē commovēre*) from the place in which they are born (§ 625). Apollonius was wont to urge (*impellere*) each man to (*ad*) the arts for which he thought him fit. He is not to be endured (*ferre*) as an accuser, who is himself caught (*dēprehendere*) in the vice, which he blames (*reprehendere*) in another. Coriolanus fled to the Volscians, a people that was at that time bitterly-hostile (*īnfestus*) to the name of Rome (*adj.*). Such is your shrewdness (*prūdentia*), that you will readily (*facile*) understand why I have not followed your advice. In the year in which Tarquin the Overbearing was exiled from Rome, the Athenians exiled Hippias. Marius having accomplished the business (*Abl. Abs.*) which he had proposed to himself, returned to Cirta. The day I heard that tyrant called (*appellāre*) a renowned (*clārus*) man, I began to distrust. The mountain, which the exiles had taken possession of (*capere*), was grassy (*herbidus*) and well-watered (*aquōsus*). Verres sent to King Antiochus to ask for (*rogāre*) the most beautiful vessels he had seen at his palace (*apud eum*). Philip subjugated (*subigere*) the Aetolians (*Aetōlī*), deserted [as they were] by the Romans, the only help to which they trusted. I see that I am deserted by those, who ought to have been the last to do so [= by whom it was least proper, *convenit*]. Being (*quum*) in the straits (*angustiae*) in which I have shown him [to have been], he resolved to resign his office. At that time they began (*coeptum est*) at Athens to choose the archons (*archontas, acc. pl.*) for ten years, a custom which remained seventy years.

G. 625, 629; A. 62, 1; A. & S. 264, 12, 280, III. (1), 264, 8; B. 1252; H. 486, 5.

234. Whichever way (*quācunque*) we turn (*sē commovēre, Perf.*), we stumble against (*offendere in*) simpletons (*stultus*) or scoundrels (*improbus*). However (*utut*) things turn out (*esse*), remember to urge as an excuse (*excūsāre*) my ill health (*valētūdo*). No matter who it is (*quīcunque*) that reaches a high-position (*fastīgium*), [he] will become dizzy (*vertīgine corripī*). We never return to our parents what we receive from them, nor will our children return to us what they receive from us. The maiden was of such extraordinary beauty (*adeō eximiā formā*) that in whatever direction (*quācunque*) she walked (*incēdere, Impf.*), she attracted (*convertere*) everybody's eyes.

235. The last battle of the war will never be effaced from (*oblītterāre in*) my mind, for I lost both [my] father and [my] uncle in it. The wall was torn down (*dīruere*), for it separated (*dirimere*) the city from the citadel. You are all of less value (*pretium*) than Albius and Atrius, for you have subjected (*subjicere*) yourselves to them. The senate held a consultation (*cōnsultāre*) about receiving Cybele, for a recent message had come that she was at Tarracina.

236. Sestius was expected day before yesterday (*nūdiustertius*), but he has not come (304), so far as I know. None of the poets, so far as I have read them, has ever equalled the silliness of Maevius. My competitors (*competītor*)—so far as they seem to be fixed (*certus*)—are Galba and Antonius. All my sister's children that I have seen have grey (*caesius*) eyes. All the provinces, so far indeed (*quidem*) as they belong (*esse*) to the mainland, have been occupied by the enemy.

G. 630–31; A. 66, 2; 67, 1, *b*; A. & S. 266; B. 1291, 1295, 1219; H. 530.

237. All men are persuaded (*persuāsum habēre*) that God is the master and regulator (*moderātor*) of all things, and that what happens, happens according to his will. Ambiorix exhorted the Nervii not to let this opportunity slip (*praetermittere* = to let slip) of taking vengeance for (*ulcisci*) the insults, which they had received from the Romans. Quintilian's precept is excellent, [namely] that parents should do nothing (§ 543, 4) that is unbecoming (*foedus*) nor (§ 450) say [any thing] that is shameful to hear (§ 437). I beg you not to spare expense (*sūmptus*) in anything that is necessary for your health. There is nothing more disgraceful than to carry on war with a man (*is*), with whom (*quīcum*) you have lived on intimate terms (*familiāriter*). In the [case of] paintings, it happens (*ūsū venit*) that those who-are unacquainted-with-the-art (*imperītī*) relish (*dēlectārī*) and praise things that are not to be praised. There is nothing that cannot be bought, if you will give as much as the seller (*vēnditor*) wants. If it were not for merchants (§ 592, R. 1), there would be no exportation of the things (195, R. 4) in which we abound (§ 517, R. 3), nor importation (*invectio*) of the things that we need. This [is what] I wonder at, that any man (§ 304) should so (*ita*) desire (*velle*) to destroy another, as to scuttle (*perforāre*) even the vessel in which he himself is sailing (*nāvigāre*). He sent [word] to the dictator that he wanted another army to oppose (*passive*) to Hannibal. "Since the colonies have rebelled," said King George, "let us send commissioners (*lēgātī*) to rebuke, not to entreat them." I have found scarcely any one who did not think that what Caesar demanded ought to be granted, rather than have a fight [about it] (*dēpugnāre*). There is no one who has equalled Hannibal in hate [= the hate of Hannibal] of the Romans.

G. 632 foll.; A. 65, 2; A. & S. 264, 5 foll.; B. 1207; H. 500.

238. The enemy (*pl.*) sent cavalry first to draw out (*ēlicere*) our men, and then to surround and attack them. The messengers, who were to bring the king the tidings that his son had fallen, were taken (*dūcere*) into the royal palace to set forth (*expōnere*) to the king in person (*ipse*) what they had seen and heard concerning the death of his son. The Carthaginians sent ambassadors to Rome to congratulate the senate and people of Rome with a present of a golden wreath, which was to be deposited (*pōnere*) in the sanctuary (*cella*) of Jupiter. There are people who forget favors (*beneficium*) received, because they are ashamed of having received favors. The Macedonians (*Macedŏnes*) felled trees which were too large for armed soldiers possibly to carry. Philistus, who imitated (*Pf.*) Thucydides, deserves being counted among (*numerāre in*, § 384, R.) the great historians (*historicī*). After almost the whole world (*orbis terrārum*) was brought into-a state-of-pacification (*pācāre*), the Roman empire was too great for it to be possible that it should be subjugated by a foreign power. The Roman race (*gēns*) is one (*is*) that cannot (*nescīre*) stay (*quiēscere*) beaten (*vincere*).

How few are those (*quotusquisque est*) who say that pleasure is not (§ 446) a blessing. You will find people who think more (§ 379) of their safety than of the state. Miltiades was [a man] of wonderful affability, so that no one was so humble as not to have free access to him (*use: patet aditus*). An old man hasn't anything even to hope for (*nē . . . quidem*). I am not ignorant that there are some who have stated (*trādere*) that Carthage was taken the year before. I meet many (*plūrimī*) people every day; for many are the gentlemen (*optimus vir*) who come here for the sake of [their] health. I know not what to answer, except this one thing, that I am sorry for what I have done (*factum*).

G. 636; A. 65, 2; A. & S. 264, 8; B. 1251; H. 517, 516, II.

239. After the battle of Allia (*Alliēnsis*) a great number of Romans fled to Veji, where they thought that they were safer than at Rome. Against the Tarentines, who live (*esse*) in Lower Italy, war was declared by the Romans for having done wrong to (*injūriā afficere*) the ambassadors of the Romans. Miserable old man! not to have perceived in so long a life that death is to be despised. The senators of Rome, thinking that they would never be free from machinations (*sine īnsidiīs esse*) so long as Hannibal was alive (*Abl. Abs.*), sent ambassadors to

Bithynia (*ȳ*) to demand of Prūsias that he should put him to death. The creditor turned (*ējicere*) the poor-fellow out of house [and home], although he had not yet buried (*efferre*) his father. Nero, although he was [a man] of unbounded debauchery, was indisposed (*languēre*) [but] three times, all-told (*omnīnō*), in (*per*) fourteen years. Atticus, wanting the community set free, paid-the-cash (*numerāre*) out of (*dē*) his own [purse]. The rascal! (*homo nēquam*) not to have awaited (*exspectāre*) your convenience (*commodum*).

I wrote in-reply (*rescrībo*) that I was worse, and that on that account I wanted her to come to me at once. Massinissa complained that Scipio had not attacked Syphax at once, for he knew to a certainty (*certum habēre*) that he would go over (*dēficere*) to the Carthaginians.

Cato, who could have held Sicily without any trouble (*nullō negōtiō*), and to whom, if he had held it, all the conservatives (*bonī*) would have flocked (*sē cōnferre*), set out from Syracuse day before yesterday (*nūdiustertius*). At the first watch, Fabius gave a signal to those who were in the citadel (*arx*) and who had the harbor in charge (*custōdia portūs*).

XCIII. Object and Causal Sentences.

G. 524 foll.; A. 70, 5; A. & S. 206 (14); B. 1258; H. 554.

240. That there is a God we conclude (*efficere*) from the fact that the belief in (*opīnio*) God is innate in all. You have done me a great (*superl.*) favor (*grātum facere*) in writing me what has happened in the city. It was a gift (*mūnus*) of fortune that Atticus was born in the city, in which was the seat (*domicilium*) of the empire of the world; it was a proof (*specimen*) of his good sense (*prūdentia*) that he was dear to the Athenians above all others (§ 317). Children do well to keep nothing secret from (*cēlāre*) their parents. Nothing destroyed the maritime cities [of] Carthage and Corinth more than that, in [their] desire for trade and navigation, they had given up (*relinquere*) agriculture (*agrōrum cultus*) and arms. The circumstance that Isocrates was hindered (§§ 547–51) from speaking in public by the weakness (*īnfirmitās*) of his voice did not prevent him from being considered a distinguished orator. As for your exhorting me to be hopeful (*spem habēre*) of recovering my former prosperity, I-would-have-you-to-know (*scīto*) that the condition of the state is now such that we must fear that it will soon succumb to the machinations (*īnsidiae*) of the revolutionists (*malī*).

G. 538 foll.; A. 63, 1; A. & S. 273, 5; B. 1250; H. 520.

241. Most seafarers (*nauta*) of antiquity were at first [≐ in the beginning] pirates (*pīrāta*), because piracy (*pīrātica*) was not regarded as a crime (§ 350). Seeing that (*quoniam*) the life which we enjoy is short, we ought to make our memory (§ 363) as long as possible. Admirably (*dīvīnus, comp.* § 441 *end*) does Plato call pleasure a bait (*esca*) for (*Gen.*) the bad, because by it men are caught as fish (*pl.*) by the hook (*hāmus*). We read that Mithridates hated the Romans because by their arrival his power had been diminished. Suetonius tells [us] that Caesar pulled down a country-house (*vīlla*) which had been built at great expense, because it did not suit him as well-as-he-could-have-desired (*ex sententiā, ex voluntāte*). We have been warned (*admonēre*) to be on our guard (*cavēre*) against being caught up (*excipere*) by highwaymen, because they will get (§ 515) to the place which we are making for (*petere*) sooner than we can. Fabius Maximus did not wish his son to be made consul, not that he lacked-confidence-in (*diffīdere* with *dat.*) his distinguished virtues, for he was an excellent man—but in order that this high office should not be kept up (*continuāre*) in one family. I wish you would write to me what answer-he-has-given (*respondēre*) in my case (*dē mē*), not that his promise will do (§ 515) me any good, but because I shall be able to say that there is nothing that I have not tried (§ 634). The [decision of the] struggle (*certāmen*) was doubtful (*anceps*), rather (*magis*) because the enemy had made a sudden charge than because he was a match in strength (*vīrēs*). A captive having (*quum*) gone from the camp by permission (*voluntās*) of Hannibal, returned soon afterwards, because, as he said, he had forgotten something. The king would not make peace because he thought that the Aetolians would never keep quiet.

XCIV Correlative Sentences.

G. 645–6; A. 22; A. & S. 206, 16; B. 706 foll.; H. 458.

242. They say that Plato had the same view (*idem sentīre*, § 45[a], R. 2) of the eternal-existence (*aeternitās*) of the soul (*animus*. *Pl.*) as Pythagoras. As you sow (*sēmentem facere*, § 236), so shall you reap (*metere*). Marcellus had taken it into his head (*in animum indūcere*) that nobody was as good a match (*tam pār*) for Hannibal as himself. Esteem other men as highly as you wish to be esteemed by them. Citizens are usually of the same character (*tālis*) as the leading-men in the state. After Hannibal had fled from home, he called his brother Mago to him, and when the Punics (*Poenī*) heard of it (*resciscere*, § 612), they visited (*afficere*) Mago with the same punishment as his brother. Hannibal had not supposed that so many nations in Italy would revolt (*dēficere*) as did revolt after the battle of Cannae (*Cannēnsis*). You have stained (*aspergere*) your character [= yourself] with a great blot (*lābēs*) by charging (*īnsimulāre*) that innocent old man with crimes such as no one will ever believe him to have committed. We have an amount (*tantum*) of leisure that it has not been our good fortune to have (*contingit alicuī*) for a long time.

The better a man is, the harder it is for him to [= with the more difficulty does he] suspect (*suspicārī*) that others are knaves (*improbus*). The more a man is furnished (*ornātus*) with virtues, the more is he to be reverenced (*colere*). Every learned man is [proportionally] modest. As I live, what my sister and I have told you, is true. As I live, my brother and myself will never desert you. Numa Pompilius was a man deeply-learned (*cōnsultissimus*) for that age in all divine and human law. If you will write to me how you are, it will be the greatest possible favor to me (§ 645, R. 5). The Romans acted prudently [as far as that was possible] in so rash an undertaking.

XCV. Comparative Sentences with Quam.

G. 647; A. 54, 5; A. & S. 256, 264, 4; B. 897; H. 417, 1, 6, 496, 2.

243. The causes of events excite (*movēre*) me more than the events themselves. He said that the causes of events excited him more than the events themselves. I am desirous of hearing Stephanus, a higher authority (*locuplēs auctor*) than Casaubon himself. I give myself up to Catullus, a poet of greater elegance (*venustus*) than any of [his] contemporaries (*aequālis*). Have you ever used a better ink (*ātrāmentum*) than mine? No castle is so lofty (*excelsus*) that a donkey (*asellus*) laden with gold cannot ascend to (*in*) it. It was evident that the tumult was too violent to be quieted (*sēdāre*). There was no desertion (*trānsitiōnem facere*), because they had already committed crimes too great (*magna dēlinquere*) to be possibly forgiven. Not less than twenty thousand men were killed or taken prisoners. [He was] not less than forty years old [when] he married. He advanced too incautiously for [his] time of life (*aetās*), for he was by that time (*jam*) sixty years old, and ten years older than his colleague. Agamemnon slew [his] daughter Īphigenīa, than whom there never was a lovelier maiden in all Greece. I have read Charles's last novel (*fābula*), than which I can imagine (*mihi substituere*) nothing more absurd.

XCVI. Ōrātio Obliqua.

Remark.—The teacher is advised to make his own exercises in Ōrātio Oblīqua from the classical texts. The exercises given here are intended only as specimens. They can be multiplied by throwing the Exercises already given into Indirect Discourse. This is specially recommended for the Conditional Sentence.

A. Ōrātio Oblīqua into Ōrātio Recta.

244 (1.) Lēgī scrīptum: esse avem quae platalea nōminārētur; eam sibi cibum quaerere advolantem ad eās avēs quae sē in mare mergerent; quae quum ēmersīssent piscemque cēpīssent usque eō premere eārum capita mordicus, dum illae captum

āmitterent, in quod ipsa invādit. Eadem haec avis scrībitur conchīs sē solēre complēre eāsque quum stomachī calōre concoxerit ēvomere atque ita ēligere quae sunt (§ 630, R. 2) esculenta. Cic. Nat. Deōr., ii. 124.

(2.) Rōmulus [raptās Sabīnās] docēbat patrum id superbiā factum, quī connūbium fīnitimīs negâssent. Illās tamen in mâtrimōniō, in societāte fortūnārum omnium cīvitātisque et quō nihil cārius hūmānō generī sit, līberum fore. Mollīrent modo īrās et quibus fors corpora dedîsset, darent animōs. Saepe ex injūriā postmodum grātiam ortam, eōque meliōribus ūsūrās virīs quod adnīsūrus pro sē quisque sit, ut parentium etiam patriaeque expleat dēsīderium. Liv., i. 9.

(3.) Idōneōs nactus hominēs per quōs ea, quae vellet, ad [Pompêjum] perferrentur, [Caesar] petit quoniam Pompēī mandāta ad sē dētulerint nē graventur sua quoque ad eum postulāta dēferre, sī (§ 462) parvō labōre magnās contrōversias tollere possint; sibi semper prīmam reīpûblicae fuîsse dignitatem vītāque potiōrem. Doluîsse quod populī Rōmānī beneficium sibi ab inimīcīs extorquerētur. Tamen hanc jactūram honōris suī reīpûblicae causā aequō animō tulîsse. [At] tōtā Italiā dēlectūs habērī, retinērī legiōnēs duo quae ab sē sint abdûctae. Quōnam haec omnia nisi ad suam perniciem pertinēre? Caesar, B. C. i. 9.

(4.) Concurrēbant lēgātī centuriōnēs tribūnīque mīlitum; nē dubitāret proelium committere. Omnium esse mīlitum parātissimōs animōs; quod sī inīquitātem locī timēret, datum īrī tamen aliquō locō pugnandī facultātem, quod certē inde dēcēdendum esset Afrāniō nec sine aquā permanēre posset . . . (Caesar respondit) . . . cūr vulnerārī paterētur optimē de sē meritōs mīlitēs? Cūr fortūnam perīclitārētur?

Caesar, B. C. i. 72.

(5.) Loquitur Āfrānius: nōn esse aut ipsīs aut mīlitibus succênsendum quod fidem ergā imperātorem suum conservāre voluerint, sed satis jam fēcîsse officiō satisque supplicīī tulîsse;

itaque sē victōs confitērī; ōrāre atque obsecrāre, sī quī locus misericordiae relinquātur, nē ad ultimum supplicium prôgredī necesse habeant. Ad ea Caesar respondit . . . prōvinciīs excēderent exercitumque dīmitterent; sī id sit factum (§ 657, R.) sē nocitūrum nēminī. Caesar, B. C. i. 84, 85.

(6.) Ad ea addidit precēs nē sē innoxiam invidiā Hierōnymī cônflagrāre sinerent. Nihil sē ex regnō illīus praeter exsilium virī habēre; neque fortūnam suam eandem vīvō Hierōnymō fuîsse quam sorōris neque interfectō eō causam eandem esse. Quid? quod, sī Andranodōrō cônsilia prōcêssîssent, illa cum virō fuerit regnātūra, sibi cum cēterīs serviendum. Sī quis Zōïppō nûntiet interfectum Hierōnymum ac līberātās Syrācūsās, cuī dubium esse quīn extemplō cônscênsurus sit nāvem atque in patriam reditūrus? At enim perīculī quidem nihil ab sē timēre: invīsam tamen stirpem rēgiam esse. Ablēgārent ergō procul ab Syrācūsīs et asportārī Alexandrīam juberent. Tum omissīs prō sē precibus, puellīs ut saltem parcerent ōrāre înstitit ā quā aetāte etiam hostēs īrātōs abstinēre; nē tyrannōs ulciscendō scelera ipsī imitārentur. Liv., xxiv. 26.

(7.) Illum equitem âjēbant sex diērum spatiō trânscurrîsse longitūdinem Italiae, et eō diē cum Hasdrubale in Galliā signīs collātīs pugnâsse, quō eum castra adversus sēsē in Āpūliā posita habēre Hannibal crēdidîsset. Nōmen Nerōnis satis fuîsse ad continendum in castrīs Hannibalem; Hasdrubalem vērō quā aliā rē quam adventū êjus obrutum atque exstinctum esse? itaque īret alter cônsul sublīmis currū multijugīs, sī vellet, equīs; ūnō equō per urbem vērum triumphum vehī Nerōnemque, etiam sī pedes incēdat, vel partā eō bello vel sprētā eō triumphō glōriā memorābilem fore. Liv., xxviii. 9.

B. Ōrātio Recta into Ōrātio Oblīqua.

(1.) Comparāte nunc cum illōrum superbiā mē hominem novum. Quae illī audīre et legere solent eōrum partem vīdī, alia egomet gessī; quae illī līterīs, ea ego mīlitandō didicī. Nunc vos existumāte, facta an dicta plūris sint. Ac sī jam ex patribus Albīnī et Bestiae quaeri posset, mēne an illōs ex sē gignī māluerint, quid responsūrōs crēditis, nisi sēsē līberōs quam optumōs voluisse?.. Plūra dīcerem sī timidīs virtūtem verba adderent. Sall., B. J. 85.

(2.) Nōlīte patī mē nepōtem Massinissae frūstrā ā vōbīs auxilium petere... Ego eīs fīnibus ējectus sum, quōs majōribus meīs populus Rōmānus dedit, unde pater et avus meus ūnā vōbīscum expulēre Syphācem et Carthāginiēnsēs. Hūcine, Micipsa pater, beneficia tua ēvāsēre ut quem tū parem cum līberīs tuīs regnīque participem fēcistī is potissimum stirpis tuae exstinctor sit? Nunquam familia nôstra quiēta erit? Semperne in sanguine, ferrō, fugā versābimur? Sall., B. J. 14.

(3.) (M. Petrōnius multīs jam vulneribus acceptīs): Quoniam, inquit, mē ūnā vōbīscum servāre nōn possum, vestrae quidem certē vītae prôspiciam, quōs cupiditāte glōriae adductus in perīculum dēdūxī, vōs datā facultāte vōbīs cônsulite. (Cōnantibus auxiliārī suīs) Frustrā, inquit, meae vītae subvenīre cōnāminī quem jam sanguis vīrēsque dēficiunt. Proinde abīte dum est facultās vōsque ad legiōnem recipite. Caes., B. G. vii. 51

XCVII. Ōrātio Oblīqua.

G. 651 foll.; A. 67; A. & S. 266, 2; B. 1295; H. 528.

245. The senate said that they did not see any reason at all why (*nihil cūr*) the welfare-of-the-state should be intrusted to soldiers, who had deserted their comrades (*commīlitōnēs*) in battle. The Roman general said that Hannibal had not attacked his camp because he was lying-torpid (*torpēre*) owing to an error, which would not last long (*diuturnum esse*). Mago was afraid that the Ligurians (*Ligurēs*) themselves, perceiving that the Punics were evacuating (*relinquere, Pass. construction*) Italy, would go over (*dēficere*) to those, in whose power they soon (*mox*) would be. Hieronymus asked the Roman ambassadors sneeringly (*per jocum*) what luck (*fortūna*) they had had (*esse*) at Cannae; for [what] the ambassadors of Hannibal told [him was] scarcely credible; he (§ 529, R. 3) wished to know what was the truth in order to determine which (§ 315) side (*partēs*) to take (*sequī*).

Amyntas informed the soldiers that the commandant (*praetor*) of Egypt had fallen in battle, that the Persian army was both without a leader and weak (*invalidus*), that the Egyptians, always hostile to their commandants, would regard (*aestimāre*) them [= Amyntas and his men] as allies. Compelled by necessity they cried out that he might lead them whithersoever he thought good (*vidētur*).

The consul made (*habēre*) a speech [in which he said] that people were mistaken if they thought that the senate had still (*etiamtum*, § 663, R. 3) any power (*posse*) in the state, that as for the Roman Knights (*equitēs vērō*) they should pay (*poenās dare*) for the day on which they met armed on the Capitoline hill (*clīvus*) [and] that the time had come for those who had been in fear—he meant (*dīcēbat*) forsooth (*vidēlicet*) the conspirators—to avenge themselves.

246. Caesar was confident that if he seized (*occupāre*) and fortified (*commūnīre*) that mound (*tumulus*), he would cut off (*interclūdere*) [his] opponents (*adversāriī*) from the town and the bridge and all the provisions (*commeātus*) that they had collected in (*cōnferre in*) the town. Inflamed (*incēnsus*) with anger and excited (*commovēre*) by the danger, King Porsenna threatened Mucius Scaevola with (*minārī alicuī aliquid*) fire and death, if he did not speedily (*properē*) disclose (*aperīre*) all the conspiracy. Cicero said that if Caesar did not kill anybody, and did not take away anything from anybody, he would be liked (*dīligere*) most by those who feared him most. I told him that I could not take the young man to my heart (*complector*), unless I was absolutely certain (*mihi explōrātum est*) that he was a friend to the conservatives (*bonī*).

They said that, if they had him for consul, their fortunes would be better. They said that if they knew that the Romans would pardon them, they would not refuse to give themselves up (*in potestātem alicūjus sē trādere*).

I think that if Philip of Macedon had not been instructed (§ 338, R. 1) in the military science of the Greeks, he would not have defeated the Greeks at Chaeronea. Vibius said that those who talked about peace and surrender (*dēditio*) did not remember what they would have done, if they had the Romans in [their] power. Pollio is very much mistaken in thinking (*existimare*) that if Caesar had lived longer, his memoirs (*commentāriī*) would have been rewritten (*rescrībo*). It seems that if they had abstained from bloodshed (*caedēs*) they could have reached the royal pavilion. I beg you to remember that you could never have attained your [present] position (*dignitās*), if you had not followed (*ūtī*) my counsels.

G. 659 foll.; A. 67, 2; A. & S. 263, R. 5; B. 1303; H. 532, 3.

247. They asked, if there was war in the province, why they were quiet, if the war was at an end (*dēbellātum est*), why they were not carried back to Italy? He said that he did not doubt that Spain was Caesar's; that Caesar was so enraged that Metellus came very near being killed, if that had been done, there would have been a great massacre (*caedēs*); that it was not done, not because Caesar was not naturally cruel, but because he thought clemency was the popular [course]; that, if he lost the enthusiastic-support (*studium*) of the people he would be cruel, because he would not have anything to gain by kindness. They said that if both consuls with their armies were before (*ad*) Nola, they would not for all that (*tamen*) be more of a match (*magis parēs*) for Hannibal than they had been at Cannae; much less (*nēdum* with *Subj.*) could one praetor with a few raw (*paucī et novī*) soldiers protect the town. The Punics strove (*nītī*) to take the Roman general alive, but he attacked (*invādere*) them so fiercely, that he could not have been spared (§208), unless they had been willing to lose many more of their men. The Campanians sent envoys to Hannibal to announce (§ 632) that the consuls were a day's march off [and] that, if he did not hasten to their aid (*properē subvenīre*), Capua would get (*venīre*) into the power of the enemy. They ordered him to be taken (*dūcere*) to prison, if he could not give security (*vas, vadis*). Syphax said that if Scipio did not keep his army away (*abstinēre*) from Africa, it would be necessary for him to fight (*dīmicāre*) for the land, in which he was born (*gigno*). The prisoners told the king that he would find out whether they were brave or no, if he were general of the Athenians [and] Chares general of the Macedonians

XCVIII. Participial Sentences.

G. 667 foll.; A. 72, 1; A. & S. 274, 3; B. 1350; H. 577–9.

248. When we behold the heaven[s], we are certain that the world is the work of God. As the consul was hastening (*festīnāre*) to Rome the enemy overtook (*cōnsequī*) his army While Cinna was lording [it] in Italy, the greater part of the nobility fled to Sulla in [= into] Achaia. After the consul had got possession of great booty, he returned to camp. After Tarquin had been exiled (*pello*) from Rome, Brutus was chosen consul. Lucius Cornelius Scipio received the surname of Asiaticus, because he had conquered Asia after the example of [his] brother, who was called Africanus for having subjugated (*domāre*) Africa. Democritus threw away (*prōjicere*) [his] wealth (*dīvitiae*) because he thought it a burden to [= of] a good mind. I never drink unless I am thirsty (*sitīre*); many men drink without being thirsty. The Stoics change the words without changing the things [= although they do not change]. Although Paullus Aemilius dissuaded [from it] Terentius Varro attacked the Carthaginians. The Greeks of Europe surrounded with cities the sea-coast (*ōra maritima*) of Asia, which they had taken in war. What general [= who among generals] is so crazy (*vēcors*) as to think that victory will perch on his lap [= fly down, *dēvolāre*, into his (*dat.*) bosom] without his doing anything? After taking Thermopylae, Xerxes immediately set out for Athens, and, as no one defended it, he destroyed (*vastāre*) it by fire (*incendium*), after killing the priests found on the Acropolis (*arx*). Lucretius triumphed over the Aequians and Volscians whom he had conquered, and as he was triumphing [his] legions followed [him]. It was announced to Q. Cincinnatus as he was ploughing that he had been made dictator. No one observes the moon except (*nisi*) when it is in eclipse (*labōrāre*).

MISCELLANEOUS EXERCISES.

XCIX. To.

219. Romulus marched out (*ēgredior*) with all [his] forces, *and* commanded a part of the soldiers *to* lie in ambush (*subsīdere in insidiīs*). It is not right (*fās*) for you *to* do that. It is the peculiar mark (*proprium*) of a well-constituted mind (*animus*) *to* rejoice in prosperity (*bonae rēs*) and *to* grieve (*dolēre*) over the opposite (*contrāriae*, i. e. *rēs*). Gâjus Duilius was the first *to* conquer the Punics (*Poenī*) on the sea (*clâssis*). I was hired (*condūco*) *to* cook [and] not *to* be beaten (*vāpulāre*). If there had been any one (*quisquam*, § 304) *to* dissuade (*revocāre*) me from so dastardly (*turpissimus*) a course (*cônsilium*), I should either have fallen (*occumbere*) honorably or should be living as a conqueror to-day. You will do me a very great favor (*pergrātum facere*) *to* send me the third volume (*tomus*) of Tennyson's poems. I am going *to* take up my lodgings (*habitāre*) at my uncle's. *To* think that you should have envied a man who had loaded you with benefits! You have done well *to* hide your life from the foolish rabble. There is nothing *to* prevent your friends from coming to your aid, unless perhaps they are afraid of an ambush. The Carthaginian senators said that Hannibal had not crossed the Alps *to* wage war on the Tarentines. What (*quae*) you are doing (*agitāre*) [so] inconsiderately (*temerē*) is [merely] *to* (§ 429, R. 2) betray the Roman people [and] give (*trādere*) the victory to Hannibal. It is hard *to* tell which was to blame (*auctorem esse*) for overthrowing the state. There is no one—*to* my knowledge—that would have received (*suscipere*) you more cordially. The Greek language lends-itself-more-readily (*facilem esse*) *to* the composition (*duplicāre*) of words.

250. **C. Without.**

I. *After a Positive Sentence.*

a. The troops crossed the river WITHOUT making any objection.

Cōpiae flūmen trānsiērunt { 1. *nihil dubitantēs.* 2. *neque quidquam dubitāvērunt.* 3. *nullā interpositā dubitātiōne.* 4. *sine ullā dubitātiōne.*

b. Divide your troops WITHOUT weakening them.

Ita dīvide cōpiās ut non (nē) dēbilitēs.

c. He divided my troops WITHOUT dividing his own.

Meās dīvīsit cōpiās cum suās nōn dīvideret (dīvīsisset) (suīs nōn dīvīsīs).

II. *After a Negative Sentence.*

a. You cannot cross the river WITHOUT dividing your forces.

Flūmen transīre nōn poteris { 1. *nisi cōpiās dīviseris.* 2. *nisi dīvīsīs copiīs.*

b. No army can be divided WITHOUT being weakened.

Nullus exercitus dīvidī potest { 1. *quīn (is) dēbilitētur.* 2. *ut nōn dēbilitētur.*

251. Is it true liberality to give money without depriving one's self of any comfort (*commodum*)? We cannot let him go without giving him a reward. Nature has given us life as a loan (*mūtuum dare*) without fixing (*dīcere*) a day [for repayment]. During the war with Pompey (*Pompējānus*) nothing happened without my foretelling it. Terentius Varro, without waiting for his colleague's aid, joined battle. That certainly would never have occurred to me (*mihi in mentem venīre*) without being reminded [of it]. The precepts of art are of little avail to form an orator without the assistance of (*Part.*) nature. Can you condemn L. Cornelius without condemning also the act of Gajus Marius? He departed without accomplishing his mission. Show yourself worthy of being believed (*fidem habeo*, I believe) without swearing. Gorgias lived-full (*complēre*) 107 years without relaxing (*cessāre*) in his enthusiasm (*studium*) for (*Gen.*) literature. Charles lived many years with his mother and sister without ever having had a difficulty (*simultās*) with them. That you should have written (*dare*) so many letters to Corinth without writing any (*quum nullās*) to me! Who ever saw a man presented (*Pres. Inf.*) with a wreath (*corōna*) without a city having been taken, or a camp of the enemy fired?

252. Sulla withdrew (*redūcere*) his forces without firing (*succendere*) the tower. Can one-of-the-two (§ 306) armies be sent to Rome without raising the siege of (*omittere*) Capua? Fulvius received (*partic.*) the letter, and (§ 667, R. 1), without opening (*resolvere*) it, laid it down. He was three miles off without any of the enemy having perceived it [= when not yet any of the enemies had perceived]. The general thought that he would not be a match for such a mass of the enemy without sending for (*accio*) auxiliary troops. A vast swarm (*vīs ingēns*) of locusts (*lōcusta*) filled (*complēre*) all the country around Capua without it appearing (*cōnstāre*) whence they came (*advenīre*).

CI. Tenses in Letters.

253. The Roman letter-writer not unfrequently puts himself in the position of the receiver, more especially at the beginning and at the end of the letter, often in the phrase "I have nothing to write." This permutation of tenses is never kept up long, and applies only to temporary situations, never to general statements.

TABLE OF PERMUTATIONS.

scrībo,	*I am writing,*	becomes	scrībēbam
	I write,		scrīpsī,
scrīpsī,	*I have written,*		scrīpseram,
	I wrote,		scrīpseram,
	or remains unchanged.		
scrībam,	*I shall write,*		scrīptūrus eram

The adverbial designations of time remain unchanged—or

Herī,	*yesterday,*	becomes	prīdiē,
hodiē,	*to-day,*	quō diē hās litterās dedī, dabam,	
crās,	*to-morrow,*	posterō diē, postrīdiē.	

254. Although I really (*sānē*) have no news, yet, as I am sending my servant back to Rome, I must write (*Ger.*) something to you. After having been (*quum*) with Pompey and at his house, I am setting out for Brundusium. Ten days after (*postquam*) leaving you (*ab aliquō discēdere*), I scratch off (*exarāre*) this note (*hoc litterulārum*) before day. I have nothing to write and sleep oppresses (*urguēre*) me. I have written to you what I think is impending, and I am now awaiting a letter from-you (*tuus*).

I write this letter at the tenth hour, immediately after (*statim ut*) reading your letter. I will give it to the postman (*tabellārius*) to-morrow. Your letter, and the expectation of a letter from you, are still (*adhūc*) keeping (*tenēre*) me at Thessalonīca. It is just (*ipse*) thirty days to-day (*quum hās dabam litterās*) that (*per quōs*) I have received no [letter] from you. A spell of sickness (*incommoda valētūdo*), from which I have not yet recovered (*ēmergo*), and (*et—et*) waiting for (*exspectātio*) Pomptinius, of whom not even a rumor has reached-me (*venīre*) yet (*adhūc*), have been detaining me for more than eleven days [= are detaining me the twelfth day] in Brundusium. We are travelling (*iter cōnficere*) by a hot (*aestuōsus*) and dusty road (*via*). I wrote (*dare*) yesterday from Ephesus; I write (*dare*) this [letter] from Tralles. I think that I shall be in my province the first of August (*Sextīlis*). We are hastening to the camp, which is two-days'-journey (*bīduī*) off. I am desirous (*cupere*) of making out (*facere*) a longer letter, but there is nothing to write about, and I cannot make fun (*jocārī*) by reason of (*prae*) [my] anxiety (*cūra*). I will send postmen to you to-morrow, and I think (*present*) that they will arrive (*venīre*) before our [friend] Saufējus. To-day, February the 2d [= February the 2d, on which day I write (*dare*) this letter], I am expecting the women in [my] Formian [villa], whither I have returned from Capua. Although when you read (*subj.*) this letter I think that I shall (*fore ut*) know what has been done (*agere*) at Brundusium, nevertheless I am harassed (*angor*) by hourly (*singulārum hōrārum*) expectation, and am wondering that not even a breath of rumor (*nihil nē—quidem*, § 404) has been brought [to me]. For there is a strange silence.

VOCABULARY.

☞ This vocabulary is intended to serve as a supplement and not as a substitute otherwise the exercise-book would defeat its own ends. Hence the absence of inflections, prepositions, numerals, and the omission of phrases and idioms explained in the appropriate sections of the grammar.

A.

Abandoned (= wretch), *perditus*.
abstain, (*sē*) *abstinēre*.
abound, *abundāre*.
absence, in my, *absente mē*.
absurd, *absurdus*.
abundance, *abundantia*.
accept, *accipere*.
acceptable, *grātus*.
accident, *cāsus*.
accomplish, *cōnficere*, *perficere*.
accuse, *accūsāre*, *arguere*.
accuser, *accūsātor*.
Achaean. *Achaeī*.
ache, *dolor*.
acknowledge (= confess) *fatērī*.
acorn, *glāns*.
acquit, *absolvere*.
act, *agere*, *facere*.
actor, *histrio*.
actually, *rē vērā*.
add, *addere*, *adjicere*.
admire, *admīrārī*.
admirable, *mīrus*, *mīrābilis*.
admit, *concēdere*.
admonish, *admonēre*, *monēre*.
adorn, *ornāre*.
adulterer, *adulter*.
advance, *prōgredī*, *prōcēdere*.
advantage, *commodum*.
advice. *cōnsilium*.
advise, *suādēre*.
affability, *cōmitās*.
affair, *rēs*, *negōtium*.
afford. *praebēre*.
afraid. to be, *metuere*, *timēre*, *verērī*.
afterwards, *post*, *posteā*, *posthāc*.
age, *aetās* (time of life), *tempora* (times).
agreeable, *grātus*, *jūcundus*.
aid, *auxilium*, *ops*, *opera*.
aid, to, *adjuvāre*.
air, *āēr*.
alive, *vīvus*.
all, *omnis*.
alleviate, *levāre*.
ally, *socius*.
almost, *prope*, *ferē*.
alone, *sōlus*.
already, *jam*.
also, *quoque*, § 444.
altar, *āra*.
alter, *mūtāre*.
always, *semper*.
Amazons, *Amazones*.
ambassador, *lēgātus*, *ōrātor*
ambush, *insidiae*.
ancestors, *majōrēs*.
ancient, *antīquus*.
and, *et*, *-que*, *atque*, § 477 foll.
anger, *īra*; *īrācundia* (angry temper).
angry, *īrātus*; to be a., *īrāscī*.
anguish, *dolor*.
announce, *nūntiāre*.
annoyance, *molestia*.
another, *alius*, *alter*, § 306.
answer, to, to make a., *respondēre*.
ant, *formica*.
Antony, *Antōnius*.
any, *ullus* (§ 304), *quīvīs* (any you choose).
ape, *simia*, *simius*.
appear, *appārēre*; (to seem) *vidērī*.
appearance, *speciēs*.
apple, *mālum*; *pōmum* (any edible fruit).
apply (to address one's self to), *adīre*.
appoint (create), *dīcere*, *creāre*.
approach, (subst.) *aditus*.
approach, to, *appropinquāre* *accēdere*, *adventare*.
approve, *probāre*, *approbāre*.
Arabians, *Arabēs*.
arm, to, *armāre*.
arm, *bracchium*, *manus*.
armor-bearer, *armiger*.
arms, *arma*.
army, *exercitus*.
arrest, *comprehendere*.
arrival, *adventus*.
arrive, *advenīre*, *pervenīre*.
arrow, *sagitta*.
art, *ars*.
artifice, *ars*, *dolus*.
ashamed, to be, *pudet*.
ashes, *cinis*.
ask, *petere*, *rogāre*; to inquire, *quaero*, *interrogo*. See p. 68.
ass, *asinus*.
assemble, *convenīre*.
assist, *adjuvāre*.
assistance, *auxilium*.
associate, *socius*.
assume, *sūmere*.
assuredly, *certō*, *profectō*.
astonished, to be, *mīrārī*.
Athenian, *Athēniēnsis*.
Athens, *Athēnae*.
attack, *impetus*.
attack, to, *adorīrī*.
attain, *adipiscī*, *assequī*, *cōnsequī*.
audacity, *audācia*.

aunt, (father's sister) *amita*; (mother's sister) *mātertera*.
author, *auctor*.
authority, *auctōritās*; authorities, *magistrātūs*
avarice, *avāritia*.
avaricious, *avārus*.
avenge, *ulcīscī*.
avoid, *vītāre*.
axe, *secūris*.
axis, *axis*.

B.

Baby, *infāns*.
back, *tergum*, *dorsum*.
bad, *malus*; *improbus* (untoward, naughty).
bag, *pēra*.
ball, *pila*.
banish, *ex urbe*, *ex cīvitāte pellere*.
bank (of a river), *rīpa*.
banquet, *convīvium*, *epulae*.
barber, *tōnsor*.
bare, *nūdus*.
bark, to, *lātrāre*.
bark (of a tree), *cortex* (outer), *liber* (inner).
barren, *sterilis*.
base, *turpis*.
bat, *vespertīlio*.
bathe, *lavāre*.
battle, *pugna*; *proelium* (engagement); to join b., *proelium committere*.
be, *esse*.
be without, *carēre*.
beam, *trabs*.
bear, *ferre*, *portāre*.
bear (subst.) *ursus*, *ursa*.
beard, *barba*.
beast, *bestia*; *bēlua* (great beast).
beat, *verberāre*, *caedere*; to be beaten, *vāpulāre* (comic); (to vanquish) *vincere*.
beautiful, *pulcher*, *formōsus*.
beauty, *pulchritūdo*.
become, to, *fierī*.
become, to (= be becoming), *decēre*.
bed, *lectus*; to go to b., *cubitum īre*.
bee, *apis*.
befall, *accidere*; *contingere* (of good luck).
before, *ante*, *anteā*, *antehāc*.
beg, *ōrāre*, *rogāre*, *petere*.
beget, *gignere*, *parere*.
beggar, *mendīcus*.
begin, *incipere*; *coepisse*, intr. with inf.
beginning, *initium*.
behold, *contemplārī*.
belief, *fidēs*.
believe, *crēdere*.
belly, *venter*, *alvus*.
bend, *flectere*.
beneficent, *beneficus*.
benefit, *beneficium*.
bereave, *prīvāre*; *orbāre*.
besiege, *obsidēre*; *oppugnāre* (assault).
best, *optimus*.
bestow, *dare*, *tribuere*, *dōnāre*.
betake one's self, *sē cōnferre*.
betray, *prōdere*.
better, *melior*.
beware, *cavēre*.
bid, *jubēre*, *imperāre*.
big, *magnus*, *grandis*.
bind, *vincīre*.
bird, *avis*.
bitch, *canis*.
bitter, *acerbus* (opp. to *mītis*), *amārus* (opp. to *dulcis*); bitter enemy, *acerbus inimīcus*, *inimīcissimus*.
black, *niger*.
blame, to, *reprehendere*; *vituperāre*.
blame (fault), *vitium*, *culpa*.
bleed, *sanguinem fundere*.
blessed, *beātus*.
blessing (boon), *bonum*; to be a blessing = to be of use.
blind, (adj.) *caecus*.
blindness, *caecitās*.
blood, *sanguis*; *cruor* (shed).
bloom, to, *flōrēre*.
blow, *plāga*.
blows, *verbera*.
boast, to, *glōriārī*.
bold, *audāx*.
boldness, *audācia*.
bone, *os*.
book, *liber*.
booty, *praeda*.
border, *margo*; (= boundary) *fīnis*.
bore, *perforāre*.
born, to be, *nāscī*.
bosom, *sinus*.
both, *ambo*, *uterque*, p. 30.
bow, *arcus*.
boy, *puer*.
bramble, *sentis*, *veprēs*.
branch, *rāmus*.
branch-of-learning, *disciplīna*.
brave, *fortis*.
bravery, *fortitūdo*.
bread, *pānis*.
break, *frangere*.
breast, *pectus*.
breath, *spīritus*, *anima*.
bribe, *pecūniā corrumpere*.
brick, *later*.
bridge, *pōns*.
brief, *brevis*.
brilliant, *splendidus*.
brilliancy, *splendor*.
brim, *margo*.
bring, *ferre*, *afferre*, *apportāre* (carry); *addūcere* (lead).
bring back, *referre*, *reportāre*; *redūcere* (lead).
bring up, *efferre*; *ēducāre*.
broad, *lātus*.
bronze, *aes*.
brook, **brooklet**, *rīvus*, *rīvulus*.
brother, *frāter*.
build, *aedificāre*; *condere*.
building, *aedificium*.
bull, *taurus*.
bundle, *fasciculus*.
burden (subst.), *onus*; (verb) *onerāre*; -some, *molestus*.
burn, to, *ūrere*; *combūrere* (alive).

burst, *rumpere*.
burial, *sepultūra*.
bury, *sepelīre*.
bush, *frutex*.
business, *negōtium*.
but, *sed*, *autem*, *vērum*, *at*. See § 485 foll.; (only), *tantum*, *modo*, *sōlum*.
butterfly, *pāpilio*.
buy, *emere*.

C.

Cage, *cavea*.
call, to, *vocāre*; call out, *ēvocāre*; call together, *convocāre*.
camel, *camēlus*.
camp, *castra*.
Campanians, *Campānī*.
can, *possum*.
capable, **capacious**, *capāx*.
captain, *centurio*.
captive, *captus*, *captīvus*.
capture, to, *capere*.
care, *cūra*, *dīligentia*.
care for, to, *cūrāre*.
careful, *dīligēns*.
careless, *incautus*.
carpenter, *faber*.
carry, *ferre*, *portāre*; carry off, *rapere*; carry a town, *expugnāre*; carry on, *gerere*.
Carthage, *Carthago*. Carthaginians, *Carthāginiēnsēs*.
cast, to, *jacere*.
castle, *arx*, *castellum*.
cat, *fēlēs*, *fēlis*.
catch, *capere*.
Catiline, *Catilīna*.
cattle, *pecus*.
cause, *causa*.
cautious, *cautus*.
cavalry, *equitātus*, *equitēs*, (adj.) *equestris*.
cave, *spēlunca*.
cease, *dēsinere*.
celebrated, *celeber* (things); *praeclārus*.
certain (fixed), *certus*; (person undefined) *quīdam*.
chain, *catēna*.
chance, *cāsus*; *opportūnitās*, *occāsio*.
change, to, *mūtāre*.
character, *mōrēs*.
charge (= attack), *impetus*.
Charles, *Carolus*.
charming, *dulcis*.
cheat, to, *fraudāre*.
child, children, *līberī* (in relation to parents); (of age) *īnfāns*, *puer*, *puella*, *parvulī*.
chokeful, *refertus*.
choose, *ēligere* (out of a number), *dēligere* (for a purpose).
circumstance, *rēs*.
citadel, *arx*, *castellum*.
citizen, *cīvis*.
city, *urbs* (capital); *oppidum* (walled town); *cīvitās* (community).
civil, *cīvīlis*.
cleanse, *pūrgāre*.
clear, *clārus*; (it is) *cōnstat*.
clemency, *clēmentia*.
clerk, *scrība*.
close, to, *claudere*.
clothes, clothing, *vestis*, *vestītus*.
cloud, *nūbēs*.
coast, *lītus*, *ōra*.
cock, *gallus*.
cohort, *cohors*.
cold (adj.), *frīgidus*.
cold (subst.), coldness, *frīgus*.
colleague, *collēga*.
collect, *colligere*.
come, *venīre*; to come up, *accēdere*; to come back, *redīre*; about, *fierī*, *accidere*.
command, to, *imperāre*.
command (subst.), *imperium*.
commit, *committere*.
common, *commūnis*.
commons, *plēbs*.
commonwealth, *rēs pūblica*.
communicate, *commūnicāre*.
companion, *comes*; (partner), *socius*; (boon companion), *sodālis*.
company (partnership), *societās*.
compassion, *misericordia*.
compel, *cōgere*.
complain, *querī*.
complete, *cōnficere*.
conceal, *cēlāre*.
conceive, *concipere*, *capere*.
concern (subst.), *cūra*.
concern, to, *cūrae esse*; *interest*, see § 177 foll.
concord, *concordia*.
condemn, *damnāre*, *condemnāre*.
confess, *fatērī*, *cōnfitērī*.
confidence, *fīdūcia*.
confident, to be, *cōnfīdere*.
congratulate, *grātulārī*.
conjunction (in) with, *cum*.
conquer, *vincere*, *superāre*.
conqueror, *victor*.
conscience, *cōnscientia*.
conscious, *cōnscius*.
consider, *habēre*, *dūcere*.
conspiracy, *conjūrātio*.
conspirators, *conjūrātī*.
constellation, *sīdus*.
constitute, *cōnstituere*.
consulship, *cōnsulātus*.
consult, *cōnsulere*.
consume, *cōnsūmere*.
contain, *continēre*.
contempt, *contemptus*, *ūs*.
content, contented, *contentus*.
contest, *certāmen*.
convict, to, *coarguere*.
convince, *persuādēre*.
convoke, *convocāre*.
cook, to, *coquere*.
cook, a, *coquus*.
cordial, *amīcus*.
Corinth, *Corinthus*.
corn, *frūmentum*.
corpse, *cadāver*.
correct, to, *corrigere*, *ēmendāre*.
corrupt, to, *corrumpere*.
corrupt (adj.), *corruptus*.
cough, a, *tussis*.

council, *concilium*.
counsel, *cōnsilium*.
count, to, *numerāre*; *habēre*, *dūcere*. § 350.
countenance. *vultus*. *ūs*.
country, *terra*; (native land) *patria*; (opposed to town.) *rūs*, *agrī*; (of a small territory), *ager*.
countryman. *rūsticus*.
courage. *animus*, *virtūs*.
course, a, *cursus*.
cover, to, *tegere*, *operīre*.
covet, *cupere*.
covetous, *avārus*.
coward, *ignāvus*.
cowardice, *ignāvia*.
craft, *calliditās*, *dolus*.
create. *creāre*.
credible, *crēdibilis*.
credit (mercantile), *fidēs*.
crime, *scelus*.
crop, *seges*.
cross (over), to, *trānsīre*.
cruel, *crūdēlis*.
crush, *opprimere*.
cry, to, *clāmāre*, *exclāmāre*.
cultivate, *colere*.
cunning (adj.), *callidus*; *dolōsus*; cunning trick, *dolus*.
cunning (subst.), *calliditās*.
cup, *pōculum*.
curse, to, *exsecrārī*; w. acc.
custody, *custōdia*.
custom, *cōnsuētūdo*, *mōs*.
cut, to, *secāre*, *caedere*.

D.

Dagger, *pūgio*, *sīca*.
daily. *quotīdiē*; *in singulōs diēs*, (when there is a progressive change.)
dance, to, *saltāre*.
danger, *perīculum*.
dangerous. *perīculōsus*.
dare, *audeo*.
dark, *obscūrus*.
daughter, *fīlia*; daughter-in-law, *nūrus*.
day (opp. to night), *diēs*; (opp. to darkness), *lūx*.
dead. *mortuus*.
dear, *cārus*.
death, *mors*; to meet death, *mortem oppetere*.
debauchery, *luxuria*.
deceive, *fallere*, (mislead); *dēcipere* (purposely).
decide. *dēcernere*.
decision, *jūdicium*.
declare. *dēclārāre*.
deed, *factum*; *facinus* (often in a bad sense).
deem, to, *dūcere*.
deep, *altus*, *profundus*.
defeat, to, *vincere*.
defeat, a, *clādēs*.
defend, *dēfendere*.
degree, to such a, *adeō*.
delight, to, *dēlectare*, *juvāre*.
deliver, *trādere*; *reddere* (what is due); *līberāre* (free).
demand, to, *postulāre*, *poscere*, *flāgitāre* (passionately).
deny, *negāre*, *recūsāre*.
depart, *abīre*, *discēdere*, *proficīscī*.
deprive, *prīvāre*.
derive, *dūcere*.
deserter, *trānsfuga*.
deserve, to, *merērī*.
deserving, *dignus*.
desire, to, } *cupere*,
desirous, to be, } *optāre*, *velle*.
desire, *cupīdo*.
desirous, *avidus*, *cupidus*.
desist, *dēsistere*, *absistere*.
despair, to, *dēspērāre*.
despise, *dēspicere* (look down on); *contemnere*, *spernere* (disdain).
despoil, *spoliāre*, *nūdāre*.
destroy, *dēlēre*, *perdere*.
detain, *retinēre*.
determine, *statuere*, *cōnstituere*, *dēcernere*.
devastate, *vastāre*.
dew, *rōs*.
dictate, *dictāre*.
die, *morī*.
different, *dīversus*, *alius*.
difficult, *difficilis*.
difficulty, *difficultās*.
dig, *fodere*.
dignity, *dignitās*.
diligence, *assiduitās*, *sēdulitās*.
diligent, *sēdulus*, *dīligēns*.
diminish, *minuere*.
dinner, *cēna*.
disadvantage, *incommodum*, *damnum*.
disagreeable, *ingrātus*, *injūcundus*.
disaster, *calamitās*.
disband, *dīmittere*.
discharge (duty), *fungī*.
discord, *discordia*.
discourse, to, *disserere*.
disease, *morbus*.
disgrace (subst.), *dēdecus*.
disgraceful, *turpis*.
disgust, to, *piget*.
dismiss, *dīmittere*.
dispense, with, *carēre*.
displease, *displicēre*.
distaff, *colus*.
distinguished, *praestāns*, *eximius*, *praeclārus*.
distribute. *distribuere*.
distrust, to, *diffīdere*.
disturb, *turbāre*.
ditch, *fossa*.
divide, to, *dīvidere*.
divine (adj.), *dīvīnus*.
do, *agere*, *facere*.
doe, *cerva*.
dog, *canis*.
door, *ōstium*, *jānua*, *fores*.
doubt, a, *dubium*.
doubt, to, *dubitāre*.
dove, *columba*.
dower, *dōs*.
dragon, *draco*.
draw, *trahere*, *dūcere*; draw off, *abdūcere*.
dress (subst.), *ornātus*, *vestītus*.
drink, to, *bibere*.
drive away, *pellere*, *abigere*
drop, a, *gutta*.
dry, *siccus*, *āridus*.
dry, to, *torrēre*.
duck, *anas*.
due, *dēbitus*.

dust, *pulvis*.
duty, *officium*, *mūnus*.
dwell, *habitāre*.

E.

Each, *quisque*. § 305.
eager, *ācer*.
eagle, *aquila*.
ear, *auris*.
early (in the morning), *māne*.
earth, *terra*; *orbis terrārum* (world).
earthly, *terrestris*.
ease, *ōtium*; at ease, *ōtiōsus*, *in ōtiō*.
easy, *facilis*.
eat, *edere*.
educate, *ēducāre*.
effeminate, *mollis*.
egg, *ōvum*.
Egyptians, *Aegyptiī*.
elephant, *elephās*, *elephantus*.
eloquent, *ēloquēns*, *disertus*.
eloquence, *ēloquentia*, *fācundia*.
embrace, to, *amplectī*, *complectī*.
emperor, *imperātor*.
empty, *vacuus*, *inānis*; to be empty, *vacāre*.
end, *fīnis*.
endeavor, to, *cōnārī*, *ēnītī*.
endowed, *praeditus*.
enemy (public), *hostis*; (at heart) *inimīcus*; (opponent) *adversārius*.
energetic, *industrius*, *strēnuus*.
energy, *industria*.
engagement, *negōtium*; *proelium*.
enjoy, *fruī*, *ūtī*.
enmity, *inimīcitia*.
enough, *satis*.
enter, *intrāre*, *inīre*.
entertain (divert), *dēlectāre*, *oblectāre*.
entrance, *aditus*.
entreat, *obsecrāre*.
enumerate, *ēnumerāre*.
envoy, *lēgātus*.
envy, *invidia*.
equal, *pār*.
equal, to, *aequāre*.
err, *errāre*.
escape, to, *effugere*; *ēvādere*.
especially, *praecipuē*, *imprīmis*, *maximē*.
esteem, to, *habēre*, *facere*, *pendere*.
even (adj.), *aequus*.
even, *etiam*.
evening, at, *vesperī*.
event (result), *ēventus* (pl. also *a*).
ever, *unquam*.
every, *omnis*, *quisque*; every-day, *cotīdiē*.
evident, to be, *appārēre*, *cōnstāre*.
example, *exemplum*.
excellent, *eximius*, *praeclārus*; *optimus*.
excite, *excitāre*, *commovēre*.
excitement, *concitātio*.
exertion, *contentio*
exhort, *hortārī*.
exile, an, *exsul*; *exsilium*.
exile, to, *pellere*.
exiled, to be, *exsulāre*.
expect, *exspectāre*.
expectation, *exspectātio*.
expense, *sūmptus*.
experienced, *perītus*; *expertus*.
expiate, *expiāre*.
explore, to, *explōrāre*.
exportation, *exportāre*.
extraordinary, *inūsitātus*, *singulāris*, *eximius*.
exult, *exsultāre*.
eye, *oculus*.

F.

Fable, *fābula*.
face, *faciēs*; *vultus*, *ōs* (countenance, looks).
fagot, *fascis*.
fail, *dēficere*.
fall, *cadere*.
fallacious *fallāx*.
fame, *fāma*.
famine, *famēs*.
famous, *clārus*, *celeber*.
farmer, *agricola*.
fast (firm), *firmus*; (swift) *celer*.
fat, *pinguis*.
father, *pater*; father in law, *socer*.
fault, *culpa*.
favor, *grātia*; a great favor, *grātissimum*.
fear (subst.), *metus*, *timor*, *formīdo*.
fear, to, *timēre*, *metuere* *verērī* (respect).
fearful, *timidus*.
feast, *convīvium*, *epulae*.
feather, *penna*.
feed, to, (act.) *pascere*; (neut.) *pascī*, *vescī*.
feel, to, *sentīre*.
feeling, *sēnsus*; feelings, *animus*, *animī*.
feign, *fingere*.
fell, to, *caedere*.
fellow, *socius*, *homo*.
ferocious, *ferōx*.
fetters, *compedēs*.
fetter, to, *vincīre*.
fever, *febris*.
few, *paucī*.
fidelity, *fidēs*.
field, *ager*.
fierce, *ferōx*.
fight, *pugna*; *proelium* (an engagement).
fight, to, *pugnāre*; *dīmicāre*.
fill, to, *implēre*.
find, to, *invenīre*, *reperīre* *comperīre*.
fine (adj.), *pulcher*.
fine (subst.), *multa*.
fine, to, *multāre*.
finger, *digitus*.
finish, to, *perficere*, *cōnficere*
fire, *ignis*.
firm, *firmus*.
first, *prīmus*.
fish, *piscis*.
fit, *aptus*, *idōneus*.
flatterer, *assentātor*.
flattery, *adūlātio*.
flee, *fugere*.
fleece, *vellus*.

fleet (subst.), *classis*.
fleet (adj.), *vēlōx*.
flesh, *caro*.
flight, *fuga*.
flight, put to, *fugāre*.
flock, a, *grex*.
flourish, *flōrēre*.
flower, *flōs*.
fly, a, *musca*.
fly, to, *volāre*; to fly away, *āvolāre*.
foliage, *frōns*.
follow, *sequor*.
following-generations, *posterī*.
folly, *stultitia*.
food, *cibus*.
fool, *stultus*.
foot, *pēs*.
foot-soldier, *pedes*.
for all that, *tamen*.
forbid, *vetāre*, *interdīcere*, *prohibēre*.
force (subst.), *vīs*, *vīrēs*.
force, to, *cōgere*.
forces, *cōpiae*.
foreign, *externus*, *exterus*.
foreigner, *peregrīnus*.
foresight, *prūdentia*.
forest, *silva*.
foretell, *praedīcere*.
forget, *oblīviscī*.
forgive, *ignōscere*, *veniam dare*.
forsake, *dēserere*, *relinquere*.
fortified, *mūnītus*.
fortune, *fortūna*.
foul, *faedus*.
found, *condere*.
fowler, *auceps*.
fox, *vulpēs*.
fraud, *fraus*, *dolus*.
free (adj.), *līber*; to be free from, *vacāre*; to set free, *līberare*.
free, to, *līberāre*, *solvere*.
freedom, *lībertās*.
fresh, *recēns*.
friend, *amīcus*.
friendship, *amīcitia*.
fright (subst.), see Fear.
frighten, to, *terrēre*.
frog, *rāna*.
fruit (of trees), *fructus*; (of the field) *frūgēs*.
fruitful, *fēcundus*, *fertilis*.
full, *plēnus*; chokeful, *refertus*.
funeral, *fūnus*; funeral pile, *rogus*.
furnish, to, *praebēre*.

G.

Gain, *lucrum*.
gall (subst.), *fel*.
game, *lūdus*, *lūsus*, *ālea*.
garment, *vestis*.
garrison, *praesidium*.
gate, *jānua*, *porta*, *ōstium*.
gather, *colligere*.
Gaul, *Gallia*; (people) *Gallī*.
general (subst.), *imperātor*.
genius, *ingenium*.
George, *Geōrgius*.
get to, *nancīscī*; *parāre*; (arrive) *advenīre*.
gift, *dōnum*.
girl, *puella*.
give, *dare*, *dōnāre*, *praebēre*; to give back, *reddere*; to give up, *trādere*; to give way, *cēdere*.
glad, *laetus*.
gladness, *laetitia*.
glory (subst.), *glōria*.
gnat, *culex*.
gnaw, to, *rōdere*, *corrōdere*.
go, to, *īre*; go off, *discēdere*, *abīre*.
goat (he,) *hircus*; goat (she,) *capra*.
God, *Deus*.
goddess, *dea*.
gold, *aurum*.
golden, *aureus*.
good, *bonus*, *probus*; (useful) *ūtilis*.
good (subst.), *bonum*.
goose, *ānser*.
govern, *regere*, *gubernāre*.
grandfather, *avus*; grandmother, *avia*; grandson, *nepōs*; grand-daughter, *neptis*.
grant, to, *concēdere*.
grape, *ūva*.
grass, *grāmen*, *herba*.
grateful, *grātus*.
grave, *gravis*.
great, *magnus*.
great-hearted, *magnanimus*.
greedy, *avidus*.
grieve, *dolēre*, *maerēre*.
ground, *humus*; (reason) *causa*.
guard, to, *custōdīre*.
guard, a, *custōdia*.
guardian, *custōs*; (legal) *tūtor*.
guilty, to declare, *damnāre* *condemnāre*.

H.

Habit, *mōs*, *consuētūdo*; to be in the h. of, *solēre*.
hair, *crīnis*, *capillus*.
half, *dīmidium*, *dīmidia pars*.
hand, *manus*.
handsome, *pulcher*.
hang, to, (act.) *suspendere*; (neut.) *pendēre*.
happen, *accidere*; *contingere* (for the better).
happy, *fēlix*, *bēatus*.
harbor, *portus*.
hard, *dūrus*; hard (to do), *difficilis*.
hare, *lepus*.
harm (subst.) *damnum*, *malum*, *incommodum*; to do harm, *nocēre*.
harmony, *concordia*.
harsh, *dūrus*.
hart, *cervus*.
hasten, *festīnāre*, *properāre*.
hate, hatred, *odium*.
hate, to, *ōdisse*; to be hated, *odiō esse*.
haughty, *superbus*.
have, *habēre*.
hawk, *accipiter*.
head, *caput*.
headlong, *praeceps*.
health, *valētūdo*.
healthy, *sānus*.

hear, *audīre.*
heart, *cor*
heaven, *caelum.*
heavy, *gravis.*
heedless, *incautus.*
heir. *hērēs.*
help (subst.), *auxilium.*
help, to, *juvāre*, *adjuvāre*
helper, *adjūtor.*
hen, *gallīna.*
herb, *herba.*
herdsman, *pastor.*
hesitate, to, *dubitāre.*
hide, to, *abdere*; to hide from, *cēlāre.*
high, *altus.*
highwayman, *latro*, *praedo.*
hill. *collis.*
hind, *cerva.*
hinder, to, *impedīre*, *obstāre*, *prohibēre.*
hinge, *cardo.*
hog, *porcus*, *sūs.*
hold, to, *tenēre.*
holidays, *fēriae.*
home, *domus.*
honey, *mel.*
honor, *honor*; to h. *colere.*
honorable, *honestus.*
hope, *spēs.*
hope, to, *spērāre.*
horn, *cornū.*
horse, *equus.*
horseman, *eques.*
hour, *hōra.*
house, *domus*, *aedēs* (pl.).
huge, *ingēns.*
human, *hūmānus*; human being, *homo.*
hunger, *famēs.*
hunter, *vēnātor.*
hurt, to, *nocēre.*
husband, *vir.*
husbandman, *agricola.*

I.

Image, *imāgo.*
imitate, *imitārī.*
imitation. *imitātio.*
immediately, *statim.*
impend, *impendēre.*
importance, to be of, *interest*, *rēfert*. § 177
impose, *impōnere.*
impudent, *impudēns*
incautious, *incautus.*
increase (act.), *augēre*; (neut.) *crēscere.*
incredible, *incrēdibilis.*
indulgence, *indulgentia.*
industry, *dīligentia*, *industria.*
industrious, *sēdulus*; *industrius.*
inexorable, *inexōrābilis.*
infantry, *peditēs*; (adj.) *pedestris.*
influence, *auctōritās.*
inform, *certiōrem facere.*
inhabitant, *incola.*
injure, to, *nocēre.*
injury, *injūria*, *damnum.*
injustice, *injūstitia*, *injūria.*
inquire, *quaerere.*
innocent, *innocēns.*
insolent, *insolēns.*
inspect, to, *inspicere.*
institution, *institūtum.*
instructed, *ēdoctus.*
insult, *contumēlia*, *injūria.*
intellect, *mēns.*
interest, *interest*, *rēfert*. § 381.
intrust, *committere.*
inventor, *inventor.*
invite, *invitāre*, *vocāre.*
iron, *ferrum*; (of iron) *ferreus.*
issue (subst.), *exitus.*
ivory, *ebur*; (of ivory) *ex ebore.*

J.

Jackdaw, *graculus.*
join, *jungere*; to join battle, *proelium committere.*
journey, *iter.*
joy, *gaudium*; *laetitia* (gladness).
judge, *jūdex.*
judgment, *jūdicium.*
just, *jūstus.*
justly, *jūre.*
justice, *jūstitia.*

K.

Keen, *ācer.*
keep, *servāre*, *custōdīre*, (keep in), *continēre*; (from), *prohibēre.*
keeper, *custōs.*
kill, to, *interficere*; *occidere*, *caedere* (slay), *necāre* (cruelly).
kind (subst.), *genus.*
kind (adj.), *benignus.*
king, *rēx.*
kingdom, *regnum.*
knee, *genū.*
knife, *culter.*
know, to, *scīre* (of things), *nōscere*; *nōsse*; *cognōscere*; not to know, *nēscīre*, *ignōrāre.*
known (well), *cognitus.*

L.

Labor, to, *labōrāre.*
labor (subst.), *labor.*
Lacedaemonian, *Lacedaemonius*, *Laco.*
lack, to, *carēre*, *egēre*, *indigēre*
laden, *onustus.*
lake, *lacus.*
lamb, *agnus.*
lame, *claudus.*
lament, to, *lāmentārī.*
land, *terra*; *patria.*
large, *magnus*; *amplus*, *ingēns* (huge).
lark, *alauda.*
laugh, to, *rīdēre.*
laugh, laughter, *rīsus*. *ūs.*
law, *lēx.*
lay down, *pōnere*, *depōnere*
laziness, *pigritia.*
lazy, *piger*, *ignāvus.*
lead (subst.), *plumbum.*
lead, to, *dūcere.*
leader, *dux.*
leading-men, *prīncipēs*
leaf, *folium.*
league, *foedus*, *eris.*
lean, to, *nītī.*
leap down, *dēsilīre.*
learn, *discere.*
learned, *doctus.*
learning, *doctrīna.*
least (adj.), *minimus.*
leave, to, *relinquere.*

left (adj.), *sinister*; (hand) *sinistra*.
leg, *crūs*.
legion, *legio*.
leisure, *ōtium*.
less (adj.), *minor*.
lever, *vectis*.
liberal, *līberālis*.
liberality, *līberālitās*.
liberate, to, *līberāre*.
lie, to, *jacēre*; to lie in wait for, *īnsidiārī alicui*.
lie, to tell a, *mentīrī*.
liar, *mendāx*.
license, *licentia*.
life, *vīta*.
light (adj.), *levis*.
light, a, *lūx*, *lūmen*.
lightning (flash of), *fulgur*; (stroke of), *fulmen*.
like (adj.), *similis*.
likeness, *imāgo*.
line (of battle), *aciēs*; (of march), *agmen*.
linger, *cunctārī*.
lion, *leo*.
lioness, *leaena*.
literature, *litterae*.
little, *parvus*; (mean) *parvus*, *pūsillus*.
live, *vīvere*; (dwell) *habitāre*.
living, *vīvus*.
load (subst.), *onus*, *eris*.
load, to, *onerāre*.
lofty, *excelsus*.
long (adj.), *longus*.
long (adv.), *diū* (a long time).
longing, *dēsīderium*.
loose, loosen, *solvere*.
lord, to, *dominārī*.
lose, *āmittere* (let go); *perdere* (waste).
loss, *damnum*, *incommodum*, *jactūra*.
lot, *sors*; *fortūna*.
loud, *clārus*; *magnus*.
love, to, *amāre*; *dīligere* (like).
love (subst.), *amor*.
lovely, see **beautiful**.
low, *humilis*.
luck, *fortūna*; good luck, (*secunda*) *fortūna*, *fēlīcitās*.
lucky, *fēlīx*, *faustus*, *fortūnātus*.
lust, *libīdo*.
luxury, *luxuria*.
Lydian, *Lȳdī*.

M.

Macedonian, *Macedo*, *ŏnis*.
mad, *īnsānus* (cracked); *furiōsus* (maniacal).
mad, to be, *īnsānīre*, *furere*.
madness, *īnsānia*, *furor*.
magistracy, magistrate, *magistrātus*.
maid, maiden, *virgo*, *puella*; maid (servant), *ancilla*.
mainland, *continēns*.
maintain, *cōnfirmare*; *cōnservāre*.
make, *facere*, *efficere*, *reddere*.
malady, *morbus*.
man, *homo* (human being); *vir* (opp. to woman); *mortālis*; man-servant, *famulus*.
mankind, *genus hūmānum*; *gēns hūmāna*.
manner, *modus*.
many, *multī*.
march, to, *proficīscī*.
maritime, *maritimus*.
mark, to, *notāre*.
market-place, *forum*.
marriage, *mātrimōnium*.
marry, to, *uxōrem dūcere* (of the man); *virō nūbere* (of the woman).
masses, *plēbs*, *multitūdo*.
master, *dominus*; *herus* (of slaves); *magister* (teacher).
master, make one's self, *potīrī*.
match, *pār*.
matter (subst.), *rēs*.
meadow, *prātum*.
measure, to, *mētīrī*.
measure (subst.), *mēnsūra*.
meat, *caro* (flesh); *cibus* (food).
meet, to, *obviam īre*, *fierī convenīre*.
member, *membrum*.
memory, *memoria*.
mention, *mentio*.
merchant, *mercātor*.
message, *nūntius*.
messenger, *nūntius*.
method, *via ratioque*, *modus*.
middle, **midst**, } *medius*, § 287 R. § 324 R. 6.
mild, *mītis*.
military, *mīlitāris*.
milk, *lac*.
mind, *animus*, *mēns*.
mindful, *memor*.
mission (object of), *rēs*.
mistaken, to be, *errāre*, *fallī*.
moderate, **moderation**, } *modestus*.
modest, **modesty**, } *modestia*.
money, *pecūnia*.
monkey, *sīmia*.
month, *mēnsis*.
moon, *lūna*.
morning, *māne*.
morose, *mōrōsus*.
morrow, the, *crās*, *crāstinus diēs*.
mortal, *mortālis*.
most (people), *plērīque*.
mother, *māter*; mother-in-law, *socrus*.
mound, *tumulus*, *agger*.
mount, to, *cōnscendere*.
mountain, *mōns*.
mourn, *lūgēre*, *maerēre*.
mouse, *mūs*.
mouth, *ōs*.
move, *movēre*, *sē movēre*.
movement, *mōtus*.
much, *multus*.
multitude, *multitūdo*.
murder, to, *interficere*.
must, *dēbēre*; *oportet*, *necesse est*.

N.

Naked, *nūdus*.
name, *nōmen*.
name, to, *nōmināre*, *appellāre*, *vocāre*.
narrow, *angustus*.
nation, *gēns*.
nature, *nātūra*.
naughty, *improbus*.
near (adj.), *propinquus*.
near, to come, § 337.
nearly, *prope*.
necessary, *necessārius*, *necesse*; *opus est*.
necessity, *necessitās*.
neck, *collum*, *cervīcēs*.
need, *opus*, *ūsus*; to be in, *egēre*, *indigēre*, *carēre*.
needle, *acus*.
nefarious, *nefārius*.
neglect, to, *negligere*.
neglect (subst.), *negligentia*.
neighbor, ing, *vīcīnus*.
neither, *neuter*.
nest, *nīdus*.
never, *nunquam*, § 482.
new, *novus* (opp. to *antīquus*); *recēns* (fresh, opp. to *vetus*).
news, *nūntius*, *aliquid novī*.
nice, = sweet, *dulcis*.
night, *nox*.
nightingale, *luscinia*.
nobility, *nōbilēs*.
noble, *nōbilis*, *generōsus*.
none, *nullus*.
noose, *laqueus*.
nose, *nāsus*.
nothing, *nihil*, *nulla rēs*.
nourish, to, *alere*.
now, *nunc*.
number, *numerus*.
Numidian, *Numida*.
nurse, to, *cūrāre*.
nut, *nux*; nut-shell, *nucis cortex*.

O.

Oak, *quercus*, *rōbur*.
oar, *rēmus*.
oath, *jūsjūrandum*.
obey, to, *obēdīre*, *obtemperāre*; *pārēre* (habitually)
obscure, to, *obscūrāre*.
obscure, *obscūrus*.
observe, *servāre*.
occupation, *negōtium*.
occupied, *occupātus*.
ocean, *ōceanus*, *mare*.
offer, to, *offerre*.
office, *magistrātus*.
often, *saepe*.
old, *vetus* (length of duration); *antīquus* (distance of origin).
old age, *senectūs*.
old man, *senex*.
omit, to, *omittere*.
once (for all), *semel*; once (on a time), *ōlim*, *quondam*.
one, *ūnus*; one day, *aliquando*.
only, *sōlus*; (adv.) *tantum*, *modo*, *sōlum*.
open, to, *aperīre*.
opportunity, *occāsio*; *opportūnitās* (convenience).
oppose, *oppōnere*.
opposite, *contrārius*.
opulent, *opulentus*.
or, *aut*, *vel*, § 495.
order (subst.), *ordo*; orders to give, *imperāre*.
order, to, *imperāre*, *jubēre*.
origin, *origo*.
ornament (subst.), *decus*.
other, *alius*, *alter*, § 306.
ought, *dēbēre*.
our, *nōster*.
overbearing, *superbus*.
overcome, *superāre* (surpass); *vincere* (vanquish).
owe, to, *dēbēre*.

P.

Pain, *dolor*.
paint, to, *pingere*.
painter, *pictor*.
painting, *pictūra*, *tabula* (*picta*).
palace, *domus*, *aedēs*.
pardon, to, *ignōscere*, *veniam dare*.
pardon (subst.), *venia*.
parent, *parēns*.
part (subst.), *pars*.
partaker, *particeps*.
partner, *socius*.
party, *pars*, *partēs*.
pass (over), *trānsīre*.
passions, *libīdinēs*.
patience, *patientia*.
pavilion, *tabernāculum*.
pay, to, *solvere*.
pay (subst.), *mercēs*.
peacock, *pāvo*.
peace, *pāx*.
peasant, *rūsticus*, *agricola*
peculiar, *proprius*.
pen, *penna*; *calamus*, *stilus*
people, *populus*; *hominēs*.
perceive, *intelligere*, *animadvertere*.
perform, *perficere*, *cōnficere* *fungī*.
perhaps, *fortasse*.
perish, *perīre*, *interīre*.
permit, *permittere*, *sinere*
perpetual, *perpetuus*.
Persian, *Persa*.
person, *homo*.
perspicuous, *perspicāx*.
persuade, *persuādēre*.
philosopher, *philosophus*.
Phoenician, *Phoenix*.
physician, *medicus*.
picture, *pictūra*, *tabula*.
pierce, *perforāre*.
pigeon, *columba*.
pine-tree, *pīnus*.
pious, *pius*.
pitch (a camp), *pōnere*.
placable, *plācābilis*.
place, *locus*.
plan, *cōnsilium*; *sententia*.
plant (subst.), *herba*.
plant, to, *serere*.
play, to, *lūdere*.
pleasant, *grātus*, *jūcundus*
please, *placēre*.
pleasure, *voluptās*.
pledge, *pignus*.
plough (subst.), *arātrum*; ploughman, *arātor*.
plough, to, *arāre*.
plunder, *spoliāre*; *dīripere*
poem, *carmen*, *poēma*.

poet, *poēta*.
point, to, *acuere*.
Pompey, *Pompējus*.
poor, *pauper*, *inops*; *miser*.
popular, *populāris*.
possession, *possessio*.
postman, *tabellārius*.
poverty, *paupertās*.
pound, *lībra*.
power, *potestās*; to be in one's power, *penes aliquem esse*.
practice, *ūsus*.
practice, to, *exercēre*.
praise (subst.), *laus*.
praise, to, *laudāre*.
precept, *praeceptum*.
prefect, *praefectus*.
prefer, *antepōnere*; *mālle*.
prepare, *parāre*.
present, to, *dōnāre*.
present (subst.), *dōnum*.
present, to be, *adesse*.
preserve, *servāre*.
pretend, *simulāre*.
pretty, *bellus*, *pulcher*.
prevent, *prohibēre*, *impedīre*, *officere*.
prey, *praeda*.
price, *pretium*.
priest, ess, *sacerdōs*.
prince, *prīnceps*.
prison, *carcer*, *custōdia*.
prisoner, *captus*; (of war) *captīvus*.
privy, *cōnscius*.
procure, *parāre*.
prodigy, *prōdigium*.
profit (subst.), *commodum*.
profit, to, *prōdesse*.
promise, to, *prōmittere*; *pollicērī* (voluntarily).
promise (subst.), *prōmissum*.
property, *rēs*, *bona*.
propose, to, *prōpōnere*.
prosperity, *fēlīcitās*.
protect, *prōtegere*, *dēfendere*, *tuērī*, *tūtārī*.
proud, *superbus*.
prove, *probāre*.
proverb, *prōverbium*.
provide, *prōvidēre*.
province, *prōvincia*.
prow, *prōra*.
prudent, *prūdēns*.
public, *hominēs*.
Punics, *Poenī*.
punish, *pūnīre*.
punishment, *poena*.
puppy, *catulus*.
pure, *pūrus*.
purify, *pūrgāre*.
put, *pōnere*, *collocāre*.

Q.

Quantity, *vīs*.
queen, *rēgīna*.
quench, *exstinguere*; *sēdāre*.
question, to, *quaerere*, *interrogāre*.
question (subst.), *quaestio*.
quick, *celer*.
quickness, *celeritās*, *vēlōcitās*.
quiet, *quiētus*.

R.

Rabble, *vulgus*.
raft, *ratis*.
raise, to, *tollere*.
ram, *ariēs*.
rampart, *vallum*.
rare, *rārus*.
rash, *temerārius*.
raven, *corvus*.
reach, *assequī*, *attingere*.
read, *legere*.
readily, *facile*.
ready, *parātus*.
rear, *tergum*.
reason, *ratio*.
recall, *revocāre*; (recollect) *recordārī*.
receive, *accipere*, *recipere*; (as a guest) *excipere*.
recollect, *recordārī*.
recommend, *commendāre*.
recover, *recuperāre*, *recipere*.
red, *ruber*.
reduce, *redigere*.
refer, *referre*.
refrain (*sē*) *abstinēre*.
refuse, to, *recūsāre*.
reign, *rēgnāre*.
rein, *frēnī*, *a*.
reject, *rejicere*, *repudiāre*.
rejoice, *gaudēre*; *laetārī* (show gladness).
region, *regio*.
relation, *propinquus*, *cognātus*.
relieve, *levāre*.
remain, *manēre*.
remember, *reminīscī*, *meminisse*.
remind, *monēre*, *commonefacere*.
remove, *movēre*, *removēre*, *tollere*.
repeat, = report, *referre*.
repent, *paenitet*.
repulse, to, *repellere*.
reputation, *fāma*.
request, see **beg**.
require, *postulāre*.
rescue, *salūs*.
resign, *abdicāre*.
resist, *resistere*.
resolve, *cōnstituere*, *dēcernere*.
rest (subst.), *quiēs*.
rest, to, *quiēscere*.
restore, *reficere*; *restituere*.
retire, *sē recipere*.
return, to (act.), *reddere*, *restituere*; (neut.) *redīre*.
return (subst.), *reditus*.
revolution, *rēs novae*.
reward (subst.), *praemium*.
Rhodes, *Rhodus*.
rich, *dīves*.
riches, *dīvitiae*, *opēs*.
right (adj.), *dexter*; *jūstus*.
right (subst.), *jūs*.
rim, *margo*.
ring, *ānulus*.
ripe, *mātūrus*.
rise, to, *surgere*; *orīrī*.
river, *fluvius*.
road, *via*.
roar (subst.), *fremitus*.
rob, *prīvāre*, *spoliāre*.
robber, *latro*, *praedo*.
rock, *saxum*, *rūpēs*.
roll, to, *volvere*.
roof, *tectum*.
root, *rādīx*.
rope, *fūnis*, *restis*; *laqueus* (halter).
rough, *asper*.
row, *ordo*.

royal, *rēgius* (of a king); *rēgālis* (like a king's).
ruin, *ruīna*; *perniciēs*.
ruin, to, *perdere*, *pessum dare*.
ruinous (act.), *perniciōsus*.
rule (subst.), *imperium*.
rule, to, *regere*, *moderārī*.
ruler, *moderātor*.
run, *currere*; *fugere*; to run up, *accurrere*.

S.

Sacred, *sacer*.
sacrifice, to, *immolāre*.
sad, *tristis*, *maestus*.
safe, *tūtus*, *salvus*, *incolumis*.
safety, *salūs*.
sail (subst.), *vēlum*.
sail, to, *nāvigāre*.
salt, *sal*.
salute, *salūtāre*.
same, *idem*, § 296.
sanctuary, *fānum*.
save, *servāre*, *cōnservāre*.
say, *dīcere*.
scarce, *vix*.
scatter, *spargere*, *dispergere*.
scholar, *discipulus*; (learned man), *doctus*.
school, *schola*, *lūdus*.
science, *scientia*.
scold, to, *vituperāre*.
scream, to, *clāmāre*, *exclāmāre*.
Scythian, *Scytha*.
sea, *mare*.
season, *tempestās*, *tempus*.
seat, *sēdēs*.
second, *secundus*.
secretly, *clam*.
see, *vidēre*.
seek, *quaerere*; seek after, *expetere*.
seem, *vidērī*.
seize, *corripere*.
sell, *vēndere*.
senate, *senātus*.
send, *mittere*; send back, *remittere*.
sensation, *mōtus*.
sense, *sēnsus*.
serious, *sērius*.
servant, *servus*; man-s. *famulus*; maid-s. *ancilla*.
servant, to be a, *servīre*.
set, *pōnere*; set on, *incitāre*; set up, *statuere*; (of the sun) *occidere*.
shade, shadow, *umbra*.
shady, *umbrōsus*.
shameful, *turpis*.
shameful deed, *facinus*.
shameless, *impudēns*, *inverēcundus*.
shape, *forma*.
share (subst.), *pars*, *portio*.
sharp, *acūtus*.
sheep, *ovis*, *pecus*.
shepherd, *pastor*.
ship, *nāvis*.
shore, *lītus*.
short, *brevis*.
shoulder, *humerus*.
show, *mōnstrāre*, *ostendere*; show one's self, *sē praestāre*.
shower, *imber*.
shrewd, *callidus*.
shrub, *frutex*.
shudder, to, *horrēre*.
shut, to, *claudere*.
Sicily, *Sicilia*.
sick, *aeger*; *aegrōtus* (physically).
sickness, *morbus*, *valētūdo*.
side, *latus*.
siege, *obsidio*.
signal, *signum*.
silent, *tacitus*; to be silent, *tacēre*.
silly, *īnsulsus*.
silliness, *īnsulsitās*.
silver, *argentum*; (of silver) *argenteus*.
simpleton, *stultus*, *fatuus*.
sing, *canere*.
sister, *soror*.
situated, *situs*.
skilled, **skilful**, *perītus*, *expertus*.
skin, *cutis*, *pellis*.
skull, *caput*.
sky, *caelum*.
slate, *tabula*.
slave, (male) *servus*; (female) *serva*; to be a slave, *servīre*.
slavery, *servitūs*.
slay, *trucīdāre*. See **kill**.
sleep (subst.), *somnus*.
sleep, to, *dormīre*.
slight, *levis*.
slow, *tardus*.
sly, *callidus*.
small, *parvus*.
smell, to, (give forth) *redolēre*; (take in) *olfacere*.
smoke, *fūmus*.
snake, *serpēns*, *anguis*, *coluber*.
snare, *laqueus*.
snow, *nix*.
so, *ita*, *sic*.
society, *societās*.
soldier, *mīles*.
sole (adj.), *sōlus*.
some, *aliquis*; *quīdam*; § 300 foll.; *nōnnullī*, some day, *aliquando*; sometimes, *nōnnunquam*; *interdum* (once in a while).
somewhat, *aliquantum*
son, *fīlius*.
son-in-law, *gener*.
song, *cantus*, *carmen*.
soon, *brevī*; *cito*.
soothe, *lēnīre*.
sorry, to be, *paenitet*.
soul, *animus*, *mēns*.
sound (adj.), *sānus*.
sound (subst.), *sonus*.
sour-tempered, *mōrōsus*.
sow, to, *serere*.
sow (subst.), *sūs*.
Spain, *Hispānia*.
spare, *parcere*.
sparrow, *passer*.
Spartan, *Spartānus*.
speak, *loquī*, *dīcere*; *verba facere*.
speech, *ōrātio*; to make a speech, *ōrātiōnem habēre*.
speed, *celeritās*, *vēlōcitās*.
spirit, *animus*.
splendid, *splendidus*

spring (season), *vēr.*
spur, *calcāria.*
stag, *cervus.*
stall, *stabulum.*
stand, to, *stāre*; to stand in the way of, *obstāre.*
standard, *signum.*
standard-bearer, *signifer.*
star, *stella.*
starling, *sturnus.*
state, *condicio*; (government) *cīvitās, res pūblica.*
statue, *signum, statua.*
stay, to, *manēre*; stay one's self, *nītī.*
steadfast, *cōnstāns.*
stern (subst.), *puppis.*
stone, *lapis.*
stork, *cicōnia.*
storm, *procella* (squall); *tempestās* (tempest).
storm, to (take by storm), *expugnāre.*
story, *fābula.*
strange (foreign), *aliēnus*; (wonderful) *mīrus.*
stranger, *peregrīnus, hospes.*
strength, *rōbur, vīrēs*; to take fresh strength, *vīrēs resūmere.*
strict, *sevērus.*
strife, *rixa.*
strip, *nūdāre.*
stroke (of lightning), *fulmen.*
strong, *validus*; *fortis.*
study, *studium.*
study, to, *studēre.*
stupid, *stultus, stupidus.*
subject, *subjectus.*
subjugate, *domāre.*
succeed, *succēdere.*
succumb, *succumbere.*
sudden, *subitus.*
suddenly, *subitō.*
suffer, *patī, perpetī.*
suffering, *dolor.*
sue for, *petere.*
sufficient, to be, *sufficere, satis esse.*
suit, to, *convenīre.*
suitable, *aptus, idōneus*
sun, *sōl.*
superstition, *superstitio.*
supplication, *supplicātio.*
supplied, bountifully (to be), *abundāre, scatēre.*
suppose, *putāre, arbitrārī, opīnārī.* See **think**.
supreme, *suprēmus, summus.*
surface (of water), *aequor.*
surname, *cognōmen.*
surpass, *superāre.*
surrender, to, *trādere, dēdere.*
surround *circumdare, cingere.*
suspicion, *suspīcio.*
swallow (subst.), *hirundo.*
swallow up, *vorāre, dēvorāre, haurīre.*
swan, *cycnus.*
sway, *imperium, dicio.*
swear, *jūrāre.*
sweet, *dulcis*; *suāvis.*
swift, *celer, vēlōx.*
swim, across, *trānāre.*
swine, *sūs, porcus.*
sword, *gladius.*
syllable, *syllaba.*
Syracuse, *Syrācūsae.*

T.

Tablet, *tabula.*
tail, *cauda.*
take, *sūmere, capere*; to take away, *adimere*; (by force), *ēripere.*
talk (subst.), *sermo.*
talk, to, *colloquī.*
tall, *prōcērus.*
talon, *unguis.*
tame, to, *domāre.*
tardy, *tardus.*
taste, to, *gustāre.*
tax (subst.), *vectīgal, tribūtum.*
tear, to pieces, *dīlaniāre.*
tear (subst.), *lacrima.*
tell, *nārrāre.*
temper, *animus.*
temple, *aedēs.*
tenacious, *tenāx.*
tender, *tener.*
testimony, *testimōnium.*
thank, to (give thanks), *grātiās agere.*
therefore, *itaque, igitur*, § 502.
thick (coarse), *crassus.*
thief, *fūr.*
thin, *tenuis.*
thing, *rēs.*
think, *putāre*; *cōgitāre* (form an idea); *arbitrārī* (judge deliberately); *opīnārī* (as an individual conviction); *sentīre* (as a view), *jūdicāre* (to judge), *cēnsēre* (to estimate); See also **remember**, **esteem**, **consider**.
thirst (subst.), *sitis.*
thirst, to, *sitīre.*
Thracian, *Thrāx.*
throat, *faucēs.*
throne, *imperium, regnum*
throw, *jacere*; off, *abjicere.*
thunder, *tonāre.*
Tiber, *Tiberis.*
tidings, *nūntius.*
time, *tempus.*
timid, *timidus.*
tire, to, *taedet.*
tongue, *lingua.*
too, *quoque.*
tooth, *dēns.*
top, *cacūmen.*
touch, *tangere.*
track, *vestīgium.*
trade, *commercium*; (handcraft) *ars.*
tragedy, *tragoedia.*
traitor, *prōditor.*
transport, *trānsportāre, trānsmittere.*
travel, to, *iter facere.*
traveller, *viātor.*
treat, *tractāre.*
treaty, *foedus.*
tribe, *gēns.*
trick, *dolus.*
triumph (subst.), *triumphus*
triumph, to, *triumphāre.*
troops, *cōpiae.*
trouble, *molestia, negōtium*

troublesome, *molestus.*
truce, *indutiae.*
true, *vērus.*
trust, *cōnfīdere.*
truth, *vērum, vēra.*
trunk, *truncus.*
try, *experīrī, tentāre, cōnārī.*
turn, *vertere;* turn out, *ēvādere.*
twins, *geminī, gemellī.*

U.

Ulysses, *Ulixēs.*
unbounded, *īnfīnītus.*
uncle (father's brother), *patruus;* (mother's brother), *avunculus.*
unburied, *īnsepultus.*
unconquered, *invictus.*
understand, *intellegere, accipere, comperīre.*
understanding, *mēns.*
undertake, *suscipere.*
undertaking, *inceptum.*
unfair, *inīquus.*
unfortunate, *īnfēlīx, miser.*
ungrateful, *ingrātus.*
uninjured, *incolumis.*
universe, *mundus.*
unjust, *inīquus, injūstus.*
unlucky, *īnfēlīx.*
unwary, *incautus.*
unwholesome, *nocēns.*
unwilling, to be, *nōlle.*
upright, *probus.*
use, to, *ūtī.*
use (subst.), *ūsus.*
usually, I am, *soleo.*
usurp, *ūsurpāre.*

V.

Vain, *vānus.*
value, *pretium.*
value, to, *aestimāre, dūcere, pendere.*
varying, *varius.*
venture, *audēre.*
vessel, *vās.*
vice, *vitium.*
victory, *victōria;* to get the victory, *vincere, victōriam reportāre.*
vigorous, *ācer.*
village, *vīcus.*
violence, *vīs.*
violent, *vehemēns, ācer.*
virtue, *virtūs.*
voice, *vōx.*
Volscians, *Volscī.*
vulture, *vultur.*

W.

Wait, for, *exspectāre.*
wait, to lie in, *īnsidiārī.*
walk, to take a walk, *ambulāre.*
wall, *mūrus; moenia* (pl.), (city); *pariēs* (party).
want, to, *carēre, egēre, indigēre;* wanted to be, *opus esse.*
want (subst.), *egestās, inopia.*
war, *bellum;* to wage war, *bellum īnferre.*
ward off, to, *dēfendere.*
warm (adj.), *calidus.*
warn, *monēre, admonēre.*
wary, *cautus.*
waste, to lay, *vastāre, populārī.*
watch, *vigilia.*
watch (-men), *custōdia, custōdēs, vigiliae, vigilēs.*
watchful, *vigil, vigilāns.*
water, *aqua.*
way, *via; modus.*
way, to give, *cēdere;* stand in the way, *obstāre.*
wayfaring man, *viātor.*
weak, *dēbilis, imbēcillus.*
weaken, *dēbilitāre.*
weal, *salūs.*
wealth, *dīvitiae, opēs.*
weary (wearied), *fessus.*
weary, to, *taedet.*
weep, *lacrimāre, flēre.*
weight, *pondus.*
welfare, *salūs.*
well (adj.), *sānus;* (adv.), *bene.*
when? *quando.*
white, *albus, candidus.*
whole, *tōtus.*
wicked, *malus, improbus.*
wide, *lātus.*
wife, *uxor.*
wild, *ferus;* wild beast, *fera.*
will, *voluntās;* good-will, *benevolentia, favor, voluntās.*
will, to, *velle.*
wind (subst.), *ventus*
window, *fenestra.*
wine, *vīnum.*
winter, *hiems.*
winter-quarters, *hīberna.*
wisdom, *sapientia, prūdentia.*
wise, *sapiēns, prūdēns.*
wish, to, *optāre, cupere, velle*
withdraw, *sē recipere.*
witness (subst.), *testis.*
wolf, *lupus;* she-wolf, *lupa.*
woman, *mulier, fēmina.*
wonderful, *mīrus.*
wont, to be, *solēre.*
wood, a, *silva;* (fuel), *lignum,* (building-wood), *māteria.*
word, *verbum.*
work (subst.), *opus.*
work, to, *labōrāre.*
world, *mundus; orbis terrārum.*
worth (subst.), *virtūs.*
worthy, *dignus;* to deem worthy, *dignārī.*
wound, to, *vulnerāre.*
wound (subst.), *vulnus.*
wreath, *corōna*
wretch (wretched), *miser; perditus.*
write, *scrībere.*
wrong, *injūria.*

Y.

Year, *annus.*
yesterday, *herī.*
yield, *cēdere.*
young (of animals), *pullus*
youth, *juvenis; juventūs*

Z.

Zeal, *studium.*
zealous, *studiōsus.*

SUPPLEMENTARY VOCABULARY.

A.

Able, to be, *posse.*
achievement, *facinus.*
act, an, *factum.*
admiration, *admīrātio.*
advice, *cōnsilium.*
Aetolian, *Aetōlus.*
affrighted, *perterritus.*
again, *rursus.*
ago, *abhinc.*
allow, *permittere, concēdere.*
although, *quanquam, quamvis.*
animal, *bestia.*
attire, *ornātus.*
avail, to be of, *juvāre.*
avert, *āvertere.*
autumn, *autumnus.*
auxiliary-troops, *auxilia.*
await, *exspectāre.*

B.

Beseech, *obsecrāre.*
boar, *aper.*
bog, *palūs.*
box, *arca, cista.*
burdensome, *molestus.*

C.

Carry, *vehere*—back, *revehere.*
cheese, *cāseus.*
Cheruscans, *Chēruscī.*
claw, *unguis.*
clearly, *perspicuē, plānē.*
clumsily, *tardē.*
color, *color.*
comfort, a, *sōlātium.*
condition, *condicio, status.*
consolation, *sōlātium.*
coverlet, *strāgulum.*
crown, wreath, *corōna;* kingly c., *diadēma.*

D.

Days, two, *biduum;* three, *triduum;* four, *quadriduum.*
deaf, *surdus.*
death, put to; see **kill**.
deer, *cervus.*
desert, to, *dēserere.*
deserve, *dignum esse.*
deter, to, *dēterrēre.*
devour, *dēvorāre.*
direction, *praeceptum.*
disappoint, *fallere.*
dissuade, *dissuādēre.*
doubtful, *dubius.*
dusty, *pulverulentus.*

E.

Emerge, *ēmergere.*
enormous, *immēnsus.*
enraged, *īrācundiā ēlātus.*
eternal, *aeternus, sempiternus.*
everybody else, *cēterī.*
evil, an, *malum.*
exclaim, *clāmāre.*
exhortation, *hortātio.*
extinguished, *exstinctus.*

F.

Fair (just), *aequus.*
falcon, *falco.*
false, *falsus.*
favor, to, *favēre.*
finery, *ornātus.*
foolish, *stultus.*
forum, *forum.*

G.

Garden, *hortus.*
general, *praetor.*
goldfinch, *acanthis.*
Greek, *Graecus.*
grove, *lūcus.*
goodwill, *benevolentia.*

H.

Heal, *medērī, sānāre.*
hence, *hinc.*
Hippocentaur, *Hippocentaurus.*
horde, *caterva.*
hostage, *obses.*
humble, *humilis.*

I.

Ignorant, *nescius.*
immortal, *immortālis.*
imprudent, *imprūdēns.*
infirmity, *infirmitās.*
innate, *innātus.*
integrity, *integritās.*
Italy, *Italia.*

J.

Jaws, *faucēs.*

K.

Kind-hearted, *benignus.*
kindness, *benignitās.*

L.

Later, adv., *post.*
let-go, *dīmittere.*
liberty, *libertās.*
lictor, *lictor.*
limb, *membrum.*

M.

Magnanimous, *magnanimus.*
magnificent, *splendidus magnificus.*
march, *iter.*
mass, *multitūdo.*

migrate, *migrāre*.
misfortunes, *incommoda*.

N.

Negligence, *neglegentia*.
nevertheless, *tamen*.

O.

Observe, *servāre*.
occur, *in mentem venīre*.
once, at (immediately), *statim*.
only, adj., *ūnicus*.
opinion, *opīnio*.
overthrow, to, *subvertere*.
ox, *bōs*.

P.

Plane-tree, *platanus*.
philosophy, *philosophia*.
pilot, *gubernātor*.
portico, *porticus*.
proconsul, *prōconsul*.
project, a, *consilium*.
propose, *intendere*.
proper, to be, *convenīre*.
pull down, *dīruere*.
put an end, *fīnem facere*.

Q.

Quickly, *cito*.
quiet, to keep, *quiescere*.

R.

Race, *gēns*.
rain, *pluvia*; *imber* (shower).
reach, to, *pervenīre ad*.
rebel, to, *dēsciscere*.
recommendation, *commendātio*.
regard, to, *habēre*.
regret, to, *dolēre*.
reign, a, *regnum*; to, *regnāre*.
rider, *eques*.
rower, *rēmex*.
rumor, *rūmor*.

S.

Set out, *proficisci*.
sharpen, *acuere*.
sin, a, *peccātum*.
size, *magnitūdo*.
sit, *sedēre*.
sod, a, *caespes*.
squander, *dissipāre*.
stability, *stabilitās*.
staff, *baculum*.
step, a, *gradus*.
strive, *nītī*.
sufficiently, *satis*.
summer, *aestās*.
sunset, *sōlis occāsus*.
swamp, *palūs*.
swiftness, *celeritās*.

T.

Tally, to, *convenīre*.
teacher, *magister*.
theatre, *theātrum*.
thwarts, *trānstra*.
toil, *labor*.
tower, *turris*.
treason, *prōditio*.
tree, *arbor*.
tremble, to, *contremiscere*
Troy, *Troja*.
tyrant, *tyrannus*.
Tyrian, *Tyrius*.

U.

Uncertain, *incertus*.
unhappy, *infēlix*.
unrest, *perturbātio*.
usefulness, *ūtilitās*

V.

Vain, in, *frūstrā*.
various, *vārius*.

W.

Wake, to, trans., *expergefacere*.
want, to (desire), *velle*.
week, *hebdomas*.
weighty, *gravis*.
Weser, *Visurgis*.
wickedness, *nēquitia*.
without, *sine*.

SUMMARY OF REFERENCES

IN THE TEXT OF THE EXERCISE-BOOK.

E. B. = *Exercise-Book.*
O. E = 1872 *Edition of Latin Grammar.*
N. E. = 1894 *Edition of Latin Grammar.*

E. B. PAGE	O. E. SEC.	N. E. SEC.	
17	286, R. 1	290, R. 1	1. The Latin language has a strong tendency to rhetorical repetition.
22	224	233	2. Imperfect of Endeavor.
26	500	498	See No. 25.
36	224	233	See No. 2.
43	586, R.	585, R.	3. **Cum**, with the Subj. is often translated by the English Participle.
46	469	467	4. The dependent interrogative is put in the Subjunctive.
	360, R. 1	362, R. 1	5. The adjective form is often preferred to the Genitive.
	345	346	6. **Prōdesse**, *to do good, to profit*, takes the Dative.
	246, R. 1	254, R. 1	7. The Roman uses the Indicative in such verbs, where we should expect the Subjunctive (Potential).
49	375	376	8. Verbs of Remembering and Forgetting take the Genitive.
	236, R. 2	244, R. 2	9. The Future Perfect is used with greater exactness in Latin than in English.
50	209	218	10. The Passive often has a reflexive signification and an intransitive translation.
51	351	351	11. **Dativus Ethicus**, or Dative of Feeling, a usage confined to the Personal Pronoun.
52	287, R.	291, R. 2	12. Superlative denoting order used partitively.
53	344	345	13. Dative with Passive.
54	298	311, 2	14. **Ipse tibi**, when **ipse** is emphatic, **ipsi tibi** when **ipsi**.
56	209	218	See No. 10.
	330, R. 2	331, R. 2	15. **Adire aliquem**, *to apply to a man*, **adire ad aliquem**, *to go up to a man.*
	625	623	16. The Pluperfect Ind. is used of antecedent iterative action in the Past.
	630	628	17. The Future Perf. Ind. is attracted into the Plupf. Subj. after a past tense in dependent discourse.
	463	461	18. *Whether . . or*, is **utrum . . . an**.
	469	467	See No. 4.
	375	376	See No. 8.
57	483	481	19. **Et** is often omitted in contrasts.
	308	293	20. **Mille** in the sing. is an indeclinable adjective, in the plur. it is a neut. subst., and must have the Genitive.
	357, R. 2	360, R. 2	21. A predicative attribute is often preferred to an abstract in the Genitive.
58	387	389	22. Place as Cause, Manner, or Instrument, needs no preposition.
	410, R. 3	337, R. 4	23. **Ad** with acc. *to the neighborhood of, siege of.*
	360, R. 1	362, R. 1	See No. 5.
60	236, R. 2	244, R. 2	See No. 9.

E. B. PAGE	O. E. SEC.	N. E. SEC.	
61	486	484	24. **Autem** is postpositive, generally after the first word.
	500, R. 2	498, N. 2	25. **Enim** is often explanatory rather than illative, and always postpositive.
62	431	430	26. Verbs of Giving and Taking take the Gerundive of the object to be effected.
	346, R. 1	347, R. 1	27. Verbs compounded with **con-(com-)** usually repeat the preposition (**cum**).
	345, R. 2	346, R. 2	28. **Persuādēre**, *to persuade* (make sweet), takes the Dat. of Person.
	612	610	29. Relative constructions are more common in Latin than in English.
63	667, R. 1	664, R. 1	30. Latin often subordinates by means of the participle where the English coördinates by means of the finite verb.
67	287, R.	291, R. 2	31. Adjective used partitively. Comp. No. 12.
68	299, R.	312, R.	32. The possessive pronouns are often peculiarly emphatic.
	236, R. 2	244, R. 2	See No. 9.
	457	455	33. **Nōnne** expects the answer: *Yes*.
69	221	230	34. The English Progressive Perfect is represented in Latin by the Present.
	388	390, 2	35. Separative Ablative after a verb of Removal.
	571	569	36. **Dum**, *so long as*, in past relations commonly takes the Perf. Ind.
70	212	221	87 Reciprocal relation is expressed by **inter sē**, **inter nōs**, &c.
71	208	217	38. A verb that takes the Dative cannot take the Passive except in an impersonal form: **Mihi invidētur**, *I am envied*, not **invideor** (poetic).
	304	317	39. A negative is involved: hence, **quidquam**.
	631	629	40. The Subj. is used in clauses which are complementary to the Subjunctive or Infinitive.
	324, R. 6	325, R. 6	41. A predicative adjective is often used instead of an adverbial phrase. See Vocabulary *s. v.* **absence**.
	346, R. 1	347, R. 1	See No. 27.
	298	311, 2	See No. 14.
72	234, R. 1	242, R. 1	See No. 126.
77	483	481	See No. 70.
78	278, R.	282, N.	42. The Perfect Participle is sometimes found where we should expect a Present.
79	208	217	See No. 38.
	195, R. 8	204, N. 8	43. Singular for Plural, collectively.
81	486	484	See No. 24.
84	586, R.	585, R.	See No. 3.
85	278	282	See No. 42.
86	277, R.	281, N.	44. **Meminī** of personal recollection usually takes the Present Inf.
87	655	652	45. The Imperative is represented in Indirect Speech by the Subjunctive.
88	623	621	46. The indefinite antecedent is commonly omitted.
	195, R. 5	204, R. 5	47. In Latin the plural of abstract nouns occurs more frequently than in English. Here the singular may be used as well.
89	521	521	48. The Reflexive is used of the principal subject in dependent sentences of design.
	586, R.	585, R.	See No. 3.
90	324, R. 7	325, R. 7	49. **Prīmus** *the first*, **prīmum** *for the first time*, **prīmō** *at first*.
	286, R. 2	290, N. 1	50. A common surname is put in the plural or repeated with each **praenōmen**.
	444	445	51. **Nē-quidem**, *not even*, strengthens a preceding negative.
	539	539	52. Subjunctive in Indirect Discourse.
91	293, R. 3	308, R. 3	53. **Is** does not represent a noun before the Genitive. Omit.
	408	409	54. Ablative Absolute.
92	236, R. 2	244, R. 2	See No. 9.
	426	425	55. After prepositions the Gerund and not the Infinitive is employed.
	469	467	See No. 4.
	349, R. 4	349, R. 4	56. The possession of qualities is expressed by **in aliquō esse** (not **alicui esse**) or **habēre**.
	634	631, 2	57. Subjunctive of Characteristic.

E. B. PAGE	O. E. SEC.	N. E. SEC.	
93	360, R. 2	362, R. 2	58. So-called Genitive of the Author.
	448, R. 2	449, R. 2	59. A negative expression is often preferred to a positive, in order to enhance the effect (Litotēs, *understatement*).
	199, R. 1	208, 2	60. Impersonals are freely formed from passives.
94	445	446	61. The Latin requires *no one ever*.
	486	484	See No. 24.
	349, R. 4	349, R. 4	See No. 56.
95	324, R. 6	325, R. 6	See No. 41.
96	548	548	62. Verbs of Forbidding take **nē** with the Subjunctive.
	370, R. 2	371, R.	63. **Uterque** is commonly used as a Substantive with pronouns, hence, **uterque nōstrum**.
97	461	459	64. *Or not* in a dependent question is commonly **necne**.
	381, R. 2	381, N. 2	65. **Meā**, etc , can not have apposition. Use the relative.
	579	577	66. **Antequam** and **priusquam** more commonly have the Subj. after positive sentences.
	195, R. 6	204, N. 6	67. Plural, because *logs*.
	344, R. 1	345, R. 2	68. **Ad**, because of the motion involved.
98	208	217	69. Impersonal Passive with Dative. See No. 38.
	483	481	70. **Et** is either omitted throughout or inserted throughout.
	221	230	See No. 34.
	497	495	71. **-Ve**, a weaker form of **vel**.
	478	476	72. **-Que** complements.
99	401, R.	399, N. 1	73. Adverbial Ablative.
	478		See No. 72.
	291	306	74. Demonstrative of Second Person.
	301	314	75. *Some or other* = **aliquis**.
	447	448	76. The negative immediately precedes the emphatic word or group.
	195, R. 8	204, N. 8	See No. 43.
100	195, R. 8	204, N. 8	See No. 43.
	612	610	See No. 29.
	286, R. 1	290, R. 1	See No. 1.
101	241	252	See E. B., p. 162.
	199, R. 1	208, 2	See No. 60.
	489	487	77. **Vērō** is generally put in the second place.
102	195, R. 5	204, N. 5	78. Pluralizing abstracts makes them concrete.
103	312	297	79. The comparative is often to be measured by the proper standard.
	357, R. 2	360, R. 2	80. Abstract with the Genitive often corresponds to English adjective and substantive.
	375, R. 1	376, R. 1	81. Neuter Accusatives are used adverbially with Verbs of Memory.
106	363	364	82. The Objective Genitive commonly takes the substantive and not the possessive form of the personal pronouns.
	350	356	83. Double Dative.
107	305	318	Better: *to each man according to his bravery*.
109	246, R. 1	254, R. 1	See No. 7.
110	646	643	84. **Atque** is used after Adjectives and Adverbs of Likeness and Unlikeness.
112	424, R. 3	423, R. 5	85. Verbs of Hope take the Fut. Inf., as a rule.
113	317	308	86. A common way of heightening a superlative.
	618	616	87. The apposition is often taken up into the Relative clause: *a tree which* becomes *which tree*.
114	292	307	88. **Ille**, of the future.
	290	305	89. **Hic** of the present.
	349, R. 4	349, R. 4	See No. 56.
115	448, R. 2	449, R. 2	See No. 59.
116	350	356	See No. 83.
117	209	218	See No. 10.
	539	539	90. **Quod** after Verbs of Emotion, takes the Subj. in Indirect Discourse.
	243	251	91. Gerundive.
118	195, R. 8	204, N. 8	See No. 43.
	486	484	See No. 24.
	210	219	92. The Passive of an action which one causes to be done to one-self.
	199, R. 1	208, 2	See No. 60.
	651, R. 1	648, R. 2	93. **Ājo** is used either as a leading verb or parenthetically.

E. B. PAGE	O. E. SEC.	N. E. SEC.	
118	448, R. 2	449, R. 2	See No. 59.
	612	610	See No. 29.
	304, R. 2	317, 2, N. 2	94. **Nullus** is used idiomatically for **nōn**.
119	212	221	See No. 37.
	331, R. 2	333, 1	95. The Cognate Accusative often appears as a Neuter Pronoun. *To ask this thing = to ask this question.*
	612	610	See No. 29.
	496	494	96. **Vel—vel** gives a choice.
	634	631, 2	See No. 57.
120	467	465	97. Deliberative Subjunctive.
	371	369	98. Partitive Genitive.
	353	355	99. Gerundive.
121	221	230	See No. 34.
	350	356	See No. 83.
122	589	588	100. **Cum** is frequently combined with **tum**. More weight is thrown on the second member.
	371	369	101. Partitive Genitive.
	390	406	102. **Opus est**.
	444	445	103. The negative may be subdivided by **neque—neque** or by **aut—aut**.
	365, R. 1	366, R. 1	104. Gen. of Property.
124	631	629	See No. 40.
125	625	623	105. Iterative Action in the Present is expressed by the Perfect Indicative in the dependent clause with the Present Indicative in the leading clause.
	627	626	106. **Qui = is enim**, takes the Indicative.
127	393	394	107. **In** with the Abl. = *in time of*.
	365, R. 1	366, R. 1	108. Genitive of Possession in the Predicate.
	250	257	109. Potential Subjunctive.
128	236, R. 2	244, R. 2	See No. 9.
	634	631, 2	See No. 57.
	551, R. 3	555, R. 3	110. **Nōn dubitāre**, with the Inf. ordinarily = *not to hesitate*.
129	208	217	See No. 38.
131	540, R. 1	541, N. 2	111. **Nōn quod** commonly takes the Subjunctive.
	208	217	See No. 38.
	365, R. 1	366, R. 1	See No. 108.
132	546, R. 2	546, R. 2	112. When Verbs of Will and Desire become Verbs of Saying and Thinking, they take the Acc. and Inf.
	623	621	See No. 46.
	199, R. 1	208, 2	See No. 60.
133	346, R. 3	546, R. 3	113. When the idea of Wishing is emphatic, the simple Subj. suffices.
134	639	636	114. Relative clauses are comparatively seldom coupled by **et** and **-que**.
	512, R. 2	512, R. 2	115. The Pure Perf. Ind. is more commonly followed by the Imperf. than by the Present Subjunctive.
	221	230	See No. 34.
135	566	563, 2	116. Of a definite interval **postquam** usually takes the Pluperfect.
	626	624	117. The Relative construction is often used to mark the temporary, transient relation.
	311, R. 4	296, R. 4	118. After **plūs**, **amplius**, and the like, **quam** may be omitted without affecting the construction.
	252	258	119. The Potential of the Past is the Imperf. Subj. generally in the Ideal Second Person. It is not changed in sequence.
136	353	355	120. Gerundive.
	302	314	121. **Quis** fainter than **aliquis**; often used after Relative forms, as, **cum quis**.
	400	403	122. Ablative of Measure of Difference
	312	297	See No. 79.
137	371	369	See No. 98.
138	462, 2	460, 1, *b*.	123. **Si**, *if*, is frequently used after Verbs and Phrases implying trial.
	515, R. 3	515, R. 3	124. After Verbs implying Hope, etc., the Periphrastic Subj. is not necessary.
	528	528	125. Give a Passive turn. *A few things seem* and Gerundive.
	548	548	See No. 62.

E. B. PAGE	O. E. SEC.	N. E. SEC.	
138	569	567	See No. 105.
	512, R. 2	512, R. 2	See No. 115.
139	234, R. 1	242, R. 1	126. The Future is used with more exactness in Latin than in English.
	348	348	127. Dat. and Accus. or Acc. and Abl.
	634	631, 2	See No. 57.
	221	230	See No. 34.
140	212	221	See No. 37.
	234, R. 1	242, R. 1	See No. 126.
	593	592	128. **Sin minus.**
	236, R. 2	244, R. 2	See No. 9.
	569	567	See No. 105.
	239	247	129. Periphrastic Active.
141	599, R. 1	597, R. 1	130. The Impf. Subj. is sometimes used in opposition to the past.
	239	247	See No. 129.
142	240, R. 1	248, R. 2	131. **Urgēre** has no Supine; hence the Periphrasis is necessary.
	639	636	132. *Who but who* is not Latin. Omit *but.*
143	515	515	133. Periphrastic Tense representing Future in a Subj. relation.
	633	631, 1	134. Subj. of Character.
	569	567	See No. 105.
	634	631, 2	See No. 57.
	246, R. 1	254, R. 1	See No. 7.
	239	247	See No. 129.
144	345, R. 1	346, N. 3	135. **Dēficere** takes the Accus.
	368, R. 2	370, R. 2	136. Where there is no partition the Genitive must not be used.
	387	380	See No. 22.
	293, R. 3	308, R. 3	See No. 53.
145	365, R. 1	366, R. 1	See No. 108.
	484, 2	482, 4	137. **Ut—ita** used adversatively.
146	625	623	See No. 105.
147	304, R. 2	317, 2, N. 2	See No. 94.
148	543, R. 4	543, 4	138. The sentence is final: hence **nē quid.**
	450	444, 2	139. **Nē** is continued by **nēve (neu).**
	437	436	140. Supine in **-ū.**
	592, R. 1	591, R. 1	141. Literally: *if merchants were not.*
	195, R. 4	204, N. 4	142. **Rēs** is better when the gender is doubtful.
	517	517	143. The conditional Imperfect Subj. attracts its dependencies into the Imperfect.
	304	317	See No. 39.
149	384, R.	385, R.	144. So Verbs of Placing with **in** and Abl.
	446	447	145. *Say not* is usually **nego.**
	379	380, 1	146. Genitive of Value.
150	317	303	See No. 86.
151	547–551	{547–549 / 554–555}	147. Verbs of Hindering take **nē** or **quōminus**; some the Inf. In order that they should take **quin** a negative must precede.
	350	356	See No. 83.
	363	364	See No. 82.
	441	440	148. Separation of adverb from verb gives stress.
	515	515	See No. 133.
	634	631, 2	See No. 57, also **Ō. O.**
152	375, R. 1	376, R. 1	See No. 95.
	236, R. 2	244, R. 2	See No. 9.
	612	610	See No. 29.
	645, R. 5	642, R. 5	149. **Quam grātissimum facere.**
154	630, R. 1	628, R. (*a*)	150. Explanations of the narrator are put in the Indicative.
	462, 2	460, 1, (*b*)	See No. 123.
155	657, R.	654, N.	151. As if a Principal Tense preceded: **Repraesentātio.**
157	527, R. 3	527, R. 3	152. The Reflexive Subject is not unfrequently omitted in **Ō. O.**
	315, R.	300, R.	153. *Which of two* = **uter.**
	663, 3	660, 3	154. **Nunc** becomes **tum** in **Ō. O.**

E. B. PAGE	O. E. SEC.	N. E. SEC.	
158	333, R. 1	339, 3, N. 4	155. Passive Verb of Teaching with Accus. of the Thing.
	208	217	See No. 38.
	632	630	156. Relative of Purpose with Subj.
160	304	317	See No. 39.
	429, R. 2	428, R. 2	157. The Genitive of the Gerundive with **esse** signifies *serves to, amounts to.*
162	306	319	158. *One of the two* = **alter**.
	667, R. 1	664, R. 1	See No. 30.
163	444	445	See No. 51.

Milton Keynes UK
Ingram Content Group UK Ltd.
UKHW021306200923
429051UK00013B/379